Faith

PHILOSOPHICAL TOPICS

PAUL EDWARDS, GENERAL EDITOR

Faith

Edited, with an Introduction,
Notes, and Bibliography by

TERENCE PENELHUM

THE UNIVERSITY OF CALGARY

Macmillan Publishing Company
New York
Collier Macmillan Publishers
London

To Edith

Copyright © 1989 by Macmillan Publishing Company,
a division of Macmillan, Inc.

Printed in the United States of America

Macmillan Publishing Company
866 Third Avenue, New York, New York 10022

Collier Macmillan Canada, Inc.

Library of Congress Cataloging-in-Publication Data

Faith / edited with an introduction, notes, and bibliography by
Terence Penelhum.
p.   cm. — (Philosophical topics)
ISBN 0-02-393721-1
1. Faith.   2. Faith and reason.   3. Belief and doubt.
I. Penelhum, Terence, 1929–   . II. Series: Philosophical topics
(New York, NY)
BD215.F35 1989
200'.1 — dc19   88–9009
                                                                                CIP

Printing: 1 2 3 4 5 6 7   Year: 9 0 1 2 3 4 5

ACKNOWLEDGMENTS

I wish to thank Mrs. Avril Dyson for innumerable forms of help in the preparation of this book, including speedy and accurate typing of my messy drafts at a busy time in the academic year. I am also indebted to Mrs. Irene Hergert for typing important parts of Section Two.

I am grateful to the series editor, Paul Edwards, for his help and encouragement.

I have dedicated the collection to my wife, who not only did the work on Section One, but has been the real source of any understanding of this subject I may have been able to come by.

T.P.

CONTENTS

SECTION THREE

SECTION FOUR

SECTION FIVE

INTRODUCTION

I

Most philosophers take it for granted that faith is a state of mind which has to be assessed by reason. If it is a state of mind they share, they will defend its rationality. If it is not, they may not claim it is *irr*ational, but they will assume that its rationality is problematic in a way that our assumption of the reality of the external world or our capacity to tell right from wrong is not. These are things that only *skeptical* philosophers have questioned. Faith, on the other hand, is thought to call for dismissal or defense by philosophers of all persuasions. (Indeed, some philosophical skeptics have made a point of defending it.)

What makes the rationality of faith problematic? To most philosophers the answer will seem obvious: the rationality of faith is problematic because faith is persistent conviction that is not founded upon adequate evidence. Briefly put, faith is certainty about matters that are *un*certain. It embodies the assurance that belongs to knowledge without the guarantees that knowledge brings with it (whatever these are). Such a state is obviously suspect, yet those who manifest faith are, puzzlingly, commended for it in their religious tradition; and the rest of us seem to be told that our salvation depends on following their example.

With the stage thus set, philosophical debate about faith and reason proceeds upon a set of received assumptions, which can be summarized as follows.

1. Faith is an intrinsically religious state of mind.

2. It consists, at least primarily, in the subject's believing in the truth of a set of doctrines. So the subject is called a *believer*.

3. This belief is whole-hearted, and its quality is shown by its persistence in the face of questions, or of events, that "test" it.

4. These tests derive their poignancy from the fact that the doctrines the believer believes are not *known* to be true. Even if there is evidence in their favor, this evidence is never conclusive.

5. The salvation of the believer is held to be due in part to the faith the believer has, and is commonly held to be impossible without it. So faith is urged upon others.

6. It follows from the preceding assumptions that failure to accept the doctrines believers believe is the primary barrier to salvation and is therefore blameworthy. If this is so, the belief the believer has and the unbeliever does not have must be voluntary.

It is not surprising, if these assumptions are correct, that faith seems to need philosophical defense. To many, it is never praiseworthy to persist in a belief when the evidence does not justify it; such persistence is therefore regarded as no more than obstinacy or self-deception. It seems inconsistent with the goodness of God that anyone's salvation should depend on a state of mind that is open to such criticism. More fundamentally still, it is not obvious that we *can* adopt a belief, or persist in it, if we ourselves do not think the evidence justifies it. Thus perhaps the only way in which faith can begin or continue is through some elaborate pretense that the evidence is better than it is. To many critics, faith is therefore a vice, not a virtue.

These objections have prompted many defenses. One defense is to say that while the doctrines held to in faith may be admitted to be beyond the power of reason to establish, they are nevertheless doctrines that are reasonable to believe, because they are natural extensions of doctrines that reason *can* establish. This view is classically represented by Aquinas. Another defense is to hold that the inconclusiveness and obscurity of religious doctrines are something that the religious tradition should make us expect, not see as a difficulty. The most famous version of this view is found in Pascal. A subtle expression of it is also found in Butler.

Defenses such as these have to contend with the difficulties expressed in arguments like those of McTaggart or Hanson. They can, however, be offered without rejecting the received assumptions about what faith is. The same is true of what might be called the prudential or pragmatic defense of faith, also historically derived from Pascal and Butler. On this view, even though the doctrines of faith cannot be rationally justified, there is still an overwhelmingly good reason for bringing oneself to *believe* them, i.e., the supreme importance of not missing one's only chance of salvation.

But many defenders of faith have sought to undermine the received assumptions on which these attacks and defenses have rested. In the first place, these assumptions are often said to overintellectualize faith, or treat it as a matter of believing, when it is primarily a matter not of the intellect but of the heart and the will. The person of faith does not believe approved doctrines *about* God, but rather *trusts* Him. Faith is a personal attitude toward God, not a set of convictions. The demand that we have faith is a personal demand to put aside our self-regarding hesitations and trust God's promises to us. The classical expression of this view of faith is in the theology of Luther. It can be extended to the point of maintaining that trust in God overrides all objective rational demands whatsoever, so that faith must necessarily make no intellectual sense, and be paradoxical to the external enquirer. This view is commonly ascribed to Kierkegaard.

In the second place, some defenders of faith have sought to make it less problematic to the philosopher by denying that it is an intrinsically religious phenomenon, and saying instead that it is a type of commitment that life demands of us in many spheres. If it is rational to make this commitment in one sphere, it needs special argument to show that it is not rational to make it in another. Tennant, who holds a similar view, speaks of faith as "venturesome supposition." (It is in connection with this understanding of faith that we find some thinkers allying it with philosophical skepticism. If reason is unable to justify the commitments life requires in secular contexts, there is nothing obviously wrong with ignoring its complaints on supernatural matters.) An impressive example of a case for faith in secular contexts that does *not* combine it with arguments for religious faith is found in Annette Baier's essay.

This second kind of apologetic defense still seems to concede that faith needs some kind of rational justification; and it says that this justification is available because religious faith resembles secular commitments that are justified by their results. This same parallel can be used in a different way, however. It can be used by suggesting that there are some commitments that need no justification whatever. This is claimed by Norman Malcolm, who likens religious faith to some basic beliefs of common sense, which, following Wittgenstein, he says it is impossible to question.

A quite different departure from the received assumptions is to be found in Richard Swinburne. He is wholly prepared to accept that religious faith should be supported by philosophical argument and is the best known practitioner of natural theology now writing. He rejects the traditional assumption that faith entails psychological certainty, even though its doctrines are beyond proof. He argues instead that faith may be a decision to found one's life on trust in a God whose being and whose promises one judges to be more *likely* realities than any religious or secular alternatives one is in a position to consider.

When the issues raised by all these contributions are taken with full seriousness, the question of the rationality of faith still remains, but is transformed. We see that before we can answer it, we have to decide what sort of phenomenon faith is: when we have an example of it, and when we do not, and how far it is an exclusively religious phenomenon. We also have to be clearer about what we have in mind when we wonder about its rationality. Neither "faith" nor "reason" are words we can assume we understand without analysis.

To add to our perplexities, we now have to take seriously the fact that most discussions of faith proceed without any analysis of the concept of *religion.* Most philosophical literature on this topic in the West addresses itself to the rationality of *Christian* faith, even though the historical roots of Christianity make it inevitable that much of what is said about it is assumed to apply also to Judaism, or at least to the pre-Christian Hebrew religious tradition. The paradigms of faith are assumed to be primarily biblical ones. But the present sophistication of religious studies makes the continuance of this monocultural restriction completely unacceptable and prompts many questions. The major religious traditions of the world are often referred to as "faiths"; but is the concept of faith properly applied, for example, to Buddhism, which is atheistic? If the world's major religions *can* all be called forms of faith, then it is not clear any longer that faith can be a form of trust, since trust seems to entail a personal object. Nor is it clear that faith can be understood as acceptance of doctrines, since the emphasis on doctrine and orthodoxy is notoriously far more central and obsessive in Christianity than it has ever been in the other religious traditions of the world. If one broadens the concept of faith in the light of these considerations, it tends to become a concept of life affirmation, perhaps with supernatural support—what Tillich has called "the courage to be." This contrasts only with the indifference of the classical Skeptics or with cosmic pessimism, though the famous essay of Russell that is included here shows that life affirmation and pessimism may not exclude one another either. If, on the other hand, one continues to restrict the concept of religious faith to commitments like those of the Judeo-Christian tradition, then the question of the rationality of faith becomes a far less central issue in the philosophy of *religion* than it has been thought to be by most philosophers.

The only writers who address this last issue in these pages are Hick and Swinburne. Problems of space have made it impossible for this anthology to include more of the relevant literature, but I shall address the question briefly in the concluding pages of this introduction. First some comments are provided on the selections.

II

SECTION ONE

Abraham and Isaac. This story is the archetypal example of faith as trusting obedience to God. Abraham's adherence to the Covenant with Yahweh is tested when he is commanded to offer his only son, Isaac, as a sacrifice. Isaac has been born after Abraham's wife, Sarah, is past the years of childbearing, as a sign from Yahweh that in return for his obedience, Abraham will indeed be the father of a great nation. The sacrifice of Isaac is at the same time a test of his obedience, and an apparent destruction of the primary sign of divine favor.

The Sayings of Jesus. The passages assembled here from the Gospels include most of those sayings in which the notion of faith *(pistis)* is explicitly used. Most of these sayings occur in the context of the stories of Jesus' healings. The major exception to this is the passage from the "Sermon on the Mount." A common theme seems to run through the former group of sayings — that faith is what enables those who seek healing to receive it. There is no suggestion that faith is a matter of assent, voluntary or otherwise, to any doctrines about God. It is rather that faith is the unreserved trust that the love of God will reach out to those who turn to it without reservation. The Sermon passage conveys a related message. The famous injunctions of the Sermon (to forgive, to do good to enemies) are said to be required of us because that is the way God behaves toward us. The unhesitating assumption that He does so behave toward us, is faith. We show whether we have faith or not by whether we are *anxious* or not. Those who have faith are not anxious; those who are anxious show that they do not trust God, and can therefore not release themselves sufficiently from fear to show love to others.

The Letter to the Hebrews. This letter is traditionally ascribed to Paul, but is thought by most scholars not to have been written by him. The famous eleventh chapter on faith is for the most part a reminder to the author's Jewish readers of those figures in their history whose lives have been governed by faith, which is seen as an assurance of an unseen realm that promises more than this world. The opening sentence is sometimes read to suggest that faith is a state of mind that itself brings about some of the reality of which it is the assurance. Tennant seems to read it in this way, but this does not seem correct. The argument seems rather to be that the assurance of the higher realm will have decisive effects on one's life in this. There is, nevertheless, some degree of intellectualization of the understanding of faith, in comparison with the Gospels.

Section Two

Aquinas. St. Thomas Aquinas (1225–1274) is commonly judged to be the greatest philosophical theologian of the Middle Ages. He is a thinker whose system has been normative in many ways for Catholic thinkers down to our own day. It is a complex and profound synthesis of Christian theology and Aristotelian philosophy. The extracts here are from the treatise on faith in the Secunda Secundae (the Second Part of Part Two) of the *Summa Theologiae,* his greatest work. Faith *(fides),* as Thomas describes it, is the believer's response of assent to the doctrinal proclamations of the Church. It is the first of the three theological virtues, the other two being hope and charity—the triad proclaimed by St. Paul at the close of his panegyric on love in 1 Corinthians 12. Faith is a virtue because assent to revelation is a voluntary act; it is voluntary because the doctrines the Church proclaims are beyond the power of reason to prove. However, although reason cannot prove the mysteries of faith, it can make it reasonable to assent to them by proving other truths that establish the credentials of the Church to speak on God's behalf—in particular, such truths as the existence of God, and the providential governance of the world. Faith so described is the cognitive component in the religious life, and it is in Thomas's account that we find the closest approximation to the received traditional assumptions listed earlier.

Luther. Martin Luther (1483–1546) has a view of faith and its relation to salvation that is always understood to be in sharp contrast to that represented by Aquinas. History identifies Luther with the insistence that salvation comes through faith alone, not through works. This insistence makes him reject the doctrine that faith is a virtue. Instead, he insists that faith, which is the acceptance of the Word of God, is itself a divine gift, and comes only when we recognize our inability to free ourselves from sin through our own righteousness. Faith liberates —when one accepts and trusts God, one is freed from self-centeredness and open to love. Faith, then, is a trusting submission that frees us from guilt and enables us to be accounted as righteous by God because we do not claim righteousness for ourselves. Whether the contrast with the position of Thomas is as great as it appears to be may be questioned (as it is by Swinburne), but at first reading Luther seems to be far less concerned with the cognitive aspects of faith, and more concerned to stress its power in personal life.

Pascal. Blaise Pascal (1623–1650) is the most powerful of Christian apologists. The work universally known as the *Pensées* consists of the notes he left for the unfinished *Apology for the Christian Religion.* The nature of the argument of that work is an issue that divides scholars, and this division naturally affects their judgments on the significance of particular fragments. Those fragments included here are numbered in the order in which they are arranged in the French edition of Louis Lafuma, in which those up to number 382 are deemed to have been classified and ordered by Pascal himself, and the remainder to be unclassified. The alternative number at the end of each fragment is that of the older French edition of Leon Brunschvicg. All the extracts here deal specifically with the nature of faith; they are not, of course, the only ones relevant to that theme. More editorial comment is necessary for this selection than for others in the book; but I am conscious of the heavy element of individual interpretation the following comments must involve.

Pascal's understanding of faith is a complex one. The first fragment is a famous expression of the anxiety of the reflective human being faced by the shock of historical contingency. This anxiety is one that we try to allay by the use of reason, but reason is not able to assure us whether our existence is meaningful, or whether there is a God who cares for us or not. To reason, nature is radically ambiguous (fragment 444), seeming both to point to God and to deny Him. The skeptics are right about the powerlessness of our intellect to solve the problems that haunt us, just as they are right to urge that reason cannot prove we are not dreaming (131). But our natures are not exhausted by the senses and the reason; there is also the heart, which teaches us those first principles that reason cannot justify, and thus enables us to live in the world in the face of the skeptic's doubts (110). The skeptic's only resource in the face of reason's limitations is frivolous indifference; but this is no antidote to despair (148, 429). We must recognize that the cure lies in the heart. But the heart is corrupted by human sinfulness, and when we see the helplessness of reason our only hope lies in recognizing that in the matters that are beyond reason, the heart must listen to God (131). When man does listen to God, and heeds the signs of Himself that God has put in the world and in the Scriptures, God will give him faith (380, 424). Faith is therefore a gift, but it is a gift we can prepare for, and receive, if we are willing to put aside the sensory pleasures in which we hide from God (816, 821). Faith, thus understood, is not contrary to reason, but is that state in which God ceases to hide himself and enables us to see that such mysteries as the Fall and the Incarnation are the only answers to human anxiety. Faith satisfies the intellect, but is not a product of it, and does not need its justification.

Most philosophical discussions of Pascal have been overobsessed by the famous *Wager* argument of fragment 418. This is especially true since William James offered his unsubtle version of it in the essay "The Will to Believe." In Pascal the argument would have had a special, but subsidiary, place. It is addressed to the skeptic who has recognized reason's limitations, but wishes to respond to the world's ambiguity by suspending judgment and filling his life with frivolities. Pascal argues that even if reason cannot tell us whether God exists or not, faith is a more rational stance than indifference. For either God does exist or He does not. Suspending judgment on this issue is equivalent in practice to wagering He does not; so one cannot *not* decide on this matter. In these circumstances, prudence makes it clear that one should bet that God does exist, and believe in Him; for the resulting losses are trivial, and we stand to gain eternal life by believing. However one judges this argument, two points are clear. First, it is only applicable to us if we judge the intellectual situation to be ambiguous in the way Pascal and the skeptic agree it is. Second, Pascal does not think we can choose to believe at will, but on the contrary that we can only induce belief indirectly by removing those habits and associations that prevent it. If we do this, he assumes faith will then follow as a gift from God. The *Wager* offers the betting man reasons for listening to Him.

Butler. In Joseph Butler (1692–1752) we return from the contrast between faith and reason to a measured case for faith's reasonableness. His great sermon "Upon the Ignorance of Man" contains in outline the main arguments of his major apologetic work, *The Analogy of Religion.* Butler's aim was to undermine the arguments of the Deists of his time. They agreed that reason requires us to believe in the existence of God, but denied the truth of the Christian revelation. They argued that a rational and perfect deity would make any message he had for us a clear and obvious one, and would not confine its reception to one nation, such as the Jews. Their form of belief in God was therefore a challenge to traditional faith, rather than a prologue to it. Using arguments that are still of interest, Butler argues that if God does exist, the obscurities in revelation and the limitations of our understanding of God are not surprising, but to be expected. It is therefore rational to take the signs of His presence that are available as guides to life. There are many similarities to the position of Pascal here.

Rousseau. It is generally held that the Deism of the seventeenth and eighteenth centuries was a halfway house on the road to the atheism and agnosticism of our own day. Though the philosophical arguments for the existence of God (which the Deists accepted as readily as their orthodox opponents) have been largely discredited by Hume and Kant, the Deists' arguments against the reliability of the Christian Scriptures have had longer influence. Also, some Deists saw themselves as representatives of a genuine religiousness that was free of superstition and sectarianism, yet quite opposed to atheism. This seems to have been true of Jean-Jacques Rousseau (1712–1778). "The Creed of a Savoyard Priest" is generally agreed to represent the author's own religious convictions, even though nominally addressed by a fictional character to a young man. It connects very loosely with the general argument of his great educational classic, *Emile* (1762), of which it forms a part. Rousseau's educational program omits formal instruction in religion until the child has almost reached adult years, and the "Creed" in the same work seems to tell us what sort of religious teaching should be provided then. It is clear that for Rousseau true religion involves veneration of a deity known through reason and through conscience to all people, together with respect for those who have served Him such as Jesus. Religion for him does not involve any special revelation, piety, or priestcraft. His position can be contrasted with that of Butler, who was arguing against similar views among his own contemporaries, and can be compared instructively with those in Section Five.

Kierkegaard. The fideism of Luther and Pascal receives its most radical expression in Søren Kierkegaard (1813–1855). In his famous panegyrics upon Abraham in *Fear and Trembling,* Kierkegaard insists that Abraham's willingness to sacrifice Isaac embodies a radical trust that can be given no coherent sense in the language of human reason. It expresses a form of affirmation that transcends the demands of human ethics and the resignation of the classical tragic hero. In the passage included here from his *Concluding Unscientific Postscript,* Kierkegaard draws a sharp contrast between what he calls the subjectivity characteristic of faith and the objectivity characteristic of scientific and philosophical thought. To demand rational justification for faith, which of its nature transcends reason's categories, is to evade the demands of God for commitment in the immediate moment, and so to intrude a detachment that postpones a passionate decision that will then go by default. There is a clear repetition here of Pascal's insistence that one cannot *not* gamble for or against God, because of each person's inescapable involvement in a unique personal situation. Kierkegaard insists, faith is necessarily absurd, or paradoxical, and any attempts to domesticate it through reason are rejections of it.

SECTION THREE

The essays included here are primarily discussions of the biblical or classical writings in Sections One and Two.

The first essay, "Faith," is a chapter from a little-known book by F. R. Tennant (1866–1957). Tennant was a philosophical theologian who sought to place theology on an intellectually acceptable footing by arguing in his *Philosophical Theology* (Cambridge, 1928–30) that faith is a reasonable extension of attitudes and commitments present in the sciences. He also sought to offer an interpretation of the Christian doctrine of sin that would provide an alternative to the classical teachings of Augustine and Luther. In the material included here, he examines the conceptions of faith found in the Gospels and in the Letter to the Hebrews. He treats the latter as expressing a view that also covers commitments of a nonreligious type. The essay "The Analysis of Faith in St. Thomas Aquinas" by this volume's editor is an attempt to analyze the Thomistic understanding of faith and to make clear some of the philosophical problems to which it gives rise. "Two of Kierkegaard's Uses of 'Paradox'" by Robert Herbert, Professor of Philosophy at the University of Oregon, provides an illuminating discussion of the difficult claims made by Kierkegaard in the *Concluding Unscientific Postscript*, especially the insistence on the paradoxical nature of faith.

SECTION FOUR

The three selections here state different cases against faith. Bertrand Russell's "A Free Man's Worship" is a classic modern expression of courage in the face of a world that gives no ground for faith whatever. It is more rhetorical in manner than was common for Russell, and he himself tells us in his *Autobiography* that he began it at a dark period in his life. It is ironic that it has itself been described as an expression of faith, in spite of the fact that it proclaims "the soul's habitation" can only be built "on the firm foundation of unyielding despair." To describe that proclamation as a form of faith is to equate faith with courage, when one of the challenges to faith is the fact that courage can exist without it.

The Cambridge philosopher John McTaggart (1866–1925), though sympathetic to some religious claims, such as the belief in immortality, denied there are adequate grounds for belief in God, or in other key Christian doctrines. In "The Establishment of Dogma," McTaggart attacks the attempt to support these doctrines by an appeal to faith.

Norwood Russell Hanson (1924–1967), at the time of his death Professor of Philosophy at Yale, was best known for his deep and original studies in the philosophy of science. His brief essay "The Agnostic's Dilemma" argues that there is no rational case for agnosticism—the view that we cannot know whether God exists or not. Hanson insists that if the case for theism and the case against it are both judged as inconclusive, we then have clear grounds for atheism. What he says here should be compared with the response to the world's ambiguity made by Pascal, and the more recent estimate of it by John Hick.

SECTION FIVE

The first two essays in our final section show, in different ways, the influence of Wittgenstein on philosophy of religion. In "Seeing-as and Religious Experience," John Hick, Danforth Professor of the Philosophy of Religion at Claremont Graduate School, attempts to illuminate the nature of faith by drawing on Wittgenstein's treatment of "seeing-as" in Part Two of the *Philosophical Investigations*. Hick argues that the believer and the skeptic experience the same world in alternative ways —the number of alternatives being further compounded by the multiplicity of religious traditions. Norman Malcolm, formerly Susan Linn Sage Professor of Philosophy at Cornell University, argues in the manner of Wittgenstein's late work *On Certainty*. In "The Groundlessness of Belief," Malcolm contends that the philosophical search for rational grounds has inevitable limits, and when this is recognized, the demand for a rational basis for faith is seen to be confused.

"The Nature of Faith" by Richard Swinburne, Nolloth Professor of the Philosophy of the Christian Religion at Oxford, is a central chapter from his book, *Faith and Reason*. This work is the third in a trilogy that has reestablished the credentials of natural theology in our time. Swinburne holds the view that the existence of God can be shown to be probable. So the faith of the Christian can be seen to be a rational commitment to base one's decisions on doctrines that are judged more likely than their real alternatives though not necessarily certain. It follows from this that the received view that faith entails certainty has to be carefully reexamined.

The essay "Secular Faith" by Annette Baier, Professor of Philosophy at the University of Pittsburgh, is not a discussion of religious faith, but an examination of what she sees as a secular counterpart of it, namely the moral agent's commitment to social responsibility. If indeed the analogy is a sound one, the received view that faith is intrinsically religious needs revision.

III

All selections require hard choices. I conclude this introduction with a brief mention of three important bodies of relevant work *not* represented here. References to each are to be found in the Bibliography.

First and foremost is the work of Wilfred Cantwell Smith. Drawing upon the erudition that has made him a world leader in religious scholarship, Smith argues that the equation of faith with belief in doctrines is not only an equation confined to Christian thinkers, but one that grossly misrepresents the Christian tradition itself. Faith is the positive response to the demands of the Transcendent, and is the central stance of all the major religious traditions; in none of them is it akin to the adoption of opinions. The fact that the verbal expression of Christian faith is "I believe" is only apparent counterevidence. Smith demonstrates, with a wealth of illustration and etymological learning, that until quite recently, to *believe* was to set one's heart upon, or to devote oneself to, not to opine. The implications of this fact are only beginning to receive the study they require, but it is essential for all serious students of religion, including philosophers, to examine them.

Second, it would be misleading to ignore what has (by one of its opponents) been called "Wittgensteinian Fideism." This position, developed in the writings of D. Z. Phillips and carried further by Don Cupitt, can best be introduced in brief space by reference to that of Norman Malcolm, who is represented in the present volume. Malcolm argues that religious beliefs are groundless, and that it is a philosophical and religious mistake to demand arguments to establish them. Phillips carries this further and maintains that it is a mistake in philosophical grammar to suppose that proclamations of faith embody supernatural doctrines at all. Talk of God is not talk of a supersensible reality, but a set of locutions that express a form of life that can only be understood by participation—such participation is what faith is. Unlike Hick, I incline to think that Wittgenstein's own fragmentary statements about religion might well be read in this way, though I agree it seems widely at variance with what most believers seem to think they are about.

Finally, I must mention a growing literature defending what might be called the Basic Belief Apologetic, associated particularly with Alvin Plantinga. Plantinga points out that we must distinguish between those beliefs of a person that are held because of other beliefs, and those that are not; the latter he calls basic beliefs. Given that no one can fail to hold some of his beliefs as basic beliefs, it seems arbitrary and question-begging to insist, as has been done in what he calls the "foundationalist" tradition, that basic beliefs must be of some favored epistemological type only. If this view is sound, there seems no compelling reason to insist that *religious* beliefs cannot be basic. Hence faith, even if groundless, may well not be irrational.

It has not been possible to represent these three major, current positions in this volume. I submit they are essential further reading, and are best considered in the light of the arguments that *are* included.

SECTION ONE

Abraham and Isaac*

As it came to pass after these things, that God did tempt Abraham, and said unto him, "Abraham": and he said, "Behold, here I am."

And he said, "Take now thy son, thine only son Isaac, whom thou lovest, and get thee into the land of Moriah; and offer him there for a burnt offering upon one of the mountains which I will tell thee of."

And Abraham rose up early in the morning, and saddled his ass, and took two of his young men with him, and Isaac his son, and clave the wood for the burnt offering, and rose up, and went unto the place of which God had told him.

Then on the third day Abraham lifted up his eyes, and saw the place afar off.

And Abraham said unto his young men, "Abide ye here with the ass; and I and the lad will go yonder and worship, and come again to you."

And Abraham took the wood of the burnt offering, and laid it upon Isaac his son; and he took the fire in his hand, and a knife; and they went both of them together.

And Isaac spake unto Abraham his father, and said, "My father": and he said, "Here am I, my son." And he said, "Behold the fire and the wood: but where is the lamb for a burnt offering?"

And Abraham said, "My son, God will provide himself a lamb for a burnt offering": so they went, both of them together.

And they came to the place which God had told him of; and Abraham

*Genesis 22, in the authorized (King James) translation of 1611.

15

built an altar there, and laid the wood in order, and bound Isaac his son, and laid him on the altar upon the wood.

And Abraham stretched for his hand, and took the knife to slay his son.

And the Angel of the Lord called unto him out of heaven, and said, "Abraham, Abraham": and he said, "Here am I."

And said, "Lay not thine hand upon the lad, neither do thou any thing unto him: for now I know that thou fearest God, seeing thou has not withheld thy son, thine only son, from me."

And Abraham lifted up his eyes, and looked, and behold behind him a ram caught in a thicket by his horns: and Abraham went and took the ram, and offered him up for a burnt offering in the stead of his son.

And Abraham called the name of that place Jehovah-jireh: as it is said to this day, in the mount of the Lord it shall be seen.

And the angel of the Lord called unto Abraham out of heaven the second time,

And said, "By myself I have sworn," saith the Lord, "for because thou has done this thing, and has not withheld thy son, thine only son, that in blessing I will bless thee, and in multiplying I will multiply thy seed as the stars of the heaven, and as the sand which is upon the seashore; and thy seed shall possess the gate of his enemies.

And in thy seed shall all the nations of the earth be blessed; because thou has obeyed my voice."

So Abraham returned unto his young men, and they rose up and went together to Beer-sheba; and Abraham dwelt at Beer-sheba.

The Sayings of Jesus*

From Mark

When he returned to Capernaum, it became known, after a few days, that he was in a house there; and so many gathered that there was no space before the door and he preached the word to them. They came bringing him a paralytic who was carried aloft by four men. When they could not reach him because of the crowd, they took away the roof from over the place where Jesus was, and when they had made an opening they lowered the bed where the paralytic lay. Jesus seeing their faith said to the paralytic: My child, your sins are forgiven. There were some of the scribes sitting by, and they said to themselves in their hearts: Why does this man talk this way? He blasphemes. Who can forgive sins, except God alone? Jesus knew at once in his mind what they were saying to themselves, and said: Why do you have such thoughts in your hearts? Which is easier, to say to the paralytic: Your sins are forgiven, or to say: Arise, take up your bed and walk about? But so that you may know that the son of man has authority to forgive sins upon earth — he said to the paralytic: I tell you, rise, take up your bed, and go to your house. And the man arose and took up his bed and went out, in the sight of all; so that all were astonished and glorified God, saying: We have never seen the like.

*The passages here are from *The Four Gospels and the Revelation*, newly translated from the Greek by Richmond Lattimore. Copyright © 1979 by Richmond Lattimore, pp. 6, 12, 13–15, 24–25, 29, 31, 59–60, 62–63, 81–82. Reprinted by permission of the publisher, Farrar Straus and Giroux, Inc.

That same day when it was evening he said to them: Let us cross over to the other side. They sent away the multitude and took him along on the ship just as he was, and there were other ships with him. There came a sudden great storm of wind, and waves dashed against the ship so that it was beginning to fill. He was in the stern asleep with his head on his pillow; and they woke him and said: Master, do you not care whether we perish? He woke and scolded the wind and said to the sea: Silence, be still. And the sea subsided and there was a great calm. Then he said to them: Why are you frightened? Do you not yet have faith? And they were seized with a great fear and said to each other: Who is this, that the wind and sea obey him?

After Jesus had crossed with his ship back to the other side, a great crowd gathered about him; and he was by the sea. And there came to him one of the leaders of the synagogue, Jairus by name, and when he saw him he fell at his feet and implored him at length, saying: My little daughter is at the point of death; so come and lay your hands upon her, so that she may recover and live. He went with him; and a great throng followed, and they were crowding against him. There was a woman who had been bleeding for twelve years, and had been treated in many ways by many physicians, and had spent all that she had, and got no benefit but rather got worse; she had heard about Jesus, and she came up behind him in the crowd and touched his mantle; for she said to herself: If I touch only his mantle I shall be healed. And immediately the source of her flow of blood dried up, and she knew in her body that she had been healed of her affliction. Immediately Jesus felt in himself that power had gone forth from him, and he turned about and said: Who touched my mantle? His disciples said to him: Do you see the throng that is crowding upon you, and yet do you ask: Who touched me? And he looked around to see who had done it. And the woman, in fear and trembling, knowing what had happened to her, threw herself down before him and told him the whole truth. He said to her: My daughter, your faith has saved you; go in peace and be healed of your affliction. While he was still talking, they came from the house of the leader of the synagogue saying: Your daughter has died; why do you continue to trouble the master? Jesus disregarded the talk that was going on and said to the leader of the synagogue: Have no fear, only have faith. And he would not let anyone follow him except Peter and James and John the brother of James. They entered the house of the leader of the synagogue, and he was aware of a great tumult, and people weeping and lamenting greatly, and going in he said to them: Why this tumult and weeping? The child has not died, she is asleep. They laughed at him. He drove out all the others, and took with him the father and mother of the child and those who were with him, and went in where the child was; and he took the child's hand, and said to her: Talitha cum; which is translated: Little girl, I say to you: Awake. At once the little girl got up and walked about, for she was twelve years old. They were seized with great amazement. And he charged them at length that no one should be told about this; and he said she should be given something to eat.

As they returned to the disciples, they saw a great crowd about them, and scribes arguing with them. And as soon as they saw him all the multitude were greatly amazed, and at once they ran up to him and greeted him. And he asked them: What are you discussing with them? A man in the crowd answered him: Master, I have brought my son to you. He has a speechless spirit. And when this seizes upon him, it batters him, and he foams and his teeth chatter, and he wastes away. I told your disciples to drive it out, and they were not able to. He answered and said to them: O generation without faith, how long shall I be with you? How long shall I endure you? Bring him to me. And they brought him to him. When he saw Jesus, the spirit at once convulsed the boy, and he fell on the ground and rolled about, foaming. Then Jesus asked the father: How long has this been happening to him? He said: Since he was little; and many times it has thrown him into fire and into water, to destroy him. But if you can, take pity on us and help us. Jesus said to him: If you can? All things are possible to him who believes. At once the father of the boy cried out and said: I believe. Help my unbelief. Jesus seeing that the crowd was growing around him admonished the unclean spirit, saying to it: You speechless deaf spirit, I command you, go forth from him, and never enter him again. And the spirit, with much screaming and struggling, went out of the boy; and he became like a corpse, so that most of the people said he had died. But Jesus took him by the hand and raised him up, and he stood. When he had gone indoors, his disciples asked him privately: Why were we not able to drive it out? He said to them: This kind cannot be made to go forth except by prayer.

And they came to Jericho. And as he was on his way out of Jericho with his disciples and a considerable multitude, Bartimaeus the son of Timaeus, a blind beggar, was sitting by the road. And hearing that it was Jesus of Nazareth, he began to cry aloud and say: Jesus, son of David, have pity on me. And many people told him angrily to be quiet, but he cried out all the more: Son of David, have pity on me. And Jesus stopped and said: Call him. And they called the blind man, saying to him: Take heart, rise up, he is calling you. He threw off his mantle and sprang to his feet and went to Jesus. Jesus spoke forth and said: What do you wish me to do for you? The blind man said to him: Master, let me see again. And Jesus said to him: Go; your faith has healed you. And at once he could see again, and he followed him on his way.

As they passed by in the morning they saw the fig tree dried up, from the roots; and Peter remembered and said to him: Master, see, the fig tree which you cursed is dried up. Jesus answered and said to them: Have faith in God. Truly I tell you, if one says to this mountain: Rise up and throw yourself into the sea, and does not deliberate in his heart but believes that what he talks about is happening, it shall be his. Therefore I tell you, all that you pray for and ask for, believe that you get it, and it shall be yours. And when you stand praying, forget anything you have against anyone, so that your father in heaven may forgive your transgressions.

From Matthew

When he came into Capernaum there came to him a centurion with a request, saying: Lord, my son is lying paralyzed in my house, in terrible pain. He said to him: I will go and treat him. But the centurion answered and said: Lord, I am not worthy that you should come under my roof; but only say it in a word, and my son will be healed. For I myself am a man under orders, and I have soldiers under me, and I say to this man: Go, and he goes, and to another: Come, and he comes, and to my slave: Do this, and he does it. Jesus hearing him was amazed and said to his followers: Truly I tell you, I have not found such faith in anyone in Israel. I tell you that many from the east and the west will come and feast with Abraham and Isaac and Jacob in the Kingdom of Heaven; but the sons of the kingdom shall be thrown into the outer darkness; and there will be weeping and gnashing of teeth. And Jesus said to the centurion: Go, as you have trusted, so let it befall you. And his son was healed in that hour.

Then Jesus left there and went away to the regions of Tyre and Sidon. And behold, a Canaanite woman from those parts came out and cried to him, saying: Pity me, son of David. My daughter is sadly vexed with a demon. But he said not a word in answer. Then his disciples came up to him and pressed him, saying: Send her away, for she follows us crying. He answered and said: I was not sent forth except after the lost sheep of the house of Israel. But she came and bowed before him, saying: Lord, help me. He answered and said: It is not well to take the bread of the children and throw it to the dogs. But she said: Yes, Lord, for even the dogs eat from the crumbs that fall from the table of their masters. Then Jesus answered and said to her: Woman, your faith is great. Let it be as you wish. And her daughter was healed from that hour.

Do not store up your treasures on earth, where the moth and rust destroy them, and where burglars dig through and steal them; but store up your treasures in heaven, where neither moth nor rust destroys them, and where burglars do not dig through or steal; for where your treasure is, there also will be your heart. The lamp of the body is the eye. Thus if your eye is clear, your whole body is full of light; but if your eye is soiled, your whole body is dark. If the light in you is darkness, how dark it is. No man can serve two masters. For either he will hate the one and love the other, or he will cling to one and despise the other; you cannot serve God and mammon. Therefore I tell you, do not take thought for your life, what you will eat, or for your body, what you will wear. Is not your life more than its food and your body more than its clothing? Consider the birds of the sky, that they do not sow or harvest or collect for their granaries, and your heavenly father feeds them. Are you not preferred above them? Which of you by taking thought can add one cubit to his growth? And why do you take thought about clothing? Study the lilies in the field, how they grow. They do not toil or spin; yet I tell you, not even Solomon in all his glory was clothed like one of these. But if God so clothes the grass of the field, which grows today and tomorrow is thrown in the oven, will he not much more clothe you, you men of little faith? Do not then worry and say: What shall we eat? Or: What shall we drink? Or: What shall we wear? For all this the Gentiles study. Your father in heaven knows that you need all these things. But seek out first his kingdom and his justice, and all these things shall be given to you. Do not then take thought of tomorrow; tomorrow will take care of itself, sufficient to the day is its own evil.

The Letter to the Hebrews*

Faith is the substance of things hoped for, the proof of things unseen; for by it our forebears were attested. By faith we understand that the ages were formed by the word of God, so that what is seen did not come from things that appear. By faith Abel brought to God a better offering than Cain, and by this he was proved righteous, with God himself bearing witness to his gifts; and by faith, though he died, he still speaks. By faith Enoch was taken up aloft, so as not to look on death, and he was never found because God had taken him; since it is attested that before his taking up he was pleasing to God, and without faith it is impossible to please him; for one who approaches God must believe that he exists and that he is the rewarder of those who seek him out. By faith Noah, divinely warned of things not yet apparent, took careful thought and built the ark for the salvation of his household; and by this he refuted the world, and became heir to that righteousness that comes through faith. By faith Abraham obeyed when he was called to go forth into that region which he was to receive as his inheritance, and he went forth not knowing where he was going. By faith he moved to the land of the promise as to a foreign land, living in tents as did also Isaac and Jacob, who shared with him the inheritance of the same promise; for he was waiting for the city with foundations, of which the architect and designer is God. By faith also Sarah herself found strength to give birth,

*From *Acts and Letters of the Apostles*, translated from the Greek by Richmond Lattimore. Copyright © 1979 by Richmond Lattimore, pp. 235–237. Reprinted by permission of the publisher, Farrar Straus and Giroux Inc.

though past her time of life, since she thought the giver of the promise was to be believed; so that from one man, even from one far gone, there came a number like the stars in the sky, or like the innumerable sands at the edge of the sea.

All of these died in faith without winning the promise, but seeing it from far off and hailing it, and confessing that they were strangers and visitors on earth. They who say such things make it clear that they are searching for their own country. If they had been remembering the country from which they came, they would have had occasion to turn back; but as it is they long for a better one, that is, the one in heaven. Therefore God is not ashamed to be called their God, for he has made ready a city for them.

By faith Abraham offered up Isaac when he was put to the test, and accepting the promise, offered up his only son, the one of whom it had been said: Your seed shall be called after Isaac; reasoning that God can even raise men from the dead; therefore symbolically he did recover him. By faith even in things to come Isaac blessed Jacob and Esau. By faith Jacob, dying, blessed each of the sons of Joseph and prayed for them over the end of his staff. By faith Joseph, dying, remembered the exodus of the sons of Israel and gave instructions concerning his bones. By faith when Moses was born he was hidden for three months by his parents, because they saw that the baby was a fine one, and they were not frightened by the edict of the King. By faith Moses, grown big, refused to be called the son of Pharaoh's daughter, choosing to suffer with the people of God rather than have the temporary enjoyment of sinfulness, considering the despised estate of the Christ a richer thing than the treasures of Egypt, since he looked forward to his reward. By faith he left Egypt, not fearing the anger of the King, for he endured as if he saw him who cannot be seen. By faith he established the Passover and the sprinkling of blood so that the destroyer of the firstborn might not strike them. By faith they walked across the Red Sea as if on dry land, which the Egyptians tried to do and were engulfed. By faith the walls of Jericho fell down when they were circled for seven days. By faith Rahab the harlot did not perish with the unbelievers, because she had received the spies in peace.

Why should I say more? My time will run out as I tell about Gideon, Barak, Samson, Jephthah, David and Samuel and the prophets. By faith they overthrew kingdoms, did works of righteousness, won promises, stopped the mouths of lions, quenched the force of fire, escaped the edge of the sword, grew strong out of weakness, proved mighty in battle, routed the lines of their opponents. Wives recovered their resurrected dead. But others were tortured, refusing release so as to win a greater resurrection; others again accepted the ordeal of mockery and whippings and even of chains and prison. They were stoned, tortured, sawn in two, slaughtered by the sword. They went about in the skins of sheep and goats, in want and affliction and abuse. The world was not worthy of them as they wandered in deserts and mountains and caves and holes in the ground.

Yet all of these, though proved through their faith, did not achieve the promise, since God for our sake contemplated something better: that they should not be perfected apart from us.

Let us also, therefore, surrounded by such a cloud of witnesses, putting aside every obstacle and the sin that easily besets us, run with tenacity the course that lies before us, looking to the originator and perfecter of faith, Jesus; who, instead of the joy that lay ready before him, endured the cross, despising the shame of it, and has sat down to the right of the throne of God.

SECTION TWO

ST. THOMAS AQUINAS

On Faith*

Secunda Secundae, Question One

ARTICLE ONE

WHETHER THE OBJECT OF FAITH IS THE FIRST TRUTH

We proceed to the first article thus:

1. It seems that the object of faith is not the first truth. For whatever is proposed for our belief would seem to be the object of faith, and there are proposed for our belief not only things pertaining to the Godhead, which is the first truth, but also things pertaining to the humanity of Christ, to the sacraments of the Church, and to the condition of creatures. Hence not only the first truth is the object of faith.

2. Again, faith and unbelief have the same object, since they are opposites. Now there can be unbelief concerning everything in sacred Scripture, since a man is called an unbeliever if he disbelieves anything which is therein contained. It follows that faith is likewise concerned with everything in sacred Scripture, which contains many things relating to men, and to other creatures also. Hence the object of faith is not only the first truth, but also the truth about creatures.

3. Again, it was said in 12ae, Q. 62, Art. 3, that faith is condivided with charity. Now by charity we not only love God, who is the supreme good, but love our neighbour also. Hence the object of faith is not only the first truth.

On the other hand: Dionysius says (7 *Div. Nom.*, lect. 5): "Faith is in the simple and eternal truth." Now this is the first truth. The object of faith is therefore the first truth.

*From A.M. Fairweather (ed. and trans.) *Nature and Grace: Selections from the Summa Theologica of St. Thomas Aquinas*, Library of Christian Classics Vol. XI, 1954, pp. 219–222, 241–242, 255–257, 268–269, 271–273, 281–282. Reprinted by permission of the Westminster Press, Philadelphia.

I answer: the object of any cognitive habit is twofold. It includes what is known materially as a material object, and also that through which it is known, this being the formal meaning of its object. In the science of geometry, for example, the conclusions are known materially, while the principles of demonstration whereby the conclusions are known are the formal meaning of the science. Now if we are thinking of the formal meaning of the object of faith, this is nothing other than the first truth. For the faith of which we are speaking does not assent to anything except on the ground that it is revealed by God. The ground upon which faith stands is therefore divine truth. But if we are thinking in a concrete way about the things to which faith gives its assent, these include not only God himself, but many other things. Such other things, however, are held in faith only because they relate to God in some way, that is to say, in so far as certain effects of the Godhead are an aid to man in his endeavour after the enjoyment of God. Thus the object of faith is still in a sense the first truth, since nothing is an object of faith unless it relates to God; just as the object of medicine is health, since nothing is considered to be medicine unless it relates to health.

On the first point: the things which pertain to the humanity of Christ, or to the sacraments of the Church, or to any creature whatsoever, are included in the object of faith in so far as we are directed by them to God, and in so far as we assent to them on account of the divine truth.

The second point, concerning all the matters related in sacred Scripture, is answered in the same way.

On the third point: by charity we love our neighbour for God's sake. Hence the object of charity is properly God, as we shall affirm later.

ARTICLE TWO

WHETHER THE OBJECT OF FAITH IS SOMETHING COMPLEX, IN THE FORM OF A PROPOSITION

We proceed to the second article thus:

1. It seems that the object of faith is not something complex, in the form of a proposition. For the object of faith is the first truth, as was maintained in the first article, and the first truth is simple. Hence the object of faith is not something complex.

2. Again, the exposition of the faith is contained in the symbol.[1] Now the symbol does not affirm the propositions, but the reality. For it does not say that God is almighty, but declares: "I believe in God . . . Almighty." Thus the object of faith is not the proposition, but the reality.

3. Again, faith is followed by vision, according to I Cor. 13:12: "For now we see through a glass, darkly; but then face to face: now I know in part; but then shall I know even as also I am known." Now the heavenly

---

[1] I.e., the Nicene Creed.

vision is of what is simple, since it is the vision of the divine essence itself. Hence the faith of the wayfarer is likewise in what is simple.

On the other hand: faith is a mean between knowledge and opinion. Now a mean and its extremes belong to the same genus, and since knowledge and opinion are about propositions, it seems that faith is also about propositions. But if faith is about propositions, the object of faith is something complex.

I answer: things known are in the knower according to the manner in which he knows them. Now the characteristic way in which the human intellect knows truth is by means of the combination and separation of ideas, as we said in Pt. I, Q. 85, Art. 5. It is therefore with a measure of complexity that the human intellect knows things which are in themselves simple; just as, conversely, the divine intellect knows without complexity things which are in themselves complex.

The object of faith may then be understood in two ways. If we are referring to the thing itself which is believed, the object of faith is something simple, namely, the thing itself in which we have faith. But from the point of view of the believer the object of faith is something complex, in the form of a proposition. Both opinions have been held true by the ancients, and both are true conditionally.

On the first point: this reasoning argues from the object of faith considered as the thing itself which is believed.

On the second point: it is clear from the very manner of speaking that the things in which faith believes are affirmed in the symbol, in so far as the act of the believer terminates in them. Now the act of the believer terminates in the reality, not in the proposition. For we formulate propositions only in order to know things by means of them, in faith no less than in science.

On the third point: the heavenly vision will be the vision of the first truth as it is in itself, according to I John 3:2: "but we know that, when he shall appear, we shall be like him; for we shall see him as he is." This vision will not then be by way of propositions, but by simple understanding. By faith, on the other hand, we do not apprehend the first truth as it is in itself. We cannot therefore argue about faith in the same way.

Question Two

ARTICLE ONE

WHETHER TO BELIEVE IS TO THINK WITH ASSENT

We proceed to the first article thus:

1. It seems that to believe is not to think with assent. For "to think" implies inquiry of some kind, the word being a contraction of "to consider together" (cogitare = coagitare = simul agitare). But the

Damascene says that "faith is assent without inquiry" (4 *De Fid. Orth.* I). It follows that the act of faith does not involve thinking.

2. Again, it will be shown in Q. 4, Art. 2, that faith belongs to reason. But it was said in Pt. I, Q. 78, Art. 4, that thinking is an act of the cogitative power, which belongs to the sensitive part of the soul.[1] It follows that faith does not involve thinking.

3. Again, belief is an act of the intellect, since the object of belief is the true. Now it was said in 12ae, Q. 15, Art. I, ad. 3 that assent is not an act of the intellect, but an act of the will, just as consent is an act of the will. It follows that to believe is not to think with assent.

On the other hand: "to believe" is thus defined by Augustine. (*De Praed. Sanct.* 2.)

I answer: "to think" can mean three things. Firstly, it means any deliberative intellectual act in general. This is what Augustine has in mind in 14 *De Trin.* 7, when he says: "what I now call understanding is that whereby we understand when we think." Secondly, and more precisely, it means the kind of intellectual deliberation which involves a degree of questioning, and which occurs before the intellect reaches perfection through the certainty of vision. This is what Augustine has in mind in 15 *De Trin.* 16, where he says: "The Son of God is not called the Thought of God, but the Word of God. When our thought has reached what we know and become formed by it, it becomes our word. The Word of God should therefore be conceived as without the thought of God, since it contains nothing which remains to be formed, and which could be unformed." In this sense, thought properly means the movement of a soul which deliberates, and which is not yet perfected by a full vision of the truth. But since such movement may be either deliberation about universal meanings, which are the concern of the intellect, or deliberation about particular meanings, which are the concern of the sensitive part of the soul, the word "to think" is used in this second sense to mean the intellectual act of deliberation, and in yet a third sense to mean an act of the cogitative power.

Now if "to think" is understood in the first or general sense, "to think with assent" does not express the whole meaning of "to believe." For a man thinks in this way even about what he knows and understands in science, and also gives his assent. But if it is understood in the second sense, then by means of this expression we understand the whole nature of the act of belief. There are some acts of the intellect, such as those whereby one contemplates what one knows and understands in science, in which assent is given with confidence, without any

---

[1]The sensitive power operates through a corporeal organ, through which it perceives things which are actually present. The cogitative power perceives and preserves the "intention" or practical significance of particular things present or absent, by means of collating ideas. It is also called the "particular reason."

deliberation. There are also others in which thought is unformed, and in which there is no firm assent. One may incline to neither alternative, as one who doubts. Or one may incline to the one rather than to the other on the strength of slight evidence, as does one who suspects. Or, again, one may choose one alternative with misgivings about the other, as does one who holds an opinion. Now the act which is "to believe" holds firmly to the one alternative. In this respect, belief is similar to science and understanding. Yet its thought is not perfected by clear vision, and in this respect belief is similar to doubt, suspicion, and opinion. To think with assent is thus the property of one who believes, and distinguishes the act of "belief" from all other acts of the intellect which are concerned with truth or falsity.

On the first point: faith does not make use of inquiry by natural reason to demonstrate what it believes. But it does inquire into the evidence by which a man is induced to believe, for example, into the circumstance that such things are spoken by God and confirmed by miracles.

On the second point: as we have said above, the word "to think" is here understood as it applies to the intellect, not as meaning an act of the cogitative power.

On the third point: the intellect of the believer is determined by the will, not by reason. Hence assent is here understood to mean the act of the intellect as determined by the will.

ARTICLE NINE

WHETHER TO BELIEVE IS MERITORIOUS

We proceed to the ninth article thus:

1. It seems that to believe is not meritorious. It was said in 12ae, Q. 114, Art. 4, that the principle of merit is charity. Now faith is a preamble to charity, just as nature is a preamble. But a natural action is not meritorious, since we merit nothing by our natural powers. Neither then is the act of faith meritorious.

2. Again, belief is a mean between opinion and science, or the study of what is known scientifically. Now the study of science is not meritorious, and neither is opinion. Neither, then, is it meritorious to believe.

3. Again, he who assents to anything by faith either has a sufficient reason for believing, or does not. If he has a sufficient reason, his assent is no credit to him, since he is not then free to believe or not to believe. If he does not have a sufficient reason, he believes lightly, in the manner referred to in Ecclesiasticus 19:4: "he that believes in haste is light in heart" — which does not appear to be meritorious. Hence in no wise is it meritorious to believe.

On the other hand: it is said in Heb. 11:33: "Who through

faith . . . obtained promises." Now this would not have been, had they not merited by believing. To believe is therefore meritorious.

I answer: as we said in 12ae, Q. 114, Arts. 3 and 4, our actions are meritorious in so far as they proceed from the free will as moved by God through grace. It follows that any human action which depends on the free will can be meritorious, provided that it is related to God. Now "to believe" is the act of the intellect as it assents to divine truth at the command of the will as moved by God through grace. It is therefore an act commanded by the free will as ordered to God. The act of faith can therefore be meritorious.

On the first point: nature is related to charity, which is the principle by which we merit, as matter is related to its form. Faith, on the other hand, is related to charity as a disposition is related to the ultimate form which it precedes. Now it is obvious that a subject, or matter, cannot act except by the power of its form. Neither can a preceding disposition act before its form is received. Once the form has been received, however, a subject and a preceding disposition alike act by the power of the form, and the form is the main principle of action. The heat of a fire, for example, acts by the power of its substantial form. Thus without charity, neither nature nor faith can produce a meritorious action. But when charity supervenes, the act of faith becomes meritorious through charity, just as a natural action thereby becomes meritorious, including a natural action of the free will.

On the second point: two things may be considered in regard to science, namely, the assent of the knower to what he knows, and his study of it. The assent of one who knows scientifically does not depend on his free will, since the cogency of demonstration compels him to give it. Hence in science, assent is not meritorious. The actual study of a scientific matter, however, does depend on his free will, since it lies within his power whether to study or not to study. The study of science can therefore be meritorious if it is referred to the end of charity, that is, to the honour of God, or to the service of one's neighbour. In faith, on the other hand, both assent and practice depend on the free will. The act of faith can therefore be meritorious in both respects. Opinion does not involve firm assent. It is indeed feeble and infirm, as the philosopher says in Post. An., text 44. Hence it does not appear to proceed from a complete volition, nor, therefore, to have much of the nature of merit in respect of its assent, although it may be meritorious in respect of actual study.

On the third point: he who believes has a sufficient reason for believing. He is induced to believe by the authority of divine teaching confirmed by miracles, and what is more, by the inward prompting of divine invitation. Hence he does not believe lightly. But he does not have a reason such as would suffice for scientific knowledge. Thus the character of merit is not taken away.

Question Four

ARTICLE THREE

WHETHER CHARITY IS THE FORM OF FAITH

We proceed to the third article thus:

1. It seems that charity is not the form of faith. The species of each thing is derived from its own form. One thing cannot then be the form of another, if the two are distinguished as separate species of one genus. Now in I Cor., ch. 13, faith and charity are distinguished as separate species of virtue. Hence charity is not the form of faith.

2. Again, a form and that of which it is the form are in the same thing, since that which arises out of them is one absolutely. But faith is in the intellect, whereas charity is in the will. Hence charity is not the form of faith.

3. Again, the form of a thing is the principle of it. Now in so far as belief is due to the will, its principle would seem to be obedience rather than charity, according to Rom. 1:5: "for obedience to the faith among all nations." Obedience is therefore the form of faith, rather than charity.

On the other hand: everything works by means of its form. Now faith worketh by love. The love of charity is therefore the form of faith.

I answer: as we explained in 12ae, Q. I, Art. 3, and Q.17, Art. 6, voluntary acts take their species from the object to which the will is directed as an end. Now things derive their species from the manner in which a form exists in natural things. The form of any voluntary act is therefore in a sense the end to which it is directed, both because it takes its species from this end, and because its manner of action is bound to correspond to the end proportionately. It is also clear from what we said in the first article that the object of will which the act of faith seeks as an end is the good, and that this good is the divine good, which is the proper object of charity. Charity is accordingly said to be the form of faith, because it is through charity that the act of faith is made perfect, and brought to its form.

On the first point: charity is said to be the form of faith in the sense that it brings the act of faith to its form. There is nothing to prevent one act being brought to its form by different habits, and consequently classified under different species when human actions in general are being discussed, as we said in 12ae, Q. 18, Arts. 6, 7; Q. 61, Art. 2.

On the second point: this objection argues from the intrinsic form. Charity is not the intrinsic form of faith, but that which brings the act of faith to its form, as we have said.

On the third point: even obedience itself, like hope and any other virtue which can precede the act of faith, is brought to its true form by charity, as we shall explain in Q. 23, Art. 8. Charity is named as the form of faith for this reason.

ARTICLE FIVE

WHETHER FAITH IS A VIRTUE

We proceed to the fifth article thus:

1. It seems that faith is not a virtue. Virtue is "that which makes its subject good," as the philosopher says in 2 *Ethics* 6, and is therefore directed to the good, whereas faith is directed to the true. It follows that faith is not a virtue.

2. Again, an infused virtue is more perfect than an acquired virtue. Now as the philosopher says in 6 *Ethics* 3, faith is not regarded as one of the acquired intellectual virtues, owing to its imperfection. Much less, then, can it be regarded as an infused virtue.

3. Again, it was said in the preceding article that formed and unformed faith are of the same species. But unformed faith is not a virtue, since it has no connection with other virtues. Hence neither is formed faith a virtue.

4. Again, the freely given graces are distinct from the virtues, and so is the fruit of the Spirit. Now in I Cor. 12:9 faith is included among the freely given graces, and in Gal. 5:22 it is included in the fruit of the Spirit. Hence faith is not a virtue.

On the other hand: a man is made just by means of the virtues. For "justice is the whole of virtue," as it is said in 5 *Ethics* 1. But he is justified by faith, according to Rom. 5:I: "Therefore being justified by faith, we have peace with God. . . ." Hence faith is a virtue.

I answer: it is plain from what we said in 12ae, Q. 55, Arts. 3 and 4, that human virtue is that which makes human actions good. Any habit which is invariably the principle of a good action may therefore be called a human virtue. Now formed faith is such a habit. Two things are necessary, however, if the act of belief is to be perfect, since it is the act wherein the intellect finally gives its assent at the command of the will. The intellect must be infallibly directed to its object, which is the truth, and the will must be infallibly directed to the ultimate end, for the sake of which assent is finally given. Now both of these conditions are fulfilled in the act of formed faith. It is of the very nature of faith that the intellect should be in the way of truth at all times, since faith cannot believe what is false, as we said in Q. 1, Art. 3. The will of the soul is likewise infallibly directed to the ultimate good by charity, which brings faith to its form. Formed faith is therefore a virtue.

Unformed faith, on the other hand, is not a virtue, since even though it should have the perfection which is necessary on the part of the intellect, it would still lack the perfection which is necessary on the part of the will; just as we said that temperance would not be a virtue if prudence were wanting in the reason, even though there should be temperance in the concupiscible element. (12ae, Q. 58, Art. 4; Q. 55, Art. 1.) An act of temperance requires an act of reason as well as an act of the concupiscible element. So likewise does the act of faith require an act of the will as well as an act of the intellect.

On the first point: "the true" is itself the good of the intellect, since it is the perfection of the intellect. Faith is consequently directed to the good in so far as the intellect is directed to truth by faith. Faith is further directed to the good in so far as it is brought to its form by charity, since the good is then the object of the will.

On the second point: the philosopher is speaking of the faith which trusts in human reason when it accepts a conclusion which does not necessarily follow, and which may be false. Faith of this kind is not a virtue. We are speaking of the faith which trusts in divine truth, which is infallible, and cannot be false. This faith can, therefore, be a virtue.

On the third point: formed and unformed faith do not differ in species as belonging to different species. They differ, however, as the perfect and the imperfect within the same species. Thus unformed faith lacks the perfect nature of a virtue because it is imperfect, virtue being a kind of perfection, as is said in 7 *Physics*, texts 17 and 18.

On the fourth point: some say that the faith included among the freely given graces is unformed faith. But this is not well said. For the graces mentioned are not common to all members of the Church, wherefore the apostle says: "there are diversities of gifts," and again, "to one is given this, to another that." Unformed faith, on the other hand, is common to all members of the Church. Lack of form is not a part of its substance, whereas a gift is gratuitous by its substance. We must therefore say that in this passage faith stands for some excellence of faith, such as constancy, as the gloss says, or the "word of faith." Faith is also included in the fruit of the Spirit, because it rejoices in its own act, on account of its certainty. As numbered with the fruits in Gal., ch. 5, faith is accordingly explained as "certainty of things not seen."

Question Five

ARTICLE TWO

WHETHER DEVILS HAVE FAITH

We proceed to the second article thus:

1. It seems that devils do not have faith. For Augustine says that "faith depends on the will of those who believe" (*De Praed. Sanct.* 5). Now the will whereby one wills to believe in God is good. But there is no deliberate good will in devils. Hence it seems that devils do not have faith.

2. Again, faith is a gift of grace, according to Eph. 2:8: "For by grace ye are saved through faith . . . it is the gift of God." Now the gloss on Hosea 3:1, "who look to other gods, and love flagons of wine," says that

the devils forfeited the gift of grace by their sin. It follows that faith did not remain in them after their sin.

3. Again, unbelief seems to be one of the more serious sins, according to what Augustine says *(Tract. 9 in Joan.)* on John 15:22: "If I had not come and spoken unto them, they had not had sin: but now they have no cloak for their sin." Now some men are guilty of the sin of unbelief. Their sin would then be worse than that of devils, if devils had faith. But this is impossible. Therefore devils do not have faith.

On the other hand: it is said in James 2:19: "the devils also believe, and tremble."

I answer: as we said in Q. 1, Art. 2, and Q. 2, Art. 1, the intellect of the believer assents to what he believes neither because he sees the thing as it is in itself, nor because he understands it through its first principles seen as they are in themselves, but because his will moves his intellect to give its assent. Now there are two ways in which the will may move the intellect to give its assent. In the first place, the will may be directed to the good, in which case belief is a praiseworthy act. Secondly, the intellect may be sufficiently convinced to judge that what is said ought to be believed, without being convinced by any evidence of the thing itself. Thus if a prophet should predict something as by the word of God, and if he should also give a sign by raising one who was dead, the intellect of one who saw would be convinced by the sign, and he would know assuredly that this was spoken by God who does not lie, even though what was predicted was not apparent. The character of faith would then remain.

Hence we must say that the faith of those who believe in Christ is praised as being of the first kind. Devils, on the other hand, do not have faith of this kind, but only of the second kind. For they see many unmistakable signs by which they know that the doctrine of the Church is given by God, although they do not see the things themselves which the Church teaches, for example, that God is Three and also One, and the like.

On the first point: the faith of devils is such as the evidence of signs compels. Their belief is therefore no credit to their will.

On the second point: even though it should be unformed, faith which is the gift of grace inclines a man to believe out of regard for what is good. The faith of devils is therefore not the gift of grace. Rather are they compelled to believe by what they perceive by their natural intellect.

On the third point: devils are displeased by the very obviousness of the signs which compel them to believe. Hence the evil in them is not diminished by their belief.

MARTIN LUTHER

The Freedom of a Christian*

Many people have considered Christian faith an easy thing, and not a few have given it a place among the virtues. They do this because they have not experienced it and have never tasted the great strength there is in faith. It is impossible to write well about it or to understand what has been written about it unless one has at one time or another experienced the courage which faith gives a man when trials oppress him. But he who has had even a faint taste of it can never write, speak, meditate, or hear enough concerning it. It is a living "spring of water welling up to eternal life," as Christ calls it in John 4 [:14].

As for me, although I have no wealth of faith to boast of and know how scant my supply is, I nevertheless hope that I have attained to a little faith, even though I have been assailed by great and various temptations; and I hope that I can discuss it, if not more elegantly, certainly more to the point, than those literalists and subtile disputants have previously done, who have not even understood what they have written.

To make the way smoother for the unlearned—for only them do I serve—I shall set down the following two propositions concerning the freedom and the bondage of the spirit:

A Christian is a perfectly free lord of all, subject to none.

A Christian is a perfectly dutiful servant of all, subject to all.

*From "The Freedom of a Christian," trans. W.A. Lambert, rev. Harold J. Grimm; in *Luther's Works*, Volume 31. Copyright © 1957, Muhlenberg Press, pp. 343–353 and 366–368. Reprinted by permission of Fortress Press, Philadelphia.

These two theses seem to contradict each other. If, however, they should be found to fit together they would serve our purpose beautifully. Both are Paul's own statements, who says in I Cor. 9 [:19], "For though I am free from all men, I have made myself a slave to all," and in Rom. 13 [:8], "Owe no one anything, except to love one another." Love by its very nature is ready to serve and be subject to him who is loved. So Christ, although he was Lord of all, was "born of woman, born under the law" [Gal. 4:4], and therefore was at the same time a free man and a servant, "in the form of God" and "of a servant" [Phil. 2:6–7].

Let us start, however, with something more remote from our subject, but more obvious. Man has a twofold nature, a spiritual and a bodily one. According to the spiritual nature, which men refer to as the soul, he is called a spiritual, inner, or new man. According to the bodily nature, which men refer to as flesh, he is called a carnal, outward, or old man, of whom the Apostle writes in II Cor. 4 [:16], "Though our outer nature is wasting away, our inner nature is being renewed every day." Because of this diversity of nature the Scriptures assert contradictory things concerning the same man, since these two men in the same man contradict each other, "for the desires of the flesh are against the Spirit, and the desires of the Spirit are against the flesh," according to Gal. 5 [:17].

First, let us consider the inner man to see how a righteous, free, and pious Christian, that is, a spiritual, new, and inner man, becomes what he is. It is evident that no external thing has any influence in producing Christian righteousness or freedom, or in producing unrighteousness or servitude. A simple argument will furnish the proof of this statement. What can it profit the soul if the body is well, free, and active, and eats, drinks, and does as it pleases? For in these respects even the most godless slaves of vice may prosper. On the other hand, how will poor health or imprisonment or hunger or thirst or any other external misfortune harm the soul? Even the most godly men, and those who are free because of clear consciences, are afflicted with these things. None of these things touch either the freedom or the servitude of the soul. It does not help the soul if the body is adorned with the sacred robes of priests or dwells in sacred places or is occupied with sacred duties or prays, fasts, abstains from certain kinds of food, or does any work that can be done by the body and in the body. The righteousness and the freedom of the soul require something far different since the things which have been mentioned could be done by any wicked person. Such works produce nothing but hypocrites. On the other hand, it will not harm the soul if the body is clothed in secular dress, dwells in unconsecrated places, eats and drinks as others do, does not pray aloud, and neglects to do all the above-mentioned things which hypocrites can do.

Furthermore, to put aside all kinds of works, even contemplation, mediation, and all that the soul can do, does not help. One thing, and only one thing, is necessary for Christian life, righteousness, and freedom. That one thing is the most holy Word of God, the gospel of Christ, as Christ says, John 11 [:25], "I am the resurrection and the life; he who believes in me, though he die, yet shall he live"; and John 8 [:36], "So if the Son makes you free, you will be free indeed"; and Matt 4 [:4], "Man shall not live by bread alone, but by every word that proceeds from the mouth of God." Let us then consider it certain and firmly established that the soul can do without anything except the Word of God and that where the Word of God is missing there is no help at all for the soul. If it has the Word of God it is rich and lacks nothing since it is the Word of life, truth, light, peace, righteousness, salvation, joy, liberty, wisdom, power, grace, glory, and of every incalculable blessing. This is why the prophet in the entire Psalm [119] and in many other places yearns and sighs for the Word of God and uses so many names to describe it.

On the other hand, there is no more terrible disaster with which the wrath of God can afflict men than a famine of the hearing of his Word, as he says in Amos [8:11]. Likewise there is no greater mercy than when he sends forth his Word, as we read in Psalm 107 [:20]: "He sent forth his word, and healed them, and delivered them from destruction." Nor was Christ sent into the world for any other ministry except that of the Word. Moreover, the entire spiritual estate — all the apostles, bishops, and priests — has been called and instituted only for the ministry of the Word.

You may ask, "What then is the Word of God, and how shall it be used, since there are so many words of God?" I answer: The Apostle explains this in Romans 1. The Word is the gospel of God concerning his Son, who was made flesh, suffered, rose from the dead, and was glorified through the Spirit who sanctifies. To preach Christ means to feed the soul, make it righteous, set it free, and save it, provided it believes the preaching. Faith alone is the saving and efficacious use of the Word of God, according to Rom. 10 [:9]: "If you confess with your lips that Jesus is Lord and believe in your heart that God raised him from the dead, you will be saved." Furthermore, "Christ is the end of the law, that every one who has faith may be justified" [Rom. 10:4]. Again, in Rom. 1 [:17], "He who through faith is righteous shall live." The Word of God cannot be received and cherished by any works whatever but only by faith. Therefore it is clear that, as the soul needs only the Word of God for its life and righteousness, so it is justified by faith alone and not any works; for if it could be justified by anything else, it would not need the Word, and consequently it would not need faith.

This faith cannot exist in connection with works — that is to say, if you at the same time claim to be justified by works, whatever their character — for that would be the same as "limping with two different opinions" [I Kings 18:21], as worshiping Baal and kissing one's own hand [Job 31:27–28], which, as Job says, is a very great iniquity. Therefore the moment you begin to have faith you learn that all things in you are altogether blameworthy, sinful, and damnable, as the Apostle says in Rom. 3 [:23], "Since all have sinned and fall short of the glory of God," and, "None is righteous, no, not one; . . . all have turned aside, together they have gone wrong" (Rom. 3:10–12). When you have learned this you will know that you need Christ, who suffered and rose again for you so that, if you believe in him, you may through this faith become a new man in so far as your sins are forgiven and you are justified by the merits of another, namely, of Christ alone.

Since, therefore, this faith can rule only in the inner man, as Rom. 10 [:10] says, "For man believes with his heart and so is justified," and since faith alone justifies, it is clear that the inner man cannot be justified, freed, or saved by any outer work or action at all, and that these works, whatever their character, have nothing to do with this inner man. On the other hand, only ungodliness and unbelief of heart, and no outer work, make him guilty and a damnable servant of sin. Wherefore it ought to be the first concern of every Christian to lay aside all confidence in works and increasingly to strengthen faith alone and through faith to grow in the knowledge, not of works, but of Christ Jesus, who suffered and rose for him, as Peter teaches in the last chapter of his first Epistle (I Pet. 5:10). No other work makes a Christian. Thus when the Jews asked Christ, as related in John 6 [:28], what they must do "to be doing the work of God," he brushed aside the multitude of works which he saw they did in great profusion and suggested one work, saying, "This is the work of God, that you believe in him whom he has sent" [John 6:29]; "for on him has God the Father set his seal" [John 6:27].

Therefore true faith in Christ is a treasure beyond comparison which brings with it complete salvation and saves man from every evil, as Christ says in the last chapter of Mark [16:16]: "He who believes and is baptized will be saved; but he who does not believe will be condemned." Isaiah contemplated this treasure and foretold it in chapter 10: "The Lord will make a small and consuming word upon the land, and it will overflow with righteousness" [Cf. Isa. 10:22]. This is as though he said, "Faith, which is a small and perfect fulfillment of the law, will fill believers with so great a righteousness that they will need nothing more to become righteous." So Paul says, Rom. 10 [:10], "For man believes with his heart and so is justified."

Should you ask how it happens that faith alone justifies and offers us such a treasure of great benefits without works in view of the fact that so many works, ceremonies, and laws are prescribed in the Scriptures, I answer: First of all, remember what has been said, namely, that faith alone, without works, justifies, frees, and saves; we shall make this clearer later on. Here we must point out that the entire Scripture of

God is divided into two parts: commandments and promises. Although the commandments teach things that are good, the things taught are not done as soon as they are taught, for the commandments show us what we ought to do but do not give us the power to do it. They are intended to teach man to know himself, that through them he may recognize his inability to do good and may despair of his own ability. That is why they are called the Old Testament and constitute the Old Testament. For example, the commandment, "You shall not covet" [Exod. 20:17], is a command which proves us all to be sinners, for no one can avoid coveting no matter how much he may struggle against it. Therefore, in order not to covet and to fulfil the commandment, a man is compelled to despair of himself, to seek the help which he does not find in himself elsewhere and from someone else, as stated in Hosea [13:9]: "Destruction is your own, O Israel: your help is only in me." As we fare with respect to one commandment, so we fare with all, for it is equally impossible for us to keep any one of them.

Now when a man has learned through the commandments to recognize his helplessness and is distressed about how he might satisfy the law — since the law must be fulfilled so that not a jot or tittle shall be lost, otherwise man will be condemned without hope — then, being truly humbled and reduced to nothing in his own eyes, he finds in himself nothing whereby he may be justified and saved. Here the second part of Scripture comes to our aid, namely, the promises of God which declare the glory of God, saying, "If you wish to fulfil the law and not covet, as the law demands, come, believe in Christ in whom grace, righteousness, peace, liberty, and all things are promised you. If you believe, you shall have all things; if you do not believe, you shall lack all things." That which is impossible for you to accomplish by trying to fulfil all the works of the law — many and useless as they all are — you will accomplish quickly and easily through faith. God our Father has made all things depend on faith so that whoever has faith will have everything, and whoever does not have faith will have nothing. "For God has consigned all men to disobedience, that he may have mercy upon all," as it is stated in Rom. 11 [:32]. Thus the promises of God give what the commandments of God demand and fulfil what the law prescribes so that all things may be God's alone, both the commandments and the fulfilling of the commandments. He alone commands, he alone fulfils. Therefore the promises of God belong to the New Testament. Indeed, they are the New Testament.

Since these promises of God are holy, true, righteous, free, and peaceful words, full of goodness, the soul which clings to them with a firm faith will be so closely united with them and altogether absorbed by them that it not only will share in all their power but will be saturated and intoxicated by them. If a touch of Christ healed, how much more will this most tender spiritual touch, this absorbing of the

Word, communicate to the soul all things that belong to the Word. This, then, is how through faith alone without works the soul is justified by the Word of God, sanctified, made true, peaceful, and free, filled with every blessing and truly made a child of God, as John 1 [:12] says: "But to all who . . . believed in his name, he gave power to become children of God."

From what has been said it is easy to see from what source faith derives such great power and why a good work or all good works together cannot equal it. No good work can rely upon the Word of God or live in the soul, for faith alone and the Word of God rule in the soul. Just as the heated iron glows like fire because of the union of fire with it, so the Word imparts its qualities to the soul. It is clear, then, that a Christian has all that he needs in faith and needs no works to justify him; and if he has no need of works, he has no need of the law; and if he has no need of the law, surely he is free from the law. It is true that "the law is not laid down for the just" [I Tim. 1:9]. This is that Christian liberty, our faith, which does not induce us to live in idleness or wickedness but makes the law and works unnecessary for any man's righteousness and salvation.

This is the first power of faith. Let us now examine also the second. It is a further function of faith that it honors him whom it trusts with the most reverent and highest regard since it considers him truthful and trustworthy. There is no other honor equal to the estimate of truthfulness and righteousness with which we honor him whom we trust. Could we ascribe to a man anything greater than truthfulness and righteousness and perfect goodness? On the other hand, there is no way in which we can show greater contempt for a man than to regard him as false and wicked and to be suspicious of him, as we do when we do not trust him. So when the soul firmly trusts God's promises, it regards him as truthful and righteous. Nothing more excellent than this can be ascribed to God. The very highest worship of God is this that we ascribe to him truthfulness, righteousness, and whatever else should be ascribed to one who is trusted. When this is done, the soul consents to his will. Then it hallows his name and allows itself to be treated according to God's good pleasure for, clinging to God's promises, it does not doubt that he who is true, just, and wise will do, dispose, and provide all things well.

Is not such a soul most obedient to God in all things by this faith? What commandment is there that such obedience has not completely fulfilled? What more complete fulfilment is there than obedience in all things? This obedience, however, is not rendered by works, but by faith alone. On the other hand, what greater rebellion against God, what greater wickedness, what greater contempt of God is there than not believing his promise? For what is this but to make God a liar or to doubt that he is truthful? — that is, to ascribe truthfulness to one's self but lying and vanity to God? Does not a man who does this deny God and set himself up as an idol in his heart? Then of what good are works done in such wickedness, even if they were the works of angels and apostles? Therefore God has rightly included all things, not under anger or lust, but under unbelief, so that they who imagine that they are fulfilling the law by doing the works of chastity and mercy required by the law (the civil and human virtues) might not be saved. They are included under the sin of unbelief and must either seek mercy or be justly condemned.

When, however, God sees that we consider him truthful and by the faith of our heart pay him the great honor which is due him, he does us that great honor of considering us truthful and righteous for the sake of our faith. Faith works truth and righteousness by giving God what belongs to him. Therefore God in turn glorifies our righteousness. It is true and just that God is truthful and just, and to consider and confess him to be so is the same as being truthful and just. Accordingly he says in I Sam. 2 [:30], "Those who honor me I will honor, and those who despise me shall be lightly esteemed." So Paul says in Rom. 4 [:3] that Abraham's faith "was reckoned to him as righteousness" because by it he gave glory most perfectly to God, and that for the same reason our faith shall be reckoned to us as righteousness if we believe.

The third incomparable benefit of faith is that it unites the soul with Christ as a bride is united with her bridegroom. By this mystery, as the Apostle teaches, Christ and the soul become one flesh [Eph. 5:31–32]. And if they are one flesh and there is between them a true marriage — indeed the most perfect of all marriages, since human marriages are but poor examples of this one true marriage — it follows that everything they have they hold in common, the good as well as the evil. Accordingly the believing soul can boast of and glory in whatever Christ has as though it were its own, and whatever the soul has Christ claims as his own. Let us compare these and we shall see inestimable benefits. Christ is full of grace, life, and salvation. The soul is full of sins, death, and damnation. Now let faith come between them and sins, death, and damnation will be Christ's, while grace, life, and salvation will be the soul's; for if Christ is a bridegroom, he must take upon himself the things which are his bride's and bestow upon her the things that are his. If he gives her his body and very self, how shall he not give her all that is his? And if he takes the body of the bride, how shall he not take all that is hers?

Here we have a most pleasing vision not only of communion but of a blessed struggle and victory and salvation and redemption. Christ is God and man in one person. He has neither sinned nor died, and is not condemned, and he cannot sin, die, or be condemned; his righteousness, life, and salvation are unconquerable, eternal, omnipotent. By the wedding ring of faith he shares in the sins, death, and pains of hell

which are his bride's. As a matter of fact, he makes them his own and
acts as if they were his own and as if he himself had sinned; he suffered,
died, and descended into hell that he might overcome them all. Now
since it was such a one who did all this, and death and hell could not
swallow him up, these were necessarily swallowed up by him in a
mighty duel; for his righteousness is greater than the sins of all men, his
life stronger than death, his salvation more invincible than hell. Thus
the believing soul by means of the pledge of its faith is free in Christ, its
bridegroom, free from all sins, secure against death and hell, and is
endowed with the eternal righteousness, life, and salvation of Christ its
bridegroom. So he takes to himself a glorious bride, "without spot or
wrinkle, cleansing her by the washing of water with the word" [Cf.
Eph. 5:26–27] of life, that is, by faith in the Word of life, righteousness, and salvation. In this way he marries her in faith, steadfast love,
and in mercies, righteousness, and justice, as Hos. 2 [:19–20] says.

Who then can fully appreciate what this royal marriage means? Who
can understand the riches of the glory of this grace? Here this rich and
divine bridegroom Christ marries this poor, wicked harlot, redeems her
from all her evil, and adorns her with all his goodness. Her sins cannot
now destroy her, since they are laid upon Christ and swallowed up by
him. And she has that righteousness in Christ, her husband, of which
she may boast as of her own and which she can confidently display
alongside her sins in the face of death and hell and say, "If I have
sinned, yet my Christ, in whom I believe, has not sinned, and all his is
mine and all mine is his," as the bride in the Song of Solomon [2:16]
says, "My beloved is mine and I am his." This is what Paul means when
he says in I Cor. 15 [:57], "Thanks be to God, who gives us the victory
through our Lord Jesus Christ," that is, the victory over sin and death,
as he also says there, "The sting of death is sin, and the power of sin is
the law" [I Cor. 15:56].

From this you once more see that much is ascribed to faith, namely,
that it alone can fulfil the law and justify without works. You see that
the First Commandment, which says, "You shall worship one God," is
fulfilled by faith alone. Though you were nothing but good works from
the soles of your feet to the crown of your head, you would still not be
righteous or worship God or fulfil the First Commandment, since God
cannot be worshiped unless you ascribe to him the glory of truthfulness
and all goodness which is due him. This cannot be done by works but
only by the faith of the heart. Not by the doing of works but by
believing do we glorify God and acknowledge that he is truthful.
Therefore faith alone is the righteousness of a Christian and the fulfilling of all the commandments, for he who fulfils the First Commandment has no difficulty in fulfilling all the rest.

So a Christian, like Christ his head, is filled and made rich by faith
and should be content with this form of God which he has obtained by

faith; only, as I have said, he should increase this faith until it is made perfect. For this faith is his life, his righteousness, and his salvation: it saves him and makes him acceptable, and bestows upon him all things that are Christ's, as has been said above, and as Paul asserts in Gal. 2 [:20] when he says, "And the life I now live in the flesh I live by faith in the Son of God." Although the Christian is thus free from all works, he ought in this liberty to empty himself, take upon himself the form of a servant, be made in the likeness of men, be found in human form, and to serve, help, and in every way deal with his neighbor as he sees that God through Christ has dealt and still deals with him. This he should do freely, having regard for nothing but divine approval.

He ought to think: "Although I am an unworthy and condemned man, my God has given me in Christ all the riches of righteousness and salvation without any merit on my part, out of pure, free mercy, so that from now on I need nothing except faith which believes that this is true. Why should I not therefore freely, joyfully, with all my heart, and with an eager will do all things which I know are pleasing and acceptable to such a Father who has overwhelmed me with his inestimable riches? I will therefore give myself as a Christ to my neighbor, just as Christ offered himself to me; I will do nothing in this life except what I see is necessary, profitable, and salutary to my neighbor, since through faith I have an abundance of all good things in Christ."

Behold, from faith thus flow forth love and joy in the Lord, and from love a joyful, willing, and free mind that serves one's neighbor willingly and takes no account of gratitude or ingratitude, of praise or blame, of gain or loss. For a man does not serve that he may put men under obligations. He does not distinguish between friends and enemies or anticipate their thankfulness or unthankfulness, but he most freely and most willingly spends himself and all that he has, whether he wastes all on the thankless or whether he gains a reward. As his Father does, distributing all things to all men richly and freely, making "his sun rise on the evil and on the good" [Matt. 5:45], so also the son does all things and suffers all things with that freely bestowing joy which is his delight when through Christ he sees it in God, the dispenser of such great benefits.

Therefore, if we recognize the great and precious things which are given us, as Paul says [Rom. 5:5], our hearts will be filled by the Holy Spirit with the love which makes us free, joyful, almighty workers and conquerors over all tribulations, servants of our neighbors, and yet lords of all. For those who do not recognize the gifts bestowed upon them through Christ, however, Christ has been born in vain; they go their way with their works and shall never come to taste or feel those things. Just as our neighbor is in need and lacks that in which we abound, so we were in need before God and lacked his mercy. Hence, as our heavenly Father has in Christ freely come to our aid, we also ought freely to help our neighbor through our body and its works, and each one should become as it were a Christ to the other that we may be Christs to one another and Christ may be the same in all, that is, that we may be truly Christians.

Who then can comprehend the riches and the glory of the Christian life? It can do all things and has all things and lacks nothing. It is lord over sin, death, and hell, and yet at the same time it serves, ministers to, and benefits all men. But alas in our day this life is unknown throughout the world; it is neither preached about nor sought after; we are altogether ignorant of our own name and do not know why we are Christians or bear the name of Christians. Surely we are named after Christ, not because he is absent from us, but because he dwells in us, that is, because we believe in him and are Christs one to another and do to our neighbors as Christ does to us. But in our day we are taught by the doctrine of men to seek nothing but merits, rewards, and the things that are ours; of Christ we have made only a taskmaster far harsher than Moses.

BLAISE PASCAL

❦

From *The Apology for the Christian Religion**

68

When I consider the short duration of my life, swallowed up in the eternity before and after ("as the remembrance of a guest that tarrieth but a day[1]") the little space which I fill, and even can see, engulfed in the infinite immensity of spaces of which I am ignorant, and which know me not, I am frightened, and am astonished at being here rather than there; for there is no reason why here rather than there, why now rather than then. Who has put me here? By whose order and direction have this space and time been allotted to me? (205)

110

We know the truth not only by the reason but also by the heart and it is in this last way that we know first principles; and reason, which has no part in it, tries in vain to impugn them. The sceptics, who have only this for their object labor to no purpose. We know that we do not dream, and however impossible it is for us to prove it by reason, this inability demonstrates only the weakness of our reason, and not, as they affirm, the uncertainty of all our knowledge. For the knowledge of first principles, as space, time, motion, number, is as sure as any of those which we

[1]Wisdom 5:15.

*From Pascal: *Pensées*. The translation is that of W.F. Trotter, with emendations by Richard Popkin and Terence Penelhum. Professor Popkin's permission is gratefully acknowledged.

get from reasoning. And reason must trust these intuitions of the heart and instinct and must base every argument on them. (We feel from the heart the tridimensional nature of space, and the infinity of number, and reason then shows that there are no two square numbers one of which is double the other. Principles are felt, propositions are inferred, all with certainty, though in different ways.) And it is as useless and absurd for reason to demand from the heart proofs of her first principles, before admitting them, as it would be for the heart to demand from reason an intuition of all demonstrated propositions before accepting them.

This inability ought, then, to serve only to humble reason, which would judge all, but not to impugn our certainty, as if only reason were capable of instructing us. Would to God, on the contrary, that we never had need of it, and that we knew everything by instinct and feeling! But nature has refused us this boon. On the contrary she has given us but very little knowledge of this kind, and all the rest can be acquired only by reasoning.

So those to whom God has imparted religion through the feeling of the heart are very fortunate and justly convinced. But to those who do not have it, we can give it only by reasoning, waiting for God to give it them through the heart without which faith is only human, and useless for salvation. (282)

131

The chief argument of the sceptics—I pass over the lesser ones—is that we have no certainty of the truth of these principles apart from faith and revelation, except in so far as we naturally perceive them in ourselves. Now this natural intuition is not a convincing proof of their truth; since, having no certainty, apart from faith, whether man was created by a good God, or by a wicked demon, or by chance, it is doubtful whether these principles given to us are true, or false or uncertain, according to our origin. Again, no person is certain, apart from faith, whether he is awake or asleep, seeing that during sleep we believe that we are awake as firmly as we do when we are awake; we believe that we see space, figure and motion; we are aware of the passage of time, we measure it; and in fact we act as if we were awake. So that half of our life being passed in sleep, we have on our own admission no idea of truth, whatever we may imagine. As all our intuitions are then illusions, who knows whether the other half of our life, in which we think we are awake, is not another sleep a little different from the former, from which we awake when we suppose ourselves asleep?

And who doubts that, if we dreamt in company, and the dreams chanced to agree, which is common enough, and if we were always alone when awake, we should believe that matters were reversed? In short, as we often dream that we dream, heaping dream upon dream, may it not be that this half of our life, wherein we think ourselves awake, is itself only a dream on which the others are grafted, from which we wake at death, during which we have as few principles of truth and good as during natural sleep, these different thoughts which disturb us being perhaps only illusions like the flight of time and the vain fancies of our dreams?

These are the chief arguments on one side and the other.

I omit minor ones, such as the sceptical talk against the impressions of custom, education, manners, country, and the like. Though these influence the majority of common folk, who dogmatize only on shallow foundations, they are upset by the least breath of the sceptics. We have only to see their books if we are not sufficiently convinced of this, and we shall very quickly become so, perhaps too much.

I notice the only strong point of the dogmatists, namely that speaking in good faith and sincerely, we cannot doubt natural principles. Against this the sceptics set up in one word the uncertainty of our origin, which includes that of our nature. The dogmatists have been trying to answer this objection ever since the world began.

So there is an open war among men, in which each must take a part, and side either with dogmatism or scepticism. For he who thinks to remain neutral is above all a sceptic. This neutrality is the essence of the sect; he who is not against them is essentially for them. In this appears their advantage. They are not for themselves; they are neutral, indifferent, in suspense as to all things, even themselves being no exception.

What then shall man do in this state? Shall he doubt everything? Shall he doubt whether he is awake, whether he is being pinched, or whether he is being burned? Shall he doubt whether he doubts? Shall he doubt whether he exists? We cannot go as far as that; and I lay it down as a fact that there never has been a real complete sceptic. Nature sustains our feeble reason, and prevents it raving to that extent.

Shall he then say, on the contrary, that he certainly possesses truth —he who then pressed ever so little, can show no title to it, and is forced to let go his hold?

What a chimera then is man! What a novelty! What a monster, what a chaos, what a contradiction, what a prodigy! Judge of all things, imbecile worm of the earth; depository of truth, a sink of uncertainty and error; the pride and refuse of the universe!

Who will unravel this tangle? Nature confutes the sceptics, and reason confutes the dogmatists. What then will you become, O men! who try to find out by your natural reason what is your true condition? You cannot avoid one of these sects, nor adhere to either of them.

Know then, proud man, what a paradox you are to yourself. Humble yourself, weak reason; be silent, foolish nature; learn that man infinitely transcends man, and learn from your Master your true condition, of which you are ignorant. Listen to God.

For in fact, if man had never been corrupt, he would enjoy in his innocence both truth and happiness with assurance; and if man had always been corrupt, he would have no idea of truth or bliss. But, wretched as we are, and more so than if there were no greatness in our condition, we have an idea of happiness, and cannot reach it. We perceive an image of truth, and possess only a lie. Incapable of absolute ignorance and of certain knowledge, we have manifestly been in a state of perfection from which we have unhappily fallen.

It is, however, an astonishing thing that the mystery furthest removed from our knowledge, namely that of the transmission of sin, should be a fact without which we can have no knowledge of ourselves. For it is beyond doubt that there is nothing which more shocks our reason than to say that the sin of the first man has rendered guilty those, who, being so removed from this source, seem incapable of participation in it. This transmission does not only seem to us impossible, it seems also very unjust. For what is more contrary to the rules of our miserable justice than to damn eternally an infant incapable of will, for a sin wherein he seems to have so little a share, that it was committed six thousand years before he was in existence? Certainly nothing offends us more rudely than this doctrine, and yet, without this mystery, the most incomprehensible of all, we are incomprehensible to ourselves. The knot of our condition takes its twists and turns in this abyss, so that man is more inconceivable without this mystery than this mystery is inconceivable to man.

Whence it seems that God, wishing to render the difficulty of our existence unintelligible to us, has concealed the knot so high, or, rather, so low, that we are quite incapable of reaching it; so that it is not by the proud exertions of our reason, but by the simple submission of reason, that we can truly know ourselves.

These foundations, solidly established on the inviolable authority of religion, make us know that there are two truths of faith equally certain: the one that man, in the state of creation, or in that of grace, is raised above all nature, made like unto God and sharing in His divinity; the other, that, in the state of corruption and sin, he is fallen from this state and made like unto the beasts.

These two propositions are equally sound and certain. Scripture manifestly declares this to us, when it says in some places: "My delights were with the sons of men[2]", and in other places, "I will pour out my spirit upon all flesh[3]", "Ye are gods[4]", and in other places, "All Flesh is

[2]Proverbs 8:31
[3]Joel 2:28
[4]Psalms 82:6

grass[5]", "Man is like the beasts that perish[6]", "I said in my heart concerning the state of the sons of men[7]".

Whence it clearly seems that man by grace is made like unto God, and a partaker in His divinity, and that without grace he is like unto the brute beasts. (434)

148

SECOND PART — THAT MAN WITHOUT FAITH
CANNOT KNOW THE TRUE GOOD, NOR JUSTICE.

All men seek happiness. This is without exception. Whatever different means they employ, they all tend to this end. The cause of some going to war, and of others avoiding it, is the same desire in both, attended with different views. They will never take the least step but for this object. This is the motive of every action of every man, even of those who hang themselves.

And yet after such a great number of years, no one without faith has ever reached the point for which all continually look. All complain: princes, and subjects, noblemen and commoners, old and young, strong and weak, learned and ignorant, healthy and sick, of all countries, all times, all ages and all conditions.

A trial so long, so continuous, and so uniform, should certainly convince us of our inability to reach the good by our own efforts. But the example teaches us little. No resemblance is ever so perfect that there is not some slight difference; and hence we expect that our hope will not be denied on this occasion as it has been before. And thus, while the present never satisfies us, experience dupes us, and from misfortune to misfortune leads us to death, their eternal crown.

What is then that this desire and this inability proclaim to us, but that there was once in man a true happiness of which there now remain in him only the mark and empty trace, which he vainly tries to fill from all his surroundings, seeking from things absent the help he does not obtain from things present? But these are all inadequate, because the infinite abyss can only be filled by an infinite and immutable object, that is to say, only by God himself.

He only is our true good, and since we have forsaken Him, it is a strange thing that there is nothing in nature which has not been serviceable in taking His place: the stars, the heavens, earth, the elements, plants, cabbages, leeks, animals, insects, calves, serpents, fever, pestilence, war, famine, vices, adultery, incest. And since man has lost the true good, everything can appear equally good to him, even his own

[5]Isaiah 11:6
[6]Psalms 49:12
[7]Ecclesiastes 3:18

destruction though so opposed to God, to reason, and to the whole course of nature.

Some seek good in authority, others in scientific research, others in pleasure. Others, who are in fact nearer the truth, have considered it necessary that the universal good, which all men desire, should not consist in any of the particular things which can only be possessed by one man, and which, when shared, afflict their possessors more by the want of the part they have not, than they please them by the possession of what they have. They have learned that the true good should be such as all can possess at once, without diminution, and without envy, and which no one can lose against his will. And their reason is that this desire is natural to man, since it is necessarily in all, and it is impossible not to have it, so they infer from it . . . (428)

185

Faith certainly tells us what the senses do not, but not the contrary of what they see. It is above them and not contrary to them. (265)

188

The last step for reason is to recognize that there is an infinity of things which are beyond it. It is only feeble if it does not see so far as to know this. But if natural things are beyond it, what will be said of supernatural ones? (267)

380

Do not wonder to see simple people believe without reasoning. God imparts to them love of Him and hatred of self. He inclines their hearts to believe. Men will never believe with a saving and real faith, unless God inclines their heart; and they will believe as soon as He inclines it. And this is what David knew well, when he said, "Incline my heart unto thy testimonies[8]". (284)

418

Infinity — nothing.   Our soul is cast into a body, where it finds number, time, dimension. Thereupon it reasons, and calls this nature necessity, and can believe nothing else.

[8]Psalm 119:36

Unity joined to infinity adds nothing to it, no more than one foot to an infinite measure. The finite is annihilated in the presence of the infinite, and becomes a pure nothing. So our spirit before God, so our justice before divine justice. There is not so great a disproportion between our justice and that of God as between unity and infinity.

The justice of God must be vast like His compassion. Now His justice to the outcast is less vast, and ought to offend our feelings less than His mercy towards the elect.

We know that there is an infinite, and are ignorant of its nature. As we know it to be false that numbers are finite, it is therefore true that there is an infinity in number. But we do not know what it is. It is false that it is even, it is false that it is odd; for the addition of a unit can make no change in its nature. Yet it is a number, and every number is odd or even (this is certainly true of every finite number). So we may well know that there is a God without knowing what He is. Is there not one substantial truth, seeing that there are so many things which are not the truth itself?

We know then the existence and nature of the finite, because we also are finite and have extension. We know the existence of the infinite, and are ignorant of its nature, because it has extension like us, but not limits like us. But we know neither the existence nor the nature of God, because He has neither extension nor limits.

But by faith we know His existence; in glory we shall know His nature. Now I have already shown that we may well know the existence of a thing without knowing its nature.

Let us now speak according to our natural lights.

If there is a God, He is infinitely incomprehensible, since, beyond having neither parts nor limits, He has no affinity to us. We are then incapable of knowing either what He is or if He is. This being so, who could undertake to decide the question? Not we, who have no affinity to Him.

Who then will blame Christians for not being able to give a reason for their belief, since they profess a religion for which they cannot give a reason? They declare, in expounding it to the world, that it is a foolishness; and then you complain that they do not prove it! If they proved it, they would not keep their word; it is in lacking proofs, that they do not lack sense. "Yes, but although this excuses those who offer it as such, and takes away from them the blame of putting it forward without reason, it does not excuse those who accept it." Let us then examine this point, and say, "God is, or He is not." But to which side shall we incline? Reason can decide nothing here. There is an infinite chaos which separates us. A game is being played at the extremity of this infinite distance where heads or tails will turn up. What will you wager? According to reason, you can do neither the one thing nor the other; according to reason, you can defend neither of the propositions.

Do not then reprove for error those who have made a choice, for you know nothing about it. "No, but I blame them for having made, not *this* choice, but any choice; for again both he who chooses heads and he who chooses tails are equally at fault, they are both in the wrong. The right course is not to wager at all."

Yes, but you must wager. It is not optional. You are embarked. Which will you choose, then? Let us see. Since you must choose, let us see which interests you least. You have two things to lose: the true and the good; and two things to stake, your reason and your will, your knowledge and your happiness; and your nature has two things to shun, error and misery. Your reason is no more offended by choosing one than the other, since you must of necessity choose. That is one point settled. But your happiness? Let us weigh the gain and the loss involved in wagering that God is. Let us estimate these two chances. If you gain, you gain all; if you lose, you lose nothing. Wager then, without hesitation that He is. "That is very fine. Yes, I must wager; but I may perhaps wager too much." Let us see. Since there is an equal risk of gain and loss, if you had only two lives, instead of one, you might still wager. But if there were three lives to gain, you would have to play (since you are under the necessity of playing), and you would be imprudent, when you are forced to play, not to chance your life to gain three in a game where there is an equal risk of loss and gain. But there is an eternity of life and happiness. And this being so, if there were an infinity of chances, of which one only would be for you, you would still be right in wagering one to win two, and you would act stupidly, being obliged to play, by refusing to stake one life against three in a game in which out of an infinity of chances there is one for you, if there were an infinity of an infinitely happy life to gain. But there is here an infinity of an infinitely happy life to gain, a chance to win against a finite number of chances of loss, and what you stake is finite. It is all divided; wherever the infinite is and there is not an infinity of chances of loss against that of gain, there is no time to hesitate, you must give all. And thus, when one is forced to play, one gives up reason if one hangs on to life, rather than risk it for an infinite gain that is as likely to happen as a loss worth nothing.

For it is no use to say it is uncertain if we will gain, and it is certain that we risk, and that the infinite distance between the *certainty* of what is staked and the *uncertainty* of what will be gained, equals the finite good which is certainly staked against the uncertain infinite. This is not so, as every player stakes a certainty to gain an uncertainty, and yet he stakes a finite certainty to gain a finite uncertainty, without transgressing against reason. There is not an infinite distance between the certainty staked and the uncertainty of the gain; that is untrue. In truth, there is an infinity between the certainty of gain and the certainty of loss. But the uncertainty of the gain is proportioned to the certainty of the stake according to the proportion of the chances of gain and loss. Hence it comes that, if there are as many risks on one side as on the other, the course is to play even; and then the certainty of the stake is equal to the uncertainty of the gain, so far is it from fact that there is an infinite distance between them. And so our proposition is of infinite force, when there is the finite to stake in a game where there are equal risks of gain and of loss, and the infinite to gain. This is demonstrable: and if men are capable of any truths, this is one.

"I confess it, I admit it. But, still, is there no means of seeing the faces of the cards?"—Yes, Scripture and the rest, etc. "Yes, but I have my hands tied and my mouth closed; I am forced to wager, and am not free. I am not released, and am so made that I cannot believe. What, then, would you have me do?"

True. But at least learn that your inability to believe comes from your passions, since reason brings you to this, and yet you cannot believe. Endeavour then to convince yourself, not by increase of proofs of God, but by the abatement of your passions. You would like to attain faith, and do not know the way; you would like to cure yourself of unbelief, and ask the remedy for it. Learn from those who have been bound like you, and who now stake all their possessions. These are people who know the way which you would follow, and who are cured of an ill of which you would be cured. Follow the way by which they began; by acting as if they believed, taking the holy water, having masses said, etc. This will naturally make you believe, and deaden your acuteness. "But this is what I am afraid of." And why? What have you to lose?

But to show you that this leads you there, it is this which will lessen the passions, which are your stumbling-blocks.

The end of this discourse. "Now what harm will befall you in taking this side? You will be faithful, honest, humble, grateful, full of good works, a sincere friend, truthful. Certainly you will not have those poisonous pleasures, glory and luxury; but will you not have others? I tell you that you will thereby gain in this life and at each step you take on this road you will see such great certainty of gain, and such nothingness in what you risk, that you will at last recognize that you have wagered for something certain and infinite, for which you have given nothing.

"Ah! This discourse transports me, charms me." etc.

If this discourse pleases you and seems impressive, know that it is made by a man who has knelt, both before and after it, in prayer to that Being infinite and without parts, before whom he lays all he has, for you also to lay before Him all you have for your own good, and for His glory, that so strength may be given to lowliness. (233)

423

The heart has its reasons that reason does not know. We feel it in a thousand things. I say that the heart naturally loves the Universal Being, and also itself naturally, according as it gives itself to them; and it hardens itself against one or the other at its will. You have rejected the one, and kept the other. Is it by reason that you love yourself? (277)

424

It is the heart which experiences God, and not the reason. This then is faith: God felt by the heart, not by the reason. (278)

429

This is what I see and what troubles me. I look on all sides, and I see only darkness everywhere. Nature presents to me nothing which is not matter of doubt and concern. If I saw nothing there which revealed a Divinity, I would come to a negative conclusion; if I saw everywhere the signs of a Creator, I would remain peacefully in faith. But, seeing too much to deny and too little to be sure, I am in a state to be pitied; wherefore I have a hundred times wished that if a God maintains nature, she should testify to Him unequivocally, and that, if the signs she gives are deceptive, she should suppress them altogether; that she should say everything or nothing, that I might see which cause I ought to follow. Whereas in my present state, ignorant of what I am or of what I ought to do, I know neither my condition nor my duty. My heart yearns wholly to know where is the true good, in order to follow it; nothing would be too dear to me for eternity.

I envy those whom I see living in the faith with such carelessness, and who make such a bad use of a gift of which it seems to me I would make such a different use. (229)

444

It is then true that everything teaches man his condition, but he must understand this well. For it is not true that all reveals God, and it is not true that all conceals God. But it is at the same time true that he hides himself from those who tempt Him, and that He reveals Himself to those who seek Him, because men are both unworthy and capable of God; unworthy by their corruption, capable by their original nature. (557)

445

What shall we conclude from all our darkness, but our unworthiness? (558)

588

Faith is a gift of God; do not believe that we said it was a gift of reasoning. Other religions do not say this about their faith. They only gave reasoning in order to arrive at it, and yet it does not bring them to it. (279)

816

"I would soon have renounced pleasure," say they, "had I faith." For my part I tell you, "You would soon have faith if you renounced pleasure." Now, it is for you to begin. If I could, I would give you faith. I cannot do so, nor therefore test the truth of what you say. But you can well renounce pleasure, and test whether what I say is true. (240)

821

For we must not misunderstand ourselves: we are as much automatic as intellectual; and hence it comes that conviction is not attained by demonstration alone. How few things are demonstrated! Proofs only convince the mind. Custom is the source of our strongest and most believed proofs. It bends the automaton, which persuades the mind without its thinking about the matter. Who has demonstrated that there will be a tomorrow, and that we shall die? And what is more believed? It is, then, custom which persuades us of it; it is custom that make so many men Christians; custom that makes them Turks, heathen, artisans, soldiers, etc. (Faith in baptism is more received among Christians than among Turks.) Finally we must have recourse to it when once the mind has seen where the truth is, in order to quench our thirst, and steep ourselves in that belief, which escapes us at every hour; for always to have proofs ready is too much trouble. We must get an easier belief, which is that of custom, which without violence, without art, without argument, makes us believe things, and inclines all our powers to this belief, so that our soul falls naturally into it. It is not enough to believe only by force of conviction, when the automaton is inclined to believe the contrary. Both our parts must be made to believe, the mind by reasons which it is sufficient to have seen once in a lifetime, and the automaton by custom, and by not allowing it to incline to the contrary. ("Incline my heart"[9].)

The reason acts slowly, with so many examinations, and on so many principles, which must be always present, so that at every hour it falls asleep, or wanders, through want of having all its principles present. Feeling does not act thus; it acts in a moment, and is always ready to act. We must then put our faith in feeling; otherwise it will always be vacillating. (252)

[9]Psalm 119:36.

JOSEPH BUTLER

⤸

Upon the Ignorance of Man*

> When I applied mine heart to know wisdom, and to see the business
> that is done upon the earth: then I beheld all the work of God, that a
> man cannot find out the work that is done under the sun: because
> though a man labour to seek it out, yet he shall not find it; yea further;
> though a wise man think to know it, yet shall he not be able to find
> it. Eccles. viii. 16, 17.

The writings of Solomon are very much taken up with reflections upon
human nature and human life; to which he hath added, in this book,
reflections upon the constitution of things. And it is not improbable,
that the little satisfaction and the great difficulties he met with in his
researches into the general constitution of nature, might be the occasion of his confining himself, so much as he hath done, to life and
conduct. However, upon that joint review he expresses great ignorance
of the works of God, and the method of his providence in the government of the world; great labour and weariness in the search and observation he had employed himself about; and great disappointment, pain,
and even vexation of mind, upon that which he had remarked of the
appearances of things, and of what was going forward upon this earth.
This whole review and inspection, and the result of it, sorrow, perplexity, a sense of his necessary ignorance, suggests various reflections to
his mind. But, notwithstanding all this ignorance and dissatisfaction,

*Sermon XV from *Fifteen Sermons Preached at the Rolls Chapel,* first published in
1726. This text is taken from *The Works of Joseph Butler,* Vol. II, ed. Samuel Halifax,
Oxford University Press, 1840, pp. 190–202.

there is somewhat upon which he assuredly rests and depends; somewhat, which is the conclusion of the whole matter, and the only concern of man. Following this his method and train of reflection, let us consider,

I. The assertion of the text, the ignorance of man; that the wisest and most knowing cannot comprehend the ways and works of God: and then,

II. What are the just consequences of this observation and knowledge of our own ignorance, and the reflections which it leads us to.

I. The wisest and most knowing cannot comprehend the works of God, the methods and designs of his providence in the creation and government of the world.

Creation is absolutely and entirely out of our depth, and beyond the extent of our utmost reach. And yet it is as certain that God made the world, as it is certain that effects must have a cause. It is indeed in general no more than effects, that the most knowing are acquainted with: for as to causes, they are as entirely in the dark as the most ignorant. What are the laws by which matter acts upon matter, but certain effects; which some, having observed to be frequently repeated, have reduced to general rules? The real nature and essence of beings likewise is what we are altogether ignorant of. All these things are so entirely out of our reach, that we have not the least glimpse of them. And we know little more of ourselves, than we do of the world about us: how we were made, how our being is continued and preserved, what the faculties of our minds are, and upon what the power of exercising them depends. *I am fearfully and wonderfully made: marvellous are thy works, and that my soul knoweth right well.* Our own nature, and the objects we are surrounded with, serve to raise our curiosity; but we are quite out of a condition of satisfying it. Every secret which is disclosed, every discovery which is made, every new effect which is brought to view, serves to convince us of numberless more which remain concealed, and which we had before no suspicion of. And what if we were acquainted with the whole creation, in the same way and as thoroughly as we are with any single object in it? What would all this natural knowledge amount to? It must be a low curiosity indeed which such superficial knowledge could satisfy. On the contrary, would it not serve to convince us of our ignorance still; and to raise our desire of knowing the nature of things themselves, the author, the cause, and the end of them?

As to the government of the world: though from consideration of the final causes which come within our knowledge; of characters, personal merit and demerit; of the favour and disapprobation, which respectively are due and belong to the righteous and the wicked, and which therefore must necessarily be in a mind which sees things as they really are; though, I say, from hence we may know somewhat concerning the designs of Providence in the government of the world, enough to enforce upon us religion and the practice of virtue: yet, since the monarchy of the universe is a dominion unlimited in extent, and everlasting in duration; the general system of it must necessarily be quite beyond our comprehension. And, since there appears such a subordination and reference of the several parts to each other, as to constitute it properly one administration or government; we cannot have a thorough knowledge of any part, without knowing the whole. This surely should convince us, that we are much less competent judges of the very small part which comes under our notice in this world, than we are apt to imagine. *No heart can think upon these things worthily: and who is able to conceive his way? It is a tempest which no man can see: for the most part of his works are hid. Who can declare the works of his justice? For his covenant is afar off, and the trial of all things is in the end:* i.e. The dealings of God with the children of men are not yet completed, and cannot be judged of by that part which is before us. *So that a man cannot say, This is worse than that: for in time they shall be well approved. Thy faithfulness, O Lord, reacheth unto the clouds: thy righteousness standeth like the strong mountains: thy judgments are like the great deep. He hath made every thing beautiful in his time: also he hath set the world in their heart; so that no man can find out the work that God maketh from the beginning to the end.* And thus St. Paul concludes a long argument upon the various dispensations of Providence: *O the depth of the riches, both of the wisdom and knowledge of God! How unsearchable are his judgments, and his ways past finding out! For who hath known the mind of the Lord?*

Thus the scheme of Providence, the ways and works of God, are too vast, of too large extent for our capacities. There is, as I may speak, such an expense of power and wisdom and goodness, in the formation and government of the world, as is too much for us to take in, or comprehend. Power and wisdom and goodness are manifest to us in all those works of God which come within our view: but there are likewise infinite stores of each poured forth throughout the immensity of the creation; no part of which can be thoroughly understood, without taking in its reference and respect to the whole: and this is what we have not faculties for.

And as the works of God, and his scheme of government, are above our capacities thoroughly to comprehend: so there possibly may be reasons which originally made it fit that many things should be concealed from us, which we have perhaps natural capacities of understanding; many things concerning the designs, methods, and ends of Divine Providence in the government of the world. There is no manner of absurdity in supposing a veil on purpose drawn over some scenes of infinite power, wisdom, and goodness, the sight of which might some way or other strike us too strongly; or that better ends are designed and served by their being concealed, than could be by their being exposed to our knowledge. The Almighty may cast clouds and darkness round about him, for reasons and purposes of which we have not the least glimpse or conception.

However, it is surely reasonable, and what might have been expected, that creatures in some stage of their being, suppose in the infancy of it, should be placed in a state of discipline and improvement, where their patience and submission is to be tried by afflictions, where temptations are to be resisted, and difficulties gone through in the discharge of their duty. Now if the greatest pleasures and pains of the present life may be overcome and suspended, as they manifestly may, by hope and fear, and other passions and affections; then the evidence of religion, and the sense of the consequences of virtue and vice, might have been such, as entirely in all cases to prevail over those afflictions, difficulties, and temptations; prevail over them so, as to render them absolutely none at all. But the very notion itself now mentioned, of a state of discipline and improvement, necessarily excludes such sensible evidence and conviction of religion, and of the consequences of virtue and vice. Religion consists in submission and resignation to the divine will. Our condition in this world is a school of exercise for this temper: and our ignorance, the shallowness of our reason, the temptations, difficulties, afflictions, which we are exposed to, all equally contribute to make it so. The general observation may be carried on; and whoever will attend to the thing will plainly see, that less sensible evidence, with less difficulty in practice, is the same, as more sensible evidence, with greater difficulty in practice. Therefore difficulties in speculation as much come into the notion of the state of discipline, as difficulties in practice: and so the same reason or account is to be given of both. Thus, though it is indeed absurd to talk of the greater merit of assent, upon little or no evidence, than upon demonstration; yet the strict discharge of our duty, with less sensible evidence, does imply in it a better character, than the same diligence in the discharge of it upon more sensible evidence. This fully accounts for and explains that assertion of our Saviour, *Blessed are they that have not seen, and yet have believed*[a]; have become Christians and obeyed the gospel, upon less sensible evidence, than that which Thomas, to whom he is speaking, insisted upon.

But after all, the same account is to be given, why we were placed in these circumstances of ignorance, as why nature has not furnished us with wings; namely, that we were designed to be inhabitants of this earth. I am afraid we think too highly of ourselves; of our rank in the

---

[a]John xx. 29.

creation, and of what is due to us. What sphere of action, what business is assigned to man, that he has not capacities and knowledge fully equal to? It is manifest he has reason and knowledge, and faculties superior to the business of the present world: faculties which appear superfluous, if we do not take in the respect which they have to somewhat further, and beyond it. If to acquire knowledge were our proper end, we should indeed be but poorly provided: but if somewhat else be our business and duty, we may, notwithstanding our ignorance, be well enough furnished for it; and the observation of our ignorance may be of assistance to us in the discharge of it.

II.   Let us then consider, what are the consequences of this knowledge and observation of our own ignorance, and the reflection it leads us to.

First, We may learn from it, with what temper of mind a man ought to inquire into the subject of religion; namely, with exception of finding difficulties, and with a disposition to take up and rest satisfied with any evidence whatever, which is real.

He should beforehand expect things mysterious, and such as he will not be able thoroughly to comprehend, or go to the bottom of. To expect a distinct comprehensive view of the whole subject, clear of difficulties and objections, is to forget our nature and condition; neither of which admit of such knowledge, with respect to any science whatever. And to inquire with this expectation, is not to inquire as a man, but as one of another order of creatures.

Due sense of the general ignorance of man would also beget in us a disposition to take up and rest satisfied with any evidence whatever, which is real. I mention this as the contrary to a disposition, of which there are not wanting instances, to find fault with and reject evidence, because it is not such as was desired. If a man were to walk by twilight, must he not follow his eyes as much as if it were broad day and clear sunshine? Or if he were obliged to take a journey by night, would he not *give heed to* any *light shining in the darkness, till the day should break and the day-star arise?* It would not be altogether unnatural for him to reflect how much better it were to have day-light; he might perhaps have great curiosity to see the country round about him; he might lament that the darkness concealed many extended prospects from his eyes, and wish for the sun to draw away the veil: but how ridiculous would it be to reject with scorn and disdain the guidance and direction which that lesser light might afford him, because it was not the sun itself! If the make and constitution of man, the circumstances he is placed in, or the reason of things affords the least hint or intimation, that virtue is the law he is born under; scepticism itself should lead him to the most strict and inviolable practice of it; that he may not make the dreadful experiment, of leaving the course of life marked out for him by nature, whatever that nature be, and entering paths of his own, of which he can know neither the dangers nor the end. For though no danger be seen, yet darkness, ignorance, and blindness are no manner of security.

Secondly, Our ignorance is the proper answer to many things, which are called objections against religion; particularly, to those which arise from the appearances of evil and irregularity in the constitution of nature and the government of the world. In all other cases it is thought necessary to be thoroughly acquainted with the whole of a scheme, even one of so narrow a compass as those which are formed by men, in order to judge of the goodness or badness of it: and the most slight and superficial view of any human contrivance comes abundantly nearer to a thorough knowledge of it, than that part, which we know of the government of the world, does to the general scheme and system of it; to the whole set of laws by which it is governed. From our ignorance of the constitution of things, and the scheme of Providence in the government of the world; from the reference the several parts have to each other, and to the whole; and from our not being able to see the end and the whole; it follows, that however perfect things are, they must even necessarily appear to us otherwise less perfect than they are[b].

Thirdly, Since the constitution of nature, and the methods and designs of Providence in the government of the world, are above our comprehension, we should acquiesce in, and rest satisfied with, our ignorance, turn our thoughts from that which is above and beyond us, and apply ourselves to that which is level to our capacities, and which is our real business and concern. Knowledge is not our proper happiness. Whoever will in the least attend to the thing will see, that it is the gaining, not the having of it, which is the entertainment of the mind. Indeed, if the proper happiness of man consisted in knowledge considered as a possession or treasure, men who are possessed of the largest share would have a very ill time of it; as they would be infinitely more sensible than others of their poverty in this respect. Thus *he who increases knowledge would* eminently *increase sorrow.* Men of deep research and curious inquiry should just be put in mind, not to mistake what they are doing. If their discoveries serve the cause of virtue and religion, in the way of proof, motive to practice, or assistance in it; or if

---

[b]Suppose some very *complicated piece of work*, some *system* or *constitution*, formed for some *general end*, to which each of the *parts* had a *reference*. The perfection or justness of this work or constitution would consist in the reference and respect, which the several parts have to the general design. This reference of parts to the general design may be infinitely various, both in degree and kind. Thus one part may only contribute and be subservient to another; this to a third; and so on through a long series, the last part of which alone may contribute immediately and directly to the general design. Or a part may have this distant reference to the general design, and may also contribute immediately to it. For instance: if the general design or end, for which the complicated frame of nature was brought into being, is happiness; whatever affords present satisfaction, and likewise tends to carry on the course of things, hath this double respect to the general design. Now suppose a spectator of that work or constitution was in a great measure ignorant of such various reference to the general end, whatever that end be; and that, upon a very slight and partial view which he had of the work, several things appeared to

they tend to render life less unhappy, and promote its satisfactions; then they are most usefully employed: but bringing things to light, alone and of itself, is of no manner of use, any otherwise than as an entertainment or diversion. Neither is this at all amiss, if it does not take up the time which should be employed in better work. But it is evident that there is another mark set up for us to aim at; another end appointed us to direct our lives to: an end, which the most knowing may fail of, and the most ignorant arrive at. *The secret things belong unto the Lord our God; but those things which are revealed belong unto us, and to our children for ever, that we may do all the words of this law.* Which reflection of Moses, put in general terms, is, that the only knowledge, which is of any avail to us, is that which teaches us our duty, or assists us in the discharge of it. The economy of the universe, the course of nature, almighty power exerted in the creation and government of the world, is out of our reach. What would be the consequence, if we could really get an insight into these things, is very uncertain; whether it would assist us in, or divert us from, what we have to do in this present state. If then there be a sphere of knowledge, of contemplation and employment, level to our capacities, and of the utmost importance to us; we ought surely to apply ourselves with all diligence to this our proper business, and esteem every thing else nothing, nothing as to us, in comparison of it. Thus Job, discoursing of natural knowledge, how much it is above us, and of wisdom in general, says, *God understandeth the way thereof, and he knoweth the place thereof. And unto man he said, Behold, the fear of the Lord, that is wisdom, and to depart from evil is understanding.* Other orders of creatures may perhaps be let into the secret counsels of Heaven; and have the designs and methods of Providence, in the creation and government of the world, communicated to them: but this does not belong to our rank or condition. *The fear of the Lord, and to depart from evil,* is the only wisdom which man should aspire after, as his work and business. The same is said, and with the same connection and context, in the conclusion of the book of Ecclesiastes. Our ignorance, and the little we can know of other things, affords a reason why we should not perplex ourselves about them; but no way invalidates that which is the *conclu-*

---

his eye disproportionate and wrong; others, just and beautiful: what would he gather from these appearances? He would immediately conclude there was a probability, if he could see the whole reference of the parts appearing wrong to the general design, that this would destroy the appearance of wrongness and disproportion: but there is no probability, that the reference would destroy the particular right appearances, though that reference might shew the things already appearing just, to be so likewise in a higher degree or another manner. There is a probability, that the right appearances were intended: there is no probability, that the wrong appearances were. We cannot suspect irregularity and disorder to be designed. The pillars of a building appear beautiful; but their being likewise its support does not destroy that beauty: there still remains a reason to believe that the architect intended the beautiful appearance, after we have found out the reference, support. It would be reasonable for a man of himself to think thus, upon the first piece of architecture he ever saw.

sion of the whole matter, Fear God, and keep his commandments; for this is the whole concern of man. So that Socrates was not the first who endeavored to draw men off from labouring after, and laying stress upon other knowledge, in comparison of that which related to morals. Our province is virtue and religion, life and manners; the science of improving the temper, and making the heart better. This is the field assigned us to cultivate: how much it has lain neglected is indeed astonishing. Virtue is demonstrably the happiness of man: it consists in good actions, proceeding from a good principle, temper, or heart. Overt acts are entirely in our power. What remains is, that we learn to *keep our heart;* to govern and regulate our passions, mind, affections: that so we may be free from the impotencies of fear, envy, malice, covetousness, ambition; that we may be clear of these, considered as vices seated in the heart, considered as constituting a general wrong temper; from which general wrong frame of mind, all the mistaken pursuits, and far the greatest part of the unhappiness of life, proceed. He, who should find out one rule to assist us in this work, would deserve infinitely better of mankind, than all the improvers of other knowledge put together.

Lastly, Let us adore that infinite wisdom and power and goodness, which is above our comprehension. *To whom hath the root of wisdom been revealed? Or who hath known her wise counsels? There is one wise and greatly to be feared; the Lord sitting upon his throne. He created her, and saw her, and numbered her, and poured her out upon all his works.* If it be thought a considerable thing to be acquainted with a few, a very few, of the effects of infinite power and wisdom; the situation, bigness, and revolution of some of the heavenly bodies; what sentiments should our minds be filled with concerning Him, who appointed to each its place and measure and sphere of motion, all which are kept with the most uniform constancy! *Who stretched out the heavens, and telleth the number of the stars, and calleth them all by their names. Who laid the foundations of the earth, who comprehendeth the dust of it in a measure, and weigheth the mountains in scales, and the hills in a balance.* And, when we have recounted all the appearances which come within our view, we must add, *Lo, these are part of his ways; but how little a portion is heard of him! Canst thou by searching find out God? Canst thou find out the Almighty unto perfection? It is as high as heaven; what canst thou do? deeper than hell; what canst thou know?*

The conclusion is, that in all lowliness of mind we set lightly by ourselves: that we form our temper to an implicit submission to the Divine Majesty; beget within ourselves an absolute resignation to all the methods of his providence, in his dealings with the children of men: that, in the deepest humility of our souls, we prostrate ourselves before him, and join in that celestial song; *Great and marvellous are thy works, Lord God Almighty! just and true are thy ways, thou King of saints! Who shall not fear thee, O Lord, and glorify thy name?*

JEAN-JACQUES ROUSSEAU

⁓

The Creed of a Savoyard Priest*

My child, do not look to me for learned speeches or profound arguments. I am no great philosopher, nor do I desire to be one. I have, however, a certain amount of common-sense and a constant devotion to truth. I have no wish to argue with you nor even to convince you; it is enough for me to show you, in all simplicity of heart, what I really think. Consult your own heart while I speak; that is all I ask. If I am mistaken, I am honestly mistaken, and therefore my error will not be counted to me as a crime; if you, too, are honestly mistaken, there is no great harm done. If I am right, we are both endowed with reason, we have both the same motive for listening to the voice of reason. Why should not you think as I do?

By birth I was a peasant and poor; to till the ground was my portion; but my parents thought it a finer thing that I should learn to get my living as a priest and they found means to send me to college. I am quite sure that neither my parents nor I had any idea of seeking after what was good, useful, or true; we only sought what was wanted to get me ordained. I learned what was taught me, I said what I was told to say, I promised all that was required, and I became a priest. But I soon discovered that when I promised not to be a man, I had promised more than I could perform.

*From Book IV of *Emile*, translated by Barbara Foxley; published by J.M. Dent and Sons, London, and E.P. Dutton and Co., New York, 1911, pp. 228–278. Reprinted, with abridgments, by permission of the publishers.

A thoughtful mind soon learns from such experiences. I found my former ideas of justice, honesty, and every duty of man overturned by these painful events, and day by day I was losing my hold on one or another of the opinions I had accepted. What was left was not enough to form a body of ideas which could stand alone, and I felt that the evidence on which my principles rested was being weakened; at last I knew not what to think, and I came to the same conclusion as yourself, but with this difference: My lack of faith was the slow growth of manhood, attained with great difficulty, and all the harder to uproot.

I was in that state of doubt and uncertainty which Descartes considers essential to the search for truth. It is a state which cannot continue, it is disquieting and painful; only vicious tendencies and an idle heart can keep us in that state. My heart was not so corrupt as to delight in it, and there is nothing which so maintains the habit of thinking as being better pleased with oneself than with one's lot.

I pondered, therefore, on the sad fate of mortals, adrift upon this sea of human opinions, without compass or rudder, and abandoned to their stormy passions with no guide but an inexperienced pilot who does not know whence he comes or whither he is going. I said to myself, "I love truth, I seek her, and cannot find her. Show me truth and I will hold her fast; why does she hide her face from the eager heart that would fain worship her?"

Although I have often experienced worse sufferings, I have never led a life so uniformly distressing as this period of unrest and anxiety, when I wandered incessantly from one doubt to another, gaining nothing from my prolonged meditations but uncertainty, darkness, and contradiction with regard to the source of my being and the rule of my duties.

I cannot understand how any one can be a sceptic sincerely and on principle. Either such philosophers do not exist or they are the most miserable of men. Doubt with regard to what we ought to know is a condition too violent for the human mind; it cannot long be endured; in spite of itself the mind decides one way or another, and it prefers to be deceived rather than to believe nothing.

My perplexity was increased by the fact that I had been brought up in a church which decides everything and permits no doubts, so that having rejected one article of faith I was forced to reject the rest; as I could not accept absurd decisions, I was deprived of those which were not absurd. When I was told to believe everything, I could believe nothing, and I knew not where to stop.

I consulted the philosophers, I searched their books and examined their various theories; I found them all alike proud, assertive, dogmatic, professing, even in their so-called scepticism, to know everything, proving nothing, scoffing at each other. This last trait, which was common to all of them, struck me as the only point in which they were right. Braggarts in attack, they are weaklings in defence. Weigh their arguments, they are all destructive; count their voices, every one speaks for himself; they are only agreed in arguing with each other. I could find no way out of my uncertainty by listening to them.

I suppose this prodigious diversity of opinion is caused, in the first place, by the weakness of the human intellect; and, in the second, by pride. We have no means of measuring this vast machine, we are unable to calculate its workings; we know neither its guiding principles nor its final purpose; we do not know ourselves, we know neither our nature nor the spirit that moves us; we scarcely know whether man is one or many; we are surrounded by impenetrable mysteries. These mysteries are beyond the region of sense, we think we can penetrate them by the light of reason, but we fall back on our imagination. Through this imagined world each forces a way for himself which he holds to be right; none can tell whether his path will lead him to the goal. Yet we long to know and understand it all. The one thing we do not know is the limit of the knowable. We prefer to trust to chance and to believe what is not true, rather than to own that not one of us can see what really is. A fragment of some vast whole whose bounds are beyond our gaze, a fragment abandoned by its Creator to our foolish quarrels, we are vain enough to want to determine the nature of that whole and our own relations with regard to it.

The first thing I learned from these considerations was to restrict my inquiries to what directly concerned myself, to rest in profound ignorance of everything else, and not even to trouble myself to doubt anything beyond what I required to know.

I also realised that the philosophers, far from ridding me of my vain doubts, only multiplied the doubts that tormented me and failed to remove any one of them. So I chose another guide and said, "Let me follow the Inner Light; it will not lead me so far astray as others have done, or if it does it will be my own fault, and I shall not go so far wrong if I follow my own illusions as if I trusted to their deceits."

Bearing thus within my heart the love of truth as my only philosophy, and as my only method a clear and simple rule which dispensed with the need for vain and subtle arguments, I returned with the help of this rule to the examination of such knowledge as concerned myself; I was resolved to admit as self-evident all that I could not honestly refuse to believe, and to admit as true all that seemed to follow directly from this; all the rest I determined to leave undecided, neither accepting nor rejecting it, nor yet troubling myself to clear up difficulties which did not lead to any practical ends.

But who am I? What right have I to decide? What is it that determines my judgments? If they are inevitable, if they are the results of the impressions I receive, I am wasting my strength in such inquiries; they would be made or not without any interference of mine. I must therefore first turn my eyes upon myself to acquaint myself with the instrument I desire to use, and to discover how far it is reliable.

I exist, and I have senses through which I receive impressions. This is the first truth that strikes me and I am forced to accept it. Have I any independent knowledge of my existence, or am I only aware of it through my sensations? This is my first difficulty, and so far I cannot solve it. For I continually experience sensations, either directly or indirectly through memory, so how can I know if the feeling of *self* is something beyond these sensations or if it can exist independently of them?

My sensations take place in myself, for they make me aware of my own existence; but their cause is outside me, for they affect me whether I have any reason for them or not, and they are produced or destroyed independently of me. So I clearly perceive that my sensation, which is within me, and its cause or its object, which is outside me, are different things.

Thus, not only do I exist, but other entities exist also, that is to say, the objects of my sensations; and even if these objects are merely ideas, still these ideas are not me.

But everything outside myself, everything which acts upon my senses, I call matter, and all the particles of matter which I suppose to be united into separate entities I call bodies. Thus all the disputes of the idealists and the realists have no meaning for me; their distinctions between the appearance and the reality of bodies are wholly fanciful.

I am now as convinced of the existence of the universe as of my own. I next consider the objects of my sensations, and I find that I have the power of comparing them, so I perceive that I am endowed with an active force of which I was not previously aware.

To perceive is to feel; to compare is to judge; to judge and to feel are not the same. Through sensation objects present themselves to me separately and singly as they are in nature; by comparing them I rearrange them, I shift them so to speak, I place one upon another to decide whether they are alike or different, or more generally to find out their relations. To my mind, the distinctive faculty of an active or intelligent being is the power of understanding this word "is." I seek in vain in the merely sensitive entity that intelligent force which compares and judges; I can find no trace of it in its nature. This passive entity will be aware of each object separately, it will even be aware of the whole formed by the two together, but having no power to place them side by side it can never compare them, it can never form a judgment with regard to them.

This power of my mind which brings my sensations together and compares them may be called by any name; let it be called attention, meditation, reflection, or what you will; it is still true that it is in me and not in things, that it is I alone who produce it, though I only produce it when I receive an impression from things. Though I am compelled to feel or not to feel, I am free to examine more or less what I feel.

Being now, so to speak, sure of myself, I begin to look at things outside myself, and I behold myself with a sort of shudder flung at random into this vast universe, plunged as it were into the vast number of entities, knowing nothing of what they are in themselves or in relation to me. I study them, I observe them; and the first object which suggests itself for comparison with them is myself.

All that I perceive through the senses is matter, and I deduce all the essential properties of matter from the sensible qualities which make me perceive it, qualities which are inseparable from it. I see it sometimes in motion, sometimes at rest, hence I infer that neither motion nor rest is essential to it, but motion, being an action, is the result of a cause of which rest is only the absence. When, therefore, there is nothing acting upon matter it does not move, and for the very reason that rest and motion are indifferent to it, its natural state is a state of rest.

I perceive two sorts of motions of bodies, acquired motion and spontaneous or voluntary motion. In the first the cause is external to the body moved, in the second it is within. I shall not conclude from that that the motion, say of a watch, is spontaneous, for if no external cause operated upon the spring it would run down and the watch would cease to go. For the same reason I should not admit that the movements of fluids are spontaneous, neither should I attribute spontaneous motion to fire which causes their fluidity.

You ask me if the movements of animals are spontaneous; my answer is, "I cannot tell," but analogy points that way. You ask me again, how do I know that there are spontaneous movements? I tell you, "I know it because I feel them." I want to move my arm and I move it without any other immediate cause of the movement but my own will. In vain would any one try to argue me out of this feeling, it is stronger than any proofs; you might as well try to convince me that I do not exist.

If there were no spontaneity in men's actions, nor in anything that happens on this earth, it would be all the more difficult to imagine a first cause for all motion. For my own part, I feel myself so thoroughly convinced that the natural state of matter is a state of rest, and that it has no power of action in itself, that when I see a body in motion I at once assume that it is either a living body or that this motion has been imparted to it. My mind declines to accept in any way the idea of inorganic matter moving of its own accord, or giving rise to any action.

Yet this visible universe consists of matter, matter diffused and dead, matter which has none of the cohesion, the organisation, the common feeling of the parts of a living body, for it is certain that we who are parts have no consciousness of the whole. This same universe is in motion, and in its movements, ordered, uniform, and subject to fixed laws, it has none of that freedom which appears in the spontaneous movements of men and animals. So the world is not some huge animal which moves of its own accord; its movements are therefore due to some external cause, a cause which I cannot perceive, but the inner voice makes this cause so apparent to me that I cannot watch the course of the sun without imagining a force which drives it, and when the earth revolves I think I see the hand that sets it in motion.

The first causes of motion are not to be found in matter; matter receives and transmits motion, but does not produce it. The more I observe the action and reaction of the forces of nature playing on one another, the more I see that we must always go back from one effect to another, till we arrive at a first cause in some will; for to assume an infinite succession of causes is to assume that there is no first cause. In a word, no motion which is not caused by another motion can take place, except by a spontaneous, voluntary action; inanimate bodies have no action but motion, and there is no real action without will. This is my first principle. I believe, therefore, that there is a will which sets the universe in motion and gives life to nature. This is my first dogma, or the first article of my creed.

If matter in motion points me to a will, matter in motion according to fixed laws points me to an intelligence; that is the second article of my creed. To act, to compare, to choose, are the operations of an active, thinking being; so this being exists. Where do you find him existing, you will say? Not merely in the revolving heavens, nor in the sun which gives us light, not in myself alone, but in the sheep that grazes, the bird that flies, the stone that falls, and the leaf blown by the wind.

I judge of the order of the world, although I know nothing of its purpose, for to judge of this order it is enough for me to compare the parts one with another, to study their cooperation, their relations, and to observe their united action. I know not why the universe exists, but I see continually how it is changed; I never fail to perceive the close connection by which the entities of which it consists lend their aid one to another. I am like a man who sees the works of a watch for the first time; he is never weary of admiring the mechanism, though he does not know the use of the instrument and has never seen its face. I do not know what this is for, says he, but I see that each part of it is fitted to the rest, I admire the workman in the details of his work, and I am quite certain that all these wheels only work together in this fashion for some common end which I cannot perceive.

Let us compare the special ends, the means, the ordered relations of every kind, then let us listen to the inner voice of feeling; what healthy mind can reject its evidence? Unless the eyes are blinded by prejudices, can they fail to see that the visible order of the universe proclaims a supreme intelligence? What sophisms must be brought together before we fail to understand the harmony of existence and the wonderful cooperation of every part for the maintenance of the rest? Say what you will of combinations and probabilities; what do you gain by reducing me to silence if you cannot gain my consent? And how can you rob me of the spontaneous feeling which, in spite of myself, continually gives you the lie? If organised bodies had come together fortuitously in all sorts of ways before assuming settled forms, if stomachs are made without mouths, feet without heads, hands without arms, imperfect organs of every kind which died because they could not preserve their life, why do none of these imperfect attempts now meet our eyes; why has nature at length prescribed laws to herself which she did not at first recognise? I must not be surprised if that which is possible should happen, and if the improbability of the event is compensated for by the number of the attempts. I grant this; yet if any one told me that printed characters scattered broadcast had produced the *Æneid* all complete, I would not condescend to take a single step to verify this falsehood. You will tell me I am forgetting the multitude of attempts. But how many such attempts must I assume to bring the combination within the bounds of probability? For my own part the only possible assumption is that the chances are infinity to one that the product is not the work of chance. In addition to this, chance combinations yield nothing but products of the same nature as the elements combined, so that life and organisation will not be produced by a flow of atoms, and a chemist when making his compounds will never give them thought and feeling in his crucible.

I believe, therefore, that the world is governed by a wise and powerful will; I see it or rather I feel it, and it is a great thing to know this. But has this same world always existed, or has it been created? Is there one source of all things? Are there two or many? What is their nature? I know not; and what concern is it of mine? When these things become of importance to me I will try to learn them; till then I abjure these idle speculations, which may trouble my peace, but cannot affect my conduct nor be comprehended by my reason.

Recollect that I am not preaching my own opinion but explaining it. Whether matter is eternal or created, whether its origin is passive or not, it is still certain that the whole is one, and that it proclaims a single intelligence; for I see nothing that is not part of the same ordered system, nothing which does not co-operate to the same end, namely, the conservation of all within the established order. This being who wills and can perform his will, this being active through his own power, this being, whoever he may be, who moves the universe and orders all things, is what I call God. To this name I add the ideas of intelligence, power, will, which I have brought together, and that of kindness which is their necessary consequence; but for all this I know no more of the being to which I ascribe them. He hides himself alike from my senses and my understanding; the more I think of him, the more perplexed I am; I know full well that he exists, and that he exists of himself alone; I know that my existence depends on his, and that everything I know depends upon him also. I see God everywhere in his works; I feel him within myself; I behold him all around me; but if I try to ponder him himself, if I try to find out where he is, what he is, what is his substance, he escapes me and my troubled spirit finds nothing.

Convinced of my unfitness, I shall never argue about the nature of God unless I am driven to it by the feeling of his relations with myself. Such reasonings are always rash; a wise man should venture on them with trembling, he should be certain that he can never sound their abysses; for the most insolent attitude towards God is not to abstain from thinking of him, but to think evil of him.

After the discovery of such of his attributes as enable me to conceive of his existence, I return to myself, and I try to discover what is my place in the order of things which he governs, and I can myself examine. At once, and beyond possibility of doubt, I discover my species; for by my own will and the instruments I can control to carry out my will, I have more power to act upon all bodies about me, either to make use of or to avoid their action at my pleasure, than any of them has power to act upon me against my will by mere physical impulsion; and through my intelligence I am the only one who can examine all the rest. What being here below, except man, can observe others, measure, calculate, forecast their motions, their effects, and unite, so to speak, the feeling of a common existence with that of his individual existence? What is there so absurd in the thought that all things are made for me, when I alone can relate all things to myself?

I am not puffed up by this thought, I am deeply moved by it; for this state was no choice of mine, it was not due to the deserts of a creature who as yet did not exist. Can I behold myself thus distinguished without congratulating myself on this post of honour, without blessing the hand which bestowed it? The first return to self has given birth to a feeling of gratitude and thankfulness to the author of my species, and this feeling calls forth my first homage to the beneficent Godhead. I worship his Almighty power and my heart acknowledges his mercies. Is it not a natural consequence of our self-love to honour our protector and to love our benefactor?

But when, in my desire to discover my own place within my species, I consider its different ranks and the men who fill them, where am I now? What a sight meets my eyes! Where is now the order I perceived? Nature showed me a scene of harmony and proportion; the human race shows me nothing but confusion and disorder. The elements agree together; men are in a state of chaos. The beasts are happy; their king alone is wretched. O Wisdom, where are thy laws? O Providence, is this thy rule over the world? Merciful God, where is thy Power? I behold the earth, and there is evil upon it.

Would you believe it, dear friend, from these gloomy thoughts and apparent contradictions, there was shaped in my mind the sublime idea of the soul, which all my seeking had hitherto failed to discover? While

I meditated upon man's nature, I seemed to discover two distinct principles in it; one of them raised him to the study of the eternal truths, to the love of justice, and of true morality, to the regions of the world of thought, which the wise delight to contemplate; the other led him downwards to himself, made him the slave of his senses, of the passions which are their instruments, and thus opposed everything suggested to him by the former principle. When I felt myself carried away, distracted by these conflicting motives, I said, No; man is not one; I will and I will not; I feel myself at once a slave and a free man; I perceive what is right, I love it, and I do what is wrong; I am active when I listen to the voice of reason; I am passive when I am carried away by my passions; and when I yield, my worst suffering is the knowledge that I might have resisted.

If man is at once active and free, he acts of his own accord; what he does freely is not part of the system marked out by Providence and it cannot be imputed to Providence. Providence does not will the evil that man does when he misuses the freedom given to him; neither does Providence prevent him doing it, either because the wrong done by so feeble a creature is as nothing in its eyes, or because it could not prevent it without doing a greater wrong and degrading his nature. Providence has made him free that he may choose the good and refuse the evil. It has made him capable of this choice if he uses rightly the faculties bestowed upon him, but it has so strictly limited his powers that the misuse of his freedom cannot disturb the general order. The evil that man does reacts upon himself without affecting the system of the world, without preventing the preservation of the human species in spite of itself. To complain that God does not prevent us from doing wrong is to complain because he has made man of so excellent a nature, that he has endowed his actions with that morality by which they are ennobled, that he has made virtue man's birthright. Supreme happiness consists in self-content; that we may gain this self-content we are placed upon this earth and endowed with freedom, we are tempted by our passions and restrained by conscience. What more could divine power itself have done on our behalf? Could it have made our nature a contradiction, and have given the prize of well-doing to one who was incapable of evil? To prevent a man from wickedness, should Providence have restricted him to instinct and made him a fool? Not so, O God of my soul, I will never reproach thee that thou hast created me in thine own image, that I may be free and good and happy like my Maker!

O Man! seek no further for the author of evil; thou art he. There is no evil but the evil you do or the evil you suffer, and both come from yourself. Evil in general can only spring from disorder, and in the order of the world I find a never-failing system. Evil in particular cases exists only in the mind of those who experience it; and this feeling is not the gift of nature, but the work of man himself. Pain has little power over those who, having thought little, look neither before nor after. Take away our fatal progress, take away our faults and our vices, take away man's handiwork, and all is well.

Where all is well, there is no such thing as injustice. Justice and goodness are inseparable; now goodness is the necessary result of boundless power and of that self-love which is innate in all sentient beings. The omnipotent projects himself, so to speak, into the being of his creatures. Creation and preservation are the everlasting work of power; it does not act on that which has no existence; God is not the God of the dead; he could not harm and destroy without injury to himself. The omnipotent can only will what is good. Therefore he who is supremely good, because he is supremely powerful, must also be supremely just, otherwise he would contradict himself; for that love of order which creates order we call goodness and that love of order which preserves order we call justice.

Men say God owes nothing to his creatures. I think he owes them all he promised when he gave them their being. Now to give them the idea of something good and to make them feel the need of it, is to promise it to them. The more closely I study myself, the more carefully I consider, the more plainly do I read these words, "Be just and you will be happy." It is not so, however, in the present condition of things, the wicked prospers and the oppression of the righteous continues. Observe how angry we are when this expectation is disappointed. Conscience revolts and murmurs against her Creator; she exclaims with cries and groans, "Thou hast deceived me."

"I have deceived thee, rash soul! Who told thee this? Is thy soul destroyed? Hast thou ceased to exist? O Brutus! O my son! let there be no stain upon the close of thy noble life; do not abandon thy hope and thy glory with thy corpse upon the plains of Philippi. Why dost thou say, 'Virtue is naught,' when thou art about to enjoy the reward of virtue? Thou art about to die! Nay, thou shalt live, and thus my promise is fulfilled."

One might judge from the complaints of impatient men that God owes them the reward before they have deserved it, that he is bound to pay for virtue in advance. Oh! let us first be good and then we shall be happy. Let us not claim the prize before we have won it, nor demand our wages before we have finished our work. "It is not in the lists that we crown the victors in the sacred games," says Plutarch, "it is when they have finished their course."

If the soul is immaterial, it may survive the body; and if it so survives, Providence is justified. Had I no other proof of the immaterial nature of the soul, the triumph of the wicked and the oppression of the righteous in this world would be enough to convince me. I should seek to resolve so appalling a discord in the universal harmony. I should say to myself, "All is not over with life, everything finds its place at death." I should still have to answer the question, "What becomes of man when all we know of him through our senses has vanished?" This question no longer presents any difficulty to me when I admit the two substances. It is easy to understand that what is imperceptible to those senses escapes me, during my bodily life, when I perceive through my senses only. When the union of soul and body is destroyed, I think one may be dissolved and the other may be preserved. Why should the destruction of the one imply the destruction of the other? On the contrary, so unlike in their nature, they were during their union in a highly unstable condition, and when this union comes to an end they both return to their natural state; the active vital substance regains all the force which it expended to set in motion the passive dead substance. Alas! my vices make me only too well aware that man is but half alive during this life; the life of the soul only begins with the death of the body.

But what is that life? Is the soul of man in its nature immortal? I know not. My finite understanding cannot hold the infinite; what is called eternity eludes my grasp. What can I assert or deny, how can I reason with regard to what I cannot conceive? I believe that the soul survives the body for the maintenance of order; who knows if this is enough to make it eternal? However, I know that the body is worn out and destroyed by the division of its parts, but I cannot conceive a similar destruction of the conscious nature, and as I cannot imagine how it can die, I presume that it does not die. As this assumption is consoling and in itself not unreasonable, why should I fear to accept it?

Having thus deduced from the perception of objects of sense and from my inner consciousness, which leads me to judge of causes by my native reason, the principal truths which I require to know, I must now seek such principles of conduct as I can draw from them, and such rules as I must lay down for my guidance in the fulfilment of my destiny in this world, according to the purpose of my Maker. Still following the same method, I do not derive these rules from the principles of the higher philosophy, I find them in the depths of my heart, traced by nature in characters which nothing can efface. I need only consult myself with regard to what I wish to do; what I feel to be right is right, what I feel to be wrong is wrong; conscience is the best casuist; and it is only when we haggle with conscience that we have recourse to the subtleties of argument. Our first duty is towards ourself; yet how often does the voice of others tell us that in seeking our good at the expense of others we are doing ill? We think we are following the guidance of nature, and we are resisting it; we listen to what she says to our senses, and we neglect what she says to our heart; the active being obeys, the passive commands. Conscience is the voice of the soul, the passions are the voice of the body. Is it strange that these voices often contradict each other? And then to which should we give heed? Too often does reason deceive us; we have only too good a right to doubt her; but conscience never deceives us; she is the true guide of man; it is to the soul what instinct is to the body; he who obeys his conscience is following nature and he need not fear that he will go astray.

Cast your eyes over every nation of the world; peruse every volume of its history; in the midst of all these strange and cruel forms of worship, among this amazing variety of manners and customs, you will everywhere find the same ideas of right and justice; everywhere the same principles of morality, the same ideas of good and evil. The old paganism gave birth to abominable gods who would have been punished as scoundrels here below, gods who merely offered, as a picture of supreme happiness, crimes to be committed and lust to be gratified. But in vain did vice descend from the abode of the gods armed with their sacred authority; the moral instinct refused to admit it into the heart of man. While the debaucheries of Jupiter were celebrated, the continence of Xenocrates was revered; the chaste Lucrece adored the shameless Venus; the bold Roman offered sacrifices to Fear; he invoked the god who mutilated his father, and he died without a murmur at the hand of his own father. The most unworthy gods were worshipped by the noblest men. The sacred voice of nature was stronger than the voice of the gods, and won reverence upon earth; it seemed to relegate guilt and the guilty alike to heaven.

There is therefore at the bottom of our hearts an innate principle of justice and virtue, by which, in spite of our maxims, we judge our own actions or those of others to be good or evil; and it is this principle that I call conscience.

To exist is to feel; our feeling is undoubtedly earlier than our intelligence, and we had feelings before we had ideas. Whatever may be the cause of our being, it has provided for our preservation by giving us feelings suited to our nature; and no one can deny that these at least are innate. These feelings, so far as the individual is concerned, are self-love, fear, pain, the dread of death, the desire for comfort. Again, if, as it is impossible to doubt, man is by nature sociable or at least fitted to become sociable, he can only be so by means of other innate feelings, relative to his kind; for if only physical well-being were considered, men would certainly be scattered rather than brought together. But the motive power of conscience is derived from the moral system formed through this twofold relation to himself and to his fellow-men. To know good is not to love it; this knowledge is not innate in man; but as soon as his reason leads him to perceive it, his conscience impels him to love it; it is this feeling which is innate.

So I do not think, my young friend, that it is impossible to explain the immediate force of conscience as a result of our own nature, independent of reason itself. And even should it be impossible, it is unnecessary; for those who deny this principle, admitted and received by everybody else in the world, do not prove that there is no such thing;

they are content to affirm, and when we affirm its existence we have quite as good grounds as they, while we have moreover the witness within us, the voice of conscience, which speaks on its own behalf. If the first beams of judgment dazzle us and confuse the objects we behold, let us wait till our feeble sight grows clear and strong, and in the light of reason we shall soon behold these very objects as nature has already showed them to us. Or rather let us be simpler and less pretentious; let us be content with the first feelings we experience in ourselves, since science always brings us back to these, unless it has led us astray.

Conscience! Conscience! Divine instinct, immortal voice from heaven; sure guide for a creature ignorant and finite indeed, yet intelligent and free; infallible judge of good and evil, making man like to God! In thee consists the excellence of man's nature and the mortality of his actions; apart from thee, I find nothing in myself to raise me above the beasts — nothing but the sad privilege of wandering from one error to another, by the help of an unbridled understanding and a reason which knows no principle.

There is an age when the heart is still free, but eager, unquiet, greedy of a happiness which is still unknown, a happiness which it seeks in curiosity and doubt; deceived by the senses it settles at length upon the empty show of happiness and thinks it has found it where it is not. In my own case these illusions endured for a long time. Alas! too late did I become aware of them, and I have not succeeded in overcoming them altogether; they will last as long as this mortal body from which they arise. If they lead me astray, I am at least no longer deceived by them; I know them for what they are, and even when I give way to them, I despise myself; far from regarding them as the goal of my happiness, I behold in them an obstacle to it. I long for the time when, freed from the fetters of the body, I shall be myself, at one with myself, no longer torn in two, when I myself shall suffice for my own happiness. Meanwhile I am happy even in this life, for I make small account of all its evils, in which I regard myself as having little or no part, while all the real good that I can get out of this life depends on myself alone.

To raise myself so far as may be even now to this state of happiness, strength, and freedom, I exercise myself in lofty contemplation. I consider the order of the universe, not to explain it by any futile system, but to revere it without ceasing, to adore the wise Author who reveals himself in it. I hold intercourse with him; I immerse all my powers in his divine essence; I am overwhelmed by his kindness, I bless him and his gifts, but I do not pray to him. What should I ask of him — to change the order of nature, to work miracles on my behalf? Should I, who am bound to love above all things the order which he has established in his wisdom and maintained by his providence, should I desire the disturbance of that order on my own account? No, that rash prayer would deserve to be punished rather than to be granted. Neither do I ask of him the power to do right; why should I ask what he has given me already? Has he not given me conscience that I may love the right, reason that I may perceive it, and freedom that I may choose it? If I do evil, I have no excuse; I do it of my own free will; to ask him to change my will is to ask him to do what he asks of me; it is to want him to do the work while I get the wages; to be dissatisfied with my lot is to wish to be no longer a man, to wish to be other than what I am, to wish for disorder and evil. Thou source of justice and truth, merciful and gracious God, in thee do I trust, and the desire of my heart is—Thy will be done. When I unite my will with thine, I do what thou doest; I have a share in thy goodness; I believe that I enjoy beforehand the supreme happiness which is the reward of goodness.

In my well-founded self-distrust the only thing that I ask of God, or rather expect from his justice, is to correct my error if I go astray, if that error is dangerous to me. To be honest I need not think myself infallible; my opinions, which seem to me true, may be so many lies; for what man is there who does not cling to his own beliefs; and how many men are agreed in everything? The illusion which deceives me may indeed have its source in myself, but it is God alone who can remove it. I have done all I can to attain to truth; but its source is beyond my reach; is it my fault if my strength fails me and I can go no further; it is for Truth to draw near to me.

The good priest had spoken with passion; he and I were overcome with emotion. It seemed to me as if I were listening to the divine Orpheus when he sang the earliest hymns and taught men the worship of the gods. I saw any number of objections which might be raised; yet I raised none, for I perceived that they were more perplexing than serious, and that my inclination took his part. When he spoke to me according to his conscience, my own seemed to confirm what he said.

"The novelty of the sentiments you have made known to me," said I, "strikes me all the more because of what you confess you do not know, than because of what you say you believe. They seem to me very like that theism or natural religion, which Christians profess to confound with atheism or irreligion which is their exact opposite. But in the present state of my faith I should have to ascend rather than descend to accept your views, and I find it difficult to remain just where you are unless I were as wise as you. That I may be at least as honest, I want time to take counsel with myself. By your own showing, the inner voice must be my guide, and you have yourself told me that when it has long been silenced it cannot be recalled in a moment. I take what you have said to heart, and I must consider it. If after I have thought things out, I am as convinced as you are, you will be my final teacher, and I will be your disciple till death. Continue your teaching however; you have only told me half what I must know. Speak to me of revelation, of the Scriptures, of those difficult doctrines among which I have strayed ever since I was a child, incapable either of understanding or believing them, unable to adopt or reject them."

"Yes, my child," said he, embracing me, "I will tell you all I think; I will not open my heart to you by halves; but the desire you express was necessary before I could cast aside all reserve. So far I have told you nothing but what I thought would be of service to you, nothing but what I was quite convinced of. The inquiry which remains to be made is very different. It seems to me full of perplexity, mystery, and darkness; I bring to it only doubt and distrust. I make up my mind with trembling, and I tell you my doubts rather than my convictions. If your own opinions were more settled I should hesitate to show you mine; but in your present condition, to think like me would be gain. Moreover, give to my words only the authority of reason; I know not whether I am mistaken. It is difficult in discussion to avoid assuming sometimes a dogmatic tone; but remember in this respect that all my assertions are but reasons to doubt me. Seek truth for yourself, for my own part I only promise you sincerity.

"In my exposition you find nothing but natural religion; strange that we should need more! How shall I become aware of this need? What guilt can be mine so long as I serve God according to the knowledge he has given to my mind, and the feelings he has put into my heart? What purity of morals, what dogma useful to man and worthy of its author, can I derive from a positive doctrine which cannot be derived without the aid of this doctrine by the right use of my faculties? Show me what you can add to the duties of the natural law, for the glory of God, for the good of mankind, and for my own welfare; and what virtue you will get from the new form of religion which does not result from mine. The grandest ideas of the Divine nature come to us from reason only. Behold the spectacle of nature; listen to the inner voice. Has not God spoken it all to our eyes, to our conscience, to our reason? What more can man tell us? Their revelations do but degrade God, by investing him with passions like our own. Far from throwing light upon the ideas of the Supreme Being, special doctrines seem to me to confuse these ideas; far from ennobling them, they degrade them; to the inconceivable mysteries which surround the Almighty, they add absurd contradictions, they make man proud, intolerant, and cruel; instead of bringing peace upon earth, they bring fire and sword. I ask myself what is the use of it all, and I find no answer. I see nothing but the crimes of men and the misery of mankind.

"They tell me a revelation was required to teach men how God would be served; as a proof of this they point to the many strange rites which men have instituted, and they do not perceive that this very diversity springs from the fanciful nature of the revelations. As soon as the nations took to making God speak, every one made him speak in his own fashion, and made him say what he himself wanted. Had they listened only to what God says in the heart of man, there would have been but one religion upon earth.

"Assuming that the divine majesty condescends so far as to make a man the channel of his sacred will, is it reasonable, is it fair, to demand that the whole of mankind should obey the voice of this minister without making him known as such? Is it just to give him as his sole credentials certain private signs, performed in the presence of a few obscure persons, signs which everybody else can only know by hearsay? If one were to believe all the miracles that the uneducated and credulous profess to have seen in every country upon earth, every sect would be in the right; there would be more miracles than ordinary events; and it would be the greatest miracle if there were no miracles wherever there were persecuted fanatics. The unchangeable order of nature is the chief witness to the wise hand that guides it; if there were many exceptions, I should hardly know what to think; for my own part I have too great a faith in God to believe in so many miracles which are so little worthy of him.

"Let a man come and say to us: Mortals, I proclaim to you the will of the Most Highest; accept my words as those of him who has sent me; I bid the sun to change his course, the stars to range themselves in a fresh order, the high places to become smooth, the floods to rise up, the earth to change her face. By these miracles who will not recognise the master of nature? She does not obey impostors, their miracles are wrought in holes and corners, in deserts, within closed doors, where they find easy dupes among a small company of spectators already disposed to believe them. Who will venture to tell me how many eye-witnesses are required to make a miracle credible? What use are your miracles, performed in proof of your doctrine, if they themselves require so much proof? You might as well have let them alone.

"There still remains the most important inquiry of all with regard to the doctrine proclaimed; for since those who tell us God works miracles in this world, profess that the devil sometimes imitates them, when we have found the best attested miracles we have got very little further; and since the magicians of Pharaoh dared in the presence of Moses to counterfeit the very signs he wrought at God's command, why should they not, behind his back, claim a like authority? So when we have proved our doctrine by means of miracles, we must prove our miracles by means of doctrine, for fear lest we should take the devil's doings for the handiwork of God. What think you of this dilemma?

"This doctrine, if it comes from God, should bear the sacred stamp of the godhead; not only should it illumine the troubled thoughts which reason imprints on our minds, but it should also offer us a form of worship, a morality, and rules of conduct in accordance with the attributes by means of which we alone conceive of God's essence. If then it teaches us what is absurd and unreasonable, if it inspires us with feelings of aversion for our fellows and terror for ourselves, if it paints us a God, angry, jealous, revengeful, partial, hating men, a God of war and battles, ever ready to strike and to destroy, ever speaking of punishment and torment, boasting even of the punishment of the innocent, my heart would not be drawn towards this terrible God, I would take good care not to quit the realm of natural religion to embrace such a religion as that; for you see plainly I must choose between them. Your God is not ours. He who begins by selecting a chosen people, and proscribing the rest of mankind, is not our common father; he who consigns to eternal punishment the greater part of his creatures, is not the merciful and gracious God revealed to me by my reason.

"Reason tells me that dogmas should be plain, clear, and striking in their simplicity. If there is something lacking in natural religion, it is with respect to the obscurity in which it leaves the great truths it teaches; revelation should teach us these truths in a way which the mind of man can understand; it should bring them within his reach, make him comprehend them, so that he may believe them. Faith is confirmed and strengthened by understanding; the best religion is of necessity the simplest. He who hides beneath mysteries and contradictions the religion that he preaches to me, teaches me at the same time to distrust that religion. The God whom I adore is not the God of darkness, he has not given me understanding in order to forbid me to use it; to tell me to submit my reason is to insult the giver of reason. The minister of truth does not tyrannise over my reason, he enlightens it.

"With regard to revelation, if I were a more accomplished disputant, or a more learned person, perhaps I should feel its truth, its usefulness for those who are happy enough to perceive it; but if I find evidence for it which I cannot combat, I also find objections against it which I cannot overcome. There are so many weighty reasons for and against that I do not know what to decide, so that I neither accept nor reject it. I only reject all obligation to be convinced of its truth; for this so-called obligation is incompatible with God's justice, and far from removing objections in this way it would multiply them, and would make them insurmountable for the greater part of mankind. In this respect I maintain an attitude of reverent doubt. I do not presume to think myself infallible; other men may have been able to make up their minds though the matter seems doubtful to myself; I am speaking for myself, not for them; I neither blame them nor follow in their steps; their judgment may be superior to mine, but it is no fault of mine that my judgment does not agree with it.

"This is the unwilling scepticism in which I rest; but this scepticism is in no way painful to me, for it does not extend to matters of practice, and I am well assured as to the principles underlying all my duties. I

serve God in the simplicity of my heart; I only seek to know what
affects my conduct. As to those dogmas which have no effect upon
action or morality, dogmas about which so many men torment themselves, I give no heed to them. I regard all individual religions as so
many wholesome institutions which prescribe a uniform method by
which each country may do honour to God in public worship; institutions which may each have its reason in the country, the government,
the genius of the people, or in other local causes which make one
preferable to another in a given time or place. I think them all good
alike, when God is served in a fitting manner. True worship is of the
heart. God rejects no homage, however offered, provided it is sincere.
Called to the service of the Church in my own religion, I fulfil as
scrupulously as I can all the duties prescribed to me, and my conscience
would reproach me if I were knowingly wanting with regard to any
point.

"Honoured with the sacred ministry, though in its lowest ranks, I will
never do or say anything which may make me unworthy to fulfil these
sublime duties. I will always preach virtue and exhort men to well-
doing; and so far as I can I will set them a good example. It will be my
business to make religion attractive; it will be my business to
strengthen their faith in those doctrines which are really useful, those
which every man must believe; but, please God, I shall never teach
them to hate their neighbour, to say to other men, You will be damned;
to say, No salvation outside the Church. If I were in a more conspicuous
position, this reticence might get me into trouble; but I am too obscure
to have much to fear, and I could hardly sink lower than I am. Come
what may, I will never blaspheme the justice of God, nor lie against the
Holy Ghost.

"My young friend, I have now repeated to you my creed as God
reads it in my heart; you are the first to whom I have told it; perhaps
you will be the last. As long as there is any true faith left among men,
we must not trouble quiet souls, nor scare the faith of the ignorant with
problems they cannot solve, with difficulties which cause them uneasi-
ness, but do not give them any guidance. But when once everything is
shaken, the trunk must be preserved at the cost of the branches. Consciences, restless, uncertain, and almost quenched like yours, require
to be strengthened and aroused; to set the feet again upon the foundation of eternal truth, we must remove the trembling supports on which
they think they rest.

"You are at that critical age when the mind is open to conviction,
when the heart receives its form and character, when we decide our
own fate for life, either for good or evil. At a later date, the material has
hardened and fresh impressions leave no trace. Young man, take the
stamp of truth upon your heart which is not yet hardened. If I were
more certain of myself, I should have adopted a more decided and

dogmatic tone; but I am a man ignorant and liable to error; what could I do? I have opened my heart fully to you; and I have told what I myself hold for certain and sure; I have told you my doubts as doubts, my opinions as opinions; I have given you my reasons both for faith and doubt. It is now your turn to judge; you have asked for time; that is a wise precaution and it makes me think well of you. Begin by bringing your conscience into that state in which it desires to see clearly; be honest with yourself. Take to yourself such of my opinions as convince you, reject the rest. You are not yet so depraved by vice as to run the risk of choosing amiss. I would offer to argue with you, but as soon as men dispute they lose their temper; pride and obstinacy come in, and there is an end of honesty. My friend, never argue; for by arguing we gain no light for ourselves or for others. So far as I myself am concerned, I have only made up my mind after many years of meditation; here I rest, my conscience is at peace, my heart is satisfied. If I wanted to begin afresh the examination of my feelings, I should not bring to the task a purer love of truth; and my mind, which is already less active, would be less able to perceive the truth. Here I shall rest, lest the love of contemplation, developing step by step into an idle passion, should make me lukewarm in the performance of my duties, lest I should fall into my former scepticism without strength to struggle out of it. More than half my life is spent; I have barely time to make good use of what is left, to blot out my faults by my virtues. If I am mistaken, it is against my will. He who reads my inmost heart knows that I have no love for my blindness. As my own knowledge is powerless to free me from this blindness, my only way out of it is by a good life; and if God from the very stones can raise up children to Abraham, every man has a right to hope that he may be taught the truth, if he makes himself worthy of it.

"If my reflections lead you to think as I do, if you share my feelings, if we have the same creed, I give you this advice: Do not continue to expose your life to the temptations of poverty and despair, nor waste it in degradation and at the mercy of strangers; no longer eat the shameful bread of charity. Return to your own country, go back to the religion of your fathers, and follow it in sincerity of heart, and never forsake it; it is very simple and very holy; I think there is no other religion upon earth whose morality is purer, no other more satisfying to the reason. Do not trouble about the cost of the journey, that will be provided for you. Neither do you fear the false shame of a humiliating return; we should blush to commit a fault, not to repair it. You are still at an age when all is forgiven, but when we cannot go on sinning with impunity. If you desire to listen to your conscience, a thousand empty objections will disappear at her voice. You will feel that, in our present state of uncertainty, it is an inexcusable presumption to profess any faith but that we were born into, while it is treachery not to practise honestly the faith we profess. If we go astray, we deprive ourselves of a great excuse before the tribunal of the sovereign judge. Will he not pardon the errors in which we were brought up, rather than those of our own choosing?

"My son, keep your soul in such a state that you always desire that there should be a God and you will never doubt it. Moreover, whatever decision you come to, remember that the real duties of religion are independent of human institutions; that a righteous heart is the true temple of the Godhead; that in every land, in every sect, to love God above all things and to love our neighbour as ourself is the whole law; remember there is no religion which absolves us from our moral duties; that these alone are really essential, that the service of the heart is the first of these duties, and that without faith there is no such thing as true virtue.

"My good youth, be honest and humble; learn how to be ignorant, then you will never deceive yourself or others. If ever your talents are so far cultivated as to enable you to speak to other men, always speak according to your conscience, without caring for their applause. The abuse of knowledge causes incredulity. The learned always despise the opinions of the crowd; each of them must have his own opinion. A haughty philosophy leads to atheism just as blind devotion leads to fanaticism. Avoid these extremes; keep steadfastly to the path of truth, or what seems to you truth, in simplicity of heart, and never let yourself be turned aside by pride or weakness. Dare to confess God before the philosophers; dare to preach humanity to the intolerant. It may be you will stand alone, but you will bear within you a witness which will make the witness of men of no account with you. Let them love or hate, let them read your writings or despise them; no matter. Speak the truth and do the right; the one thing that really matters is to do one's duty in this world; and when we forget ourselves we are really working for ourselves. My child, self-interest misleads us; the hope of the just is the only sure guide."

SØREN KIERKEGAARD

Truth and Subjectivity*

In an attempt to make clear the difference of way that exists between an objective and a subjective reflection, I shall now proceed to show how a subjective reflection makes its way inwardly in inwardness. Inwardness in an existing subject culminates in passion; corresponding to passion in the subject the truth becomes a paradox; and the fact that the truth becomes a paradox is rooted precisely in its having a relationship to an existing subject. Thus the one corresponds to the other. By forgetting that one is an existing subject, passion goes by the board and the truth is no longer a paradox; the knowing subject becomes a fantastic entity rather than a human being, and the truth becomes a fantastic object for the knowledge of this fantastic entity.

When the question of truth is raised in an objective manner, reflection is directed objectively to the truth, as an object to which the knower is related. Reflection is not focussed upon the relationship, however, but upon the question of whether it is the truth to which the knower is related. If only the object to which he is related is the truth, the subject is accounted to be in the truth. When the question of the truth is raised subjectively, reflection is directed subjectively to the nature of the individual's relationship; if only the mode of this relationship is in the truth, the individual is in the truth even if he should happen to be thus related to what is not true.[1] Let us take as an example the knowledge of God. Objectively, reflection is directed to the problem of whether this object is the true God; subjectively, reflection is directed to the question whether the individual is related to a something *in such a manner* that his relationship is in truth a God-relationship. On which side is the truth now to be found? Ah, may we not here resort to a mediation, and say: It is on neither side, but in the mediation of both? Excellently well said, provided we might have it explained how an existing individual manages to be in a state of mediation. For to be in a state of mediation is to be finished, while to exist is to become. Nor can an existing individual be in two places at the same time—he cannot be an identity of subject and object. When he is nearest to being in two places at the same time he is in passion; but passion is momentary, and passion is also the highest expression of subjectivity.

The existing individual who chooses to pursue the objective way enters upon the entire approximation-process by which it is proposed to bring God to light objectively. But this is in all eternity impossible, because God is a subject, and therefore exists only for subjectivity in inwardness. The existing individual who chooses the subjective way apprehends instantly the entire dialectical difficulty involved in having to use some time, perhaps a long time, in finding God objectively; and he feels this dialectical difficulty in all its painfulness, because every moment is wasted in which he does not have God. That very instant he has God, not by virtue of any objective deliberation, but by virtue of the infinite passion of inwardness. The objective inquirer, on the other hand, is not embarrassed by such dialectical difficulties as are involved in devoting an entire period of investigation to finding God—since it is possible that the inquirer may die tomorrow; and if he lives he can scarcely regard God as something to be taken along if convenient, since God is precisely that which one takes *a tout prix*, which in the understanding of passion constitutes the true inward relationship to God.

It is at this point, so difficult dialectically, that the way swings off for everyone who knows what it means to think, and to think existentially; which is something very different from sitting at a desk and writing about what one has never done, something very different from writing *de omnibus dubitandum* and at the same time being as credulous existentially as the most sensuous of men. Here is where the way swings off, and the change is marked by the fact that while objective knowledge rambles comfortably on by way of the long road of approximation without being impelled by the urge of passion, subjective knowledge counts every delay a deadly peril, and the decision so infinitely impor-

---

[1]The reader will observe that the question here is about essential truth, or about the truth which is essentially related to existence, and that it is precisely for the sake of clarifying it as inwardness or as subjectivity that this contrast is drawn.

tant and so instantly pressing that it is as if the opportunity had already passed.

Now when the problem is to reckon up on which side there is most truth, whether on the side of one who seeks the true God objectively, and pursues the approximate truth of the God-idea; or on the side of one who, driven by the infinite passion of his need of God, feels an infinite concern for his own relationship to God in truth (and to be at one and the same time on both sides equally, is as we have noted not possible for an existing individual, but is merely the happy delusion of an imaginary I-am-I): the answer cannot be in doubt for anyone who has not been demoralized with the aid of science. If one who lives in the midst of Christendom goes up to the house of God, the house of the true God, with the true conception of God in his knowledge, and prays, but prays in a false spirit; and one who lives in an idolatrous community prays with the entire passion of the infinite, although his eyes rest upon the image of an idol: where is there most truth? The one prays in truth to God though he worships an idol; the other prays falsely to the true God, and hence worships in fact an idol.

When one man investigates objectively the problem of immortality, and another embraces an uncertainty with the passion of the infinite: where is there most truth, and who has the greater certainty? The one has entered upon a never-ending approximation, for the certainty of immortality lies precisely in the subjectivity of the individual; the other is immortal, and fights for his immortality by struggling with the uncertainty. Let us consider Socrates. Nowadays everyone dabbles in a few proofs; some have several such proofs, others fewer. But Socrates! He puts the question objectively in a problematic manner: *if* there is an immortality. He must therefore be accounted a doubter in comparison with one of our modern thinkers with the three proofs? By no means. On this "if" he risks his entire life, he has the courage to meet death, and he has with the passion of the infinite so determined the pattern of his life that it must be found acceptable — *if* there is an immortality. Is any better proof capable of being given for the immortality of the soul? But those who have the three proofs do not at all determine their lives in conformity therewith; if there is an immortality it must feel disgust over their manner of life: can any better refutation be given of the three proofs? The bit of uncertainty that Socrates had, helped him because he himself contributed the passion of the infinite; the three proofs that the others have do not profit them at all, because they are dead to spirit and enthusiasm, and their three proofs, in lieu of proving anything else, prove just this. A young girl may enjoy all the sweetness of love on the basis of what is merely a weak hope that she is beloved, because she rests everything on this weak hope; but many a wedded matron more than once subjected to the strongest expressions of love, has in so far indeed had proofs, but strangely enough has not enjoyed *quod erat demonstrandum.* The Socratic ignorance, which Socrates held fast with the entire passion of his inwardness, was thus an expression for the principle that the eternal truth is related to an existing individual, and that this truth must therefore be a paradox for him as long as he exists; and yet it is possible that there was more truth in the Socratic ignorance as it was in him, than in the entire objective truth of the System, which flirts with what the times demand and accommodates itself to *Privatdocents.*

The objective accent falls on WHAT is said, the subjective accent on HOW it is said. This distinction holds even in the aesthetic realm, and receives definite expression in the principle that what is in itself true may in the mouth of such and such a person become untrue. In these times this distinction is particularly worthy of notice, for if we wish to express in a single sentence the difference between ancient times and our own, we should doubtless have to say: "In ancient times only an individual here and there knew the truth; now all know it, except that the inwardness of its appropriation stands in an inverse relationship to the extent of its dissemination." Aesthetically the contradiction that truth becomes untruth in this or that person's mouth, is best construed comically: In the ethico-religious sphere, accent is again on the "how." But this is not to be understood as referring to demeanor, expression, or the like; rather it refers to the relationship sustained by the existing individual, in his own existence, to the content of his utterance. Objectively the interest is focussed merely on the thought-content, subjectively on the inwardness. At its maximum this inward "how" is the passion of the infinite, and the passion of the infinite is the truth. But the passion of the infinite is precisely subjectivity, and thus subjectivity becomes the truth. Objectively there is no infinite decisiveness, and hence it is objectively in order to annul the difference between good and evil, together with the principle of contradiction, and therewith also the infinite difference between the true and the false. Only in subjectivity is there decisiveness, to seek objectivity is to be in error. It is the passion of the infinite that is the decisive factor and not its content, for its content is precisely itself. In this manner subjectivity and the subjective "how" constitute the truth.

But the "how" which is thus subjectively accentuated precisely because the subject is an existing individual, is also subject to a dialectic with respect to time. In the passionate moment of decision, where the road swings away from objective knowledge, it seems as if the infinite decision were thereby realized. But in the same moment the existing individual finds himself in the temporal order, and the subjective "how" is transformed into a striving, a striving which receives indeed its impulse and a repeated renewal from the decisive passion of the infinite, but is nevertheless a striving.

When subjectivity is the truth, the conceptual determination of the truth must include an expression for the antithesis to objectivity, a memento of the fork in the road where the way swings off; this expression will at the same time serve as an indication of the tension of the subjective inwardness. Here is such a definition of truth: *An objective uncertainty held fast in an appropriation–process of the most passionate inwardness is the truth,* the highest truth attainable for an *existing* individual. At the point where the way swings off (and where this is cannot be specified objectively, since it is a matter of subjectivity), there objective knowledge is placed in abeyance. Thus the subject merely has, objectively, the uncertainty; but it is this which precisely increases the tension of that infinite passion which constitutes his inwardness. The truth is precisely the venture which chooses an objective uncertainty with the passion of the infinite. I contemplate the order of nature in the hope of finding God, and I see omnipotence and wisdom; but I also see much else that disturbs my mind and excites anxiety. The sum of all this is an objective uncertainty. But it is for this very reason that the inwardness becomes as intense as it is, for it embraces this objective uncertainty with the entire passion of the infinite. In the case of a mathematical proposition the objectivity is given, but for this reason the truth of such a proposition is also an indifferent truth.

But the above definition of truth is an equivalent expression for faith. Without risk there is no faith. Faith is precisely the contradiction between the infinite passion of the individual's inwardness and the objective uncertainty. If I am capable of grasping God objectively, I do not believe, but precisely because I cannot do this I must believe. If I wish to preserve myself in faith I must constantly be intent upon holding fast the objective uncertainty, so as to remain out upon the deep, over seventy thousand fathoms of water, still preserving my faith.

In the principle that subjectivity, inwardness, is the truth, there is comprehended the Socratic wisdom, whose everlasting merit it was to have become aware of the essential significance of existence, of the fact that the knower is an existing individual. For this reason Socrates was in the truth by virtue of his ignorance, in the highest sense in which this was possible within paganism. To attain to an understanding of this, to comprehend that the misfortune of speculative philosophy is again and again to have forgotten that the knower is an existing individual, is in our objective age difficult enough. But to have made an advance upon Socrates without even having understood what he understood, is at any rate not "Socratic."

Let us now start from this point, and as was attempted in the *Fragments,* seek a determination of thought which will really carry us further. I have nothing here to do with the question of whether this proposed thought-determination is true or not, since I am merely experimenting; but it must at any rate be clearly manifest that the Socratic thought is understood within the new proposal, so that at least I do not come out behind Socrates.

When subjectivity, inwardness, is the truth, the truth becomes objectively a paradox; and the fact that the truth is objectively a paradox shows in its turn that subjectivity is the truth. For the objective situation is repellent; and the expression for the objective repulsion constitutes the tension and the measure of the corresponding inwardness. The paradoxical character of the truth is its objective uncertainty; this uncertainty is an expression for the passionate inwardness, and this passion is precisely the truth. So far the Socratic principle. The eternal and essential truth, the truth which has an essential relationship to an existing individual because it pertains essentially to existence (all other knowledge being from the Socratic point of view accidental, its scope and degree a matter of indifference), is a paradox. But the eternal essential truth is by no means in itself a paradox; but it becomes paradoxical by virtue of its relationship to an existing individual. The Socratic ignorance gives expression to the objective uncertainty attaching to the truth, while his inwardness in existing is the truth. To anticipate here what will be developed later, let me make the following remark. The Socratic ignorance is an analogue to the category of the absurd, only that there is still less of objective certainty in the absurd, and in the repellent effect that the absurd exercises. It is certain only that it is absurd, and precisely on that account it incites to an infinitely greater tension in the corresponding inwardness. The Socratic inwardness in existing is an analogue to faith; only that the inwardness of faith, corresponding as it does, not to the repulsion of the Socratic ignorance, but to the repulsion exerted by the absurd, is infinitely more profound.

Socratically the eternal essential truth is by no means in its own nature paradoxical, but only in its relationship to an existing individual. This finds expression in another Socratic proposition, namely, that all knowledge is recollection. This proposition is not for Socrates a cue to the speculative enterprise, and hence he does not follow it up; essentially it becomes a Platonic principle. Here the way swings off; Socrates concentrates essentially upon accentuating existence, while Plato forgets this and loses himself in speculation. Socrates' infinite merit is to have been an *existing* thinker, not a speculative philosopher who forgets what it means to exist. For Socrates therefore the principle that all knowledge is recollection has at the moment of his leave-taking and as the constantly rejected possibility of engaging in speculation, the following two-fold significance: (1) that the knower is essentially *integer*, and that with respect to the knowledge of the eternal truth he is confronted with no other difficulty than the circumstance that he exists; which difficulty, however, is so essential and decisive for him that it means that existing, the process of transformation to inwardness in existing and by existing, is the truth; (2) that existence in time does not have any decisive significance, because the possibility of taking oneself back into eternity through recollection is always there, though this possibility is constantly nullified by utilizing the time, not for speculation, but for the transformation to inwardness in existing.

The infinite merit of the Socratic position was precisely to accentuate the fact that the knower is an existing individual, and that the task of existing is his essential task. Making an advance upon Socrates by failing to understand this, is quite a mediocre achievement. This Socratic principle we must therefore bear in mind, and then inquire whether the formula may not be so altered as really to make an advance beyond the Socratic position.

Subjectivity, inwardness, has been posited as the truth; can any expression for the truth be found which has a still higher degree of inwardness? Aye, there is such an expression, provided the principle that subjectivity or inwardness is the truth begins by positing the opposite principle: that subjectivity is untruth. Let us not at this point succumb to such haste as to fail in making the necessary distinctions. Speculative philosophy also says that subjectivity is untruth, but says it in order to stimulate a movement in precisely the opposite direction, namely, in the direction of the principle that objectivity is the truth. Speculative philosophy determines subjectivity negatively as tending toward objectivity. This second determination of ours, however, places a hindrance in its own way while proposing to begin, which has the effect of making the inwardness far more intensive. Socratically speaking, subjectivity is untruth if it refuses to understand that subjectivity is truth, but, for example, desires to become objective. Here, on the other hand, subjectivity in beginning upon the task of becoming the truth through a subjectifying process, is in the difficulty that it is already untruth. Thus, the labor of the task is thrust backward, backward, that is, in inwardness. So far is it from being the case that the way tends in the direction of objectivity, that the beginning merely lies still deeper in subjectivity.

But the subject cannot be untruth eternally, or eternally be presupposed as having been untruth; it must have been brought to this condition in time, or here become untruth in time. The Socratic paradox consisted in the fact that the eternal was related to an existing individual, but now existence has stamped itself upon the existing individual a second time. There has taken place so essential an alteration in him that he cannot now possibly take himself back into the eternal by way of recollection. To do this is to speculate; to be able to do this, but to reject the possibility by apprehending the task of life as a realization of inwardness in existing, is the Socratic position. But now the difficulty is that what followed Socrates on his way as a rejected possibility, has become an impossibility. If engaging in speculation was a dubious merit even from the point of view of the Socratic, it is now neither more nor less than confusion.

The paradox emerges when the eternal truth and existence are placed in juxtaposition with one another; each time the stamp of existence is brought to bear, the paradox becomes more clearly evident. Viewed Socratically the knower was simply an existing individual, but now the existing individual bears the stamp of having been essentially altered by existence.

Let us now call the untruth of the individual *Sin*. Viewed eternally he cannot be sin, nor can he be eternally presupposed as having been in sin. By coming into existence therefore (for the beginning was that subjectivity is untruth), he becomes a sinner. He is not born as a sinner in the sense that he is presupposed as being a sinner before he is born, but he is born in sin and as a sinner. This we might call *Original Sin*. But if existence has in this manner acquired a power over him, he is prevented from taking himself back into the eternal by way of recollection. If it was paradoxical to posit the eternal truth in relationship to an existing individual, it is now absolutely paradoxical to posit it in relationship to such an individual as we have here defined. But the more difficult it is made for him to take himself out of existence by way of recollection, the more profound is the inwardness that his existence may have in existence; and when it is made impossible for him, when he is held so fast in existence that the back door of recollection is forever closed to him, then his inwardness will be the most profound possible. But let us never forget that the Socratic merit was to stress the fact that the knower is an existing individual; for the more difficult the matter becomes, the greater the temptation to hasten along the easy road of speculation, away from fearful dangers and crucial decisions, to the winning of renown and honors and property, and so forth. If even Socrates understood the dubiety of taking himself speculatively out of existence back into the eternal, although no other difficulty confronted the existing individual except that he existed, and that existing was his essential task, now it is impossible. Forward he must, backward he cannot go.

Subjectivity is the truth. By virtue of the relationship subsisting between the eternal truth and the existing individual, the paradox came into being. Let us now go further, let us suppose that the eternal essential truth is itself a paradox. How does the paradox come into being? By putting the eternal essential truth into juxtaposition with existence. Hence when we posit such a conjunction within the truth itself, the truth becomes a paradox. The eternal truth has come into being in time: this is the paradox. If in accordance with the determinations just posited, the subject is prevented by sin from taking himself back into the eternal, now he need not trouble himself about this; for now the eternal essential truth is not behind him but in front of him, through its being in existence or having existed, so that if the individual does not existentially and in existence lay hold of the truth, he will never lay hold of it.

Existence can never be more sharply accentuated than by means of these determinations. The evasion by which speculative philosophy attempts to recollect itself out of existence has been made impossible. With reference to this, there is nothing for speculation to do except to arrive at an understanding of this impossibility; every speculative attempt which insists on being speculative shows *eo ipso* that it has not understood it. The individual may thrust all this away from him, and take refuge in speculation; but it is impossible first to accept it, and then to revoke it by means of speculation, since it is definitely calculated to prevent speculation.

When the eternal truth is related to an existing individual it becomes a paradox. The paradox repels in the inwardness of the existing individual, through the objective uncertainty and the corresponding Socratic ignorance. But since the paradox is not in the first instance itself paradoxical (but only in its relationship to the existing individual), it does not repel with a sufficient intensive inwardness. For without risk there is no faith, and the greater the risk the greater the faith; the more objective security the less inwardness (for inwardness is precisely subjectivity), and the less objective security the more profound the possible inwardness. When the paradox is paradoxical in itself, it repels the individual by virtue of its absurdity, and the corresponding passion of inwardness is faith. But subjectivity, inwardness, is the truth; for otherwise we have forgotten what the merit of the Socratic position is. But there can be no stronger expression for inwardness than when the retreat out of existence into the eternal by way of recollection is impossible; and when, with truth confronting the individual as a paradox, gripped in the anguish and pain of sin, facing the tremendous risk of the objective insecurity, the individual believes. But without risk no faith, not even the Socratic form of faith, much less the form of which we here speak.

When Socrates believed that there was a God, he held fast to the objective uncertainty with the whole passion of his inwardness, and it is precisely in this contradiction and in this risk, that faith is rooted. Now it is otherwise. Instead of the objective uncertainty, there is here a certainty, namely, that objectively it is absurd; and this absurdity, held fast in the passion of inwardness, is faith. The Socratic ignorance is as a witty jest in comparison with the earnestness of facing the absurd; and the Socratic existential inwardness is as Greek light-mindedness in comparison with the grave strenuosity of faith.

What now is the absurd? The absurd is—that the eternal truth has come into being in time, that God has come into being, has been born, has grown up, and so forth, precisely like any other individual human being, quite indistinguishable from other individuals.

SECTION THREE

F.R. TENNANT

⤎

Faith*

The word "faith," when it does not mean either The Faith (Christian Beliefs) or trust, has been used down the ages to the present day, with very few exceptions, as a synonym for religious belief. In other words, faith and belief have been regarded almost universally as identical. There is a need, however, for the term "faith" in addition to "belief," in order to give a name to an attitude of mind that is akin to belief yet distinct from it. Both terms signify mental states or acts belonging to the cognitive side of experience; but while "belief" emphasises almost exclusively the intellectual element in assent, and has reference to an objective situation, "faith" rather lays stress on the conative factor of the subjective attitude. Belief is more or less constrained by fact or actuality which already exists in complete independence of any desiring or striving on our part, and which in some degree compels our assent. Faith, as it is here conceived, is, on the other hand, not concerned with actuality that is or was, but with the possible, which may or may not prove to be actual. Belief is assent to data; faith, in the first instance, is not confronted with data, but creates its objects, which are ideas, just as the mathematician posits the entities with which he deals —for instance, spaces of different numbers of dimensions. By practical activity, or living as if its ideal creations were also real, faith may go on to discover their actuality. Though not knowledge, it is possibly, and

*Chapter VI of F.R. Tennant, *The Nature of Belief*, Centenary Press, London, 1943, pp. 62–78.

often actually, a step towards knowledge, and to knowledge otherwise unattainable.

There has already been occasion, in the foregoing pages, to allude to this faith. It is involved, the reader will remember, in Science's adoption of the metaphysical principles which must underlie the whole process of the inductive method if that method is to be understood to yield certain knowledge, as distinct from probable Beliefs. It is also involved in what has been called the "primitive credulity" of early mankind. And now it may be added that it is generally involved in the invention of all kinds of machines. The engine or machine desired by a mechanician is first imagined or conceived; it does not as yet exist as an actuality; steps are then taken to construct an actual copy of what was supposed to be possible; and if these steps meet with success, what was hoped for is actualised. Besides invention, discovery of what already exists but has hitherto remained unknown may be the outcome of the venture of faith: the outstanding instance is the discovery of America by Columbus.

It has been remarked by one of the very few writers who have discerned the difference between this faith and belief, and the function of faith as a means to knowledge, that there is an analogy between man's acquisition of knowledge by realisation of the hoped-for and Nature's production of higher from lower forms of organic life in the course of the evolutionary process. Almost every forward step in that process, he says, could be formulated as an adoption of a line of conduct not warranted by present facts: each of such steps was "an act of faith not warranted by aught within the ken of the savant at that point. There was little, for example, in all that the wisest fish could know to justify the belief that there was more scope for existence on the earth than in the water and that persistent attempts to live on land would issue in the transformation of his swim-bladder into lungs."[1] Whether or not this analogy seems at all fanciful, it is a fact that much of the belief which underlies knowledge, or what we commonly account knowledge, is the outcome of faith which ventures beyond the apprehension and treatment of data to supposition, imagination and creation of ideal objects, and justifies its audacity and irrationality (in accounting them to be also real) by practical actualisation. Many theoretical propositions were preceded by practical maxims, and much of our learning has issued out of doing. Not only is there "more in life than logic"; there is more in knowledge than logic, and more in reasonableness than ratiocination and rationality. Faith-venture is a cause of belief, and is dictated by human interest. And it is not confined to the realms of morality and religion, but is involved in theoretical and existential knowledge as well. Hence it is that theory of knowledge needs the word "faith," with

[1] J. Ward, *Essays in Philosophy*, 1927, p. 106.

a different signification from that of "belief," as well as does religion. Faith involves the determination to be guided by such experience as we have, rather than by none at all, and to experiment in the realm of the merely possible or ideal.

There is, of course, nothing in the nature of faith to guarantee that its adventurousness will always be crowned with success. Hopeful experimenting succeeded when an engineer invented the steam-engine, but not when faith-inspired mechanicians tried to produce machines capable of perpetual motion. Faith as to the possibility of squaring the circle, again, has never issued in aught but futile labour on the part of amateurs lacking due respect for the judgment of experts. And if Columbus had steered for Utopia with the same sanguine faith that urged him to cross the Atlantic, he would not have found it. Not every imagination or idea that the mind of man can shape has its counterpart in the actual world, though there are probably more existing things than the human mind has dreamed of. Faith has always to take the risk of disappointment and defeat.

It has been stated above that science must have had its origin in primitive faith. Mankind did not begin its intellectual career with innate ideas or knowledge, or with reminiscence of what it knew in a previous state of existence. It began by learning, and after acquiring the modicum of learning sufficient to enable it to act otherwise than by inherited instinct, it learned largely by doing. Learning came out of both success and failure: in either case man ventured before he could have. The causal law, or the principle of uniformity, is not written so large or so legibly on natural phenomena that, in the time of man's primitiveness, he who ran could read it off. On the other hand, had it not been hoped for, expected, and tentatively assumed, here a little and there a little and line upon line, the principle would not have become known. "Nothing venture, nothing have" must have been the habit of mind in virtue of which the "rationality" of the world such as science, with its "reign of law," describes, was gradually discerned. There is no *a priori* reason why the world should be amenable to scientific reasoning: a world conceivably might be of such a nature that any kind of event in it succeeded on any other kind of happening. But science has approached the world with the quasi-religious faith that the world is thus amenable, and has maintained its hope against the world itself, throughout its struggle to reduce brute facts to order and law. The "father of the faithful," in leaving his Mesopotamian home, forsaking the Nature-worship of his ancestors, and hearkening to the inward summons to go out *not knowing* whither he went, was not only a prophetic type of the religious history of Israel but also an allegory of the intellectual progress of the human race. If he had been a mere adventurer, without any inward "call," this analogy would be still more apt. Had not man similarly trusted the regularity of Nature while as yet it was unknown or unverified, the unseen but hoped-for truth would never have been substantiated.

These last sentences will have recalled the eleventh chapter of the *Epistle to the Hebrews;* and as that passage contains the earliest and the classical exposition of what faith, as distinct from belief or assent, is, it calls here for some consideration. The word for faith ($\pi\iota\sigma\tau\iota\varsigma$ — pistis) used by the unknown author of the Epistle, is the same as that which in other books of the New Testament is translated by "faith," though in them it never has the same connotation. In the Synoptic Gospels it is used for confidence in the power of Christ to heal, as contrasted with the unbelief on account of which He could not heal some sick persons, and for the spontaneously adopted attitude towards Christ which would be involved in acceptance of His words as truth. The faith which can remove mountains would seem to be belief in God or trust in Christ and His claims, rather than an attitude towards unknown objects, and to be equivalent to the belief with which, our Lord said, "all things are possible." In classical Greek, again, $\pi\iota\sigma\tau\iota\varsigma$ means either trust, fidelity, or unverified conviction as contrasted with knowledge, but apparently never anything akin to what is defined by the author of the Epistle to the Hebrews. In the fourth Gospel the verb corresponding to $\pi\iota\sigma\tau\iota\varsigma$ ($\pi\iota\sigma\tau\epsilon\upsilon\epsilon\iota\nu$ — pisteuein) is used for believing that Jesus is the divine Logos, for believing on His name (probably a reference to the profession required at baptism), and for allegiance to Him as a means to eternal life. The faith through which, as St. Paul teaches, a man is justified by God, consists in accepting the unmerited and free gift of God's justifying grace, and involves previous belief as to God's existence; and the word, as this Apostle uses it in its subjective sense, again denotes an attitude towards *known* beings — God or Christ. When he says (2 Cor. v. 7) that we (Christians) "walk by faith," he might seem to be contemplating faith such as creates ideas of intrinsically invisible things and assumes their reality, but the preceding verse shows that he only means that during our earthly embodied life the actual ascended Christ is hidden from our eyes.

Besides belief and trust, or confidence, there is one other meaning of $\pi\iota\sigma\tau\iota\varsigma$ to be mentioned in connexion with the New Testament. In the Pauline Epistles, and more commonly in Acts of the Apostles, the word is used in its objective sense, in which it denotes Beliefs. In the phrase "stand fast in the faith," for instance, "faith" means the body of facts and doctrines as to which believers were instructed. When, in later times, rules of faith or creeds were formulated, they were regarded as summaries of "the faith once delivered to the saints," or of truth having apostolic authority.

Such being the meanings of $\pi\iota\sigma\tau\iota\varsigma$ in the New Testament, it will be seen that the faith described by the writer of the Epistle to the Hebrews is of a unique kind. He uses the noun without its article, signifying that he speaks of faith in the abstract, or as a general psychical attitude, and not of faith of the peculiarly Christian kind. Indeed he regards faith as a mental functioning that may be found in any human mind; for among his instances of the faithful culled from the Old Testament he includes the heathen Rahab, one "who believed not in the God of Israel." This faith is defined in words which admit of the two different translations given respectively in the text and the margin of the Revised Version. The one runs thus: "faith is the assurance of [things] hoped for, the proving of things not seen." Here the words "assurance" and "proving" denote a subjective state (certitude) and a subjective act — that of putting to the test. The other translation, apparently considered less suitable by the translators in that it is a marginal reading, is: "faith is the giving substance to [things] hoped for, the test of things not seen." As it stands, this latter translation seems to imply that the "giving" of substance, and therefore of reality, is done by the faithful person; in which case the Greek (hypostasis) would denote a subjective act. If Liddell and Scott's abridged Greek Lexicon is exhaustive in its list of meanings borne by hypostasis, the word never means "giving substance," but merely "substance"; it is substance itself which gives reality to things. The word "giving" would thus appear to be a translator's gloss. If we expunge the word "giving," the second of the translations would state that faith is not the substantiation, but the substance, of things hoped for. But such a view as that, implying that ultimate realities are the creation of the human mind, is the opposite of what a Platonist would hold. And the writer seems to be somewhat of a Platonist: not only do "things hoped for" and "unseen" suggest the "universals," or abstract "ideas," of Plato's philosophical system, but several distinctions drawn in this Epistle are expressed, after the manner of Plato, in terms of the contrast between archetype and copy, substance and shadow, reality and appearance; and there are numerous coincidences of vocabulary with that of Philo, a Platonising Alexandrian Jew. This translation is in keeping with the interpretation put upon it by Greek patristic writers; and Westcott regarded the use of the Greek word for "proving" or "test" as decisive in its favour. It seems to be generally held by commentators that the word for "substance," like that for "test," has an objective signification, and does not mean a subject's act such as "giving," though they generally translate hypostasis by "giving substance" rather than by "substance" alone. Dr. Inge[2] quotes Chrysostom as saying "whereas things that are matters of hope seem to be unsubstantial, Faith gives them substance; or rather, does not give it, but is itself their being." He also cites the words of Du Bose: "Faith is not only assurance; it is the present possession, the very substance and reality of its object. Assurance is substance, Faith is fact,

[2]Faith, 1909, pp. 16, 17.

promise is fulfilment, hope is possession and fruition. . . ." The quotation from Chrysostom, however, continues thus: "For instance, the resurrection has not taken place, and is not in substance, but Faith gives it reality (ὑφίστησιν) in our soul." The last three words of this sentence find a parallel in those which are here italicised in the following interpretation given in Westcott's work on the Epistle to the Hebrews: "Nor is it a valid objection that ὑπόστασις [substance] is not in this case strictly 'essence' as applied to the several objects of hope, but (generally) that which gives reality to them. For it is in virtue of Faith that things hoped for *are*[3] now, so that Faith is their essence *in regard to the actual experience of the believer.* Thus the general scope of the statement [in Heb. xi 1] is to show that the future, and the unseen can be *made real for men* by faith. Things which in the succession of time are still 'hoped for' as future have a true existence in the eternal order; and this existence Faith *brings home to the believer* as a real fact."

Now reality "in our soul," essence "in regard to the experience of the believer," reality "for men," and existence "brought home to the believer" are very different from existence *per se,* and from essence, substantiality or reality, in the plain and usual sense of the words; and all the interpretations which have been quoted overlook this difference. The several authors of them would fain take the writer of the Epistle to mean that reality in the true sense — i.e., reality the same as that of God or of Christ, which is wholly independent of human states of mind — is conferred on the hoped for and unseen by man's faith; whereas their own phrases utter the contrary to all who are able to discern the difference between reality proper and so-called reality. Faith, of course, cannot confer existence on the non-existent, such as the future which as yet *is* not; it cannot create things out of nothing; such substantiation as lies within its capacity consists in treating hoped for and unseen things, which as yet are only known as possibilities, or as matters of its own conceiving, *as if* they were real, in the proper sense of the word, and then acting accordingly. Interpreters, by the unconscious use of rhetoric, or by confounding the literal with a metaphorical meaning, have endeavoured to annihilate the difference between faith and knowledge. But as they finally allow that the substantiality which faith confers upon its objects is but "substantiality" (in the sense of significance) for the believer, it follows that the two translations of Heb. xi 1, given respectively in the text and the margin of the Revised Version, are identical in meaning.

Faith, then, as described in this *locus classicus,* is *in itself* efficacious, and not because, as elsewhere in the New Testament, of its being faith in Christ or in God. And its objects are things hoped for and unseen, whatever these may be. Possibly the writer has in mind what ancient

---

[3]The italics, in the case of this word, are Westcott's.

philosophers, *e.g.*, Plato, regarded as thought-given realities—few modern philosophers would grant that there are any such things—or "timeless existents," such as now generally deemed to be impossibilities, but of which things temporal were regarded as shadows: *e.g.*, Plato described time as the moving shadow of eternity. The sacred writer does not mean that the *esse* of the unseen things is their *percipi* by faith, or that their reality consists in their being believed by human subjects; for they then might be comparable to dream-objects or fancy-bred entities, destined never to enter the realm of actuality. Their so called "reality," before faith proves them pragmatically to have also true reality, is their efficacy, when certitude is entertained as to their actuality, to mould belief and to determine conduct.

The substantiating or realising which faith effects is, in fact, what is meant by our word "realise," when used in one of its colloquial senses. We are familiar with the difference between the aspect of an event which has just happened or is about to happen, before we have discerned its import or the implications with which it may be fraught, and its aspect after its purport, significance and consequences have come within our ken. What was "nothing to us" becomes "something for us": something, that is to say, with which we have to reckon, or which may influence our thought and action. When that is the case, we speak of having "realised" what an event or a situation is, and mean that its significance has been brought home to us. Faith similarly "realises" hoped for and unseen things when it assumes their as yet unproved actuality and, acting on the certitude that they are real existents, establishes practical relations with them. Faith thus extends our intellectual horizon so that it includes the unknown Beyond and brings it within reach of experiment. As has been already observed, faith may fail to prove the reality of its objects, and the classical exposition of the nature of faith given in the Epistle to the Hebrews is insufficient in that it does not explicitly recognise this possibility. Successful faith, however, is defined with psychological accuracy, and is illustrated by numerous examples of the gaining of material and moral advantages, the surmounting of trials and afflictions, and the attainment of heroic life, by men of old who were inspired by faith. It is thus that faith is pragmatically "verified" and that certitude as to the unseen is established. It should be observed, however, that such verification is only for certitude, not a proving of certainty as to external reality. The fruitfulness of a belief or of faith for the moral and religious life is one thing, and the reality or existence of what is ideated and assumed is another. There are instances in which a belief that is not true, in the sense of corresponding with fact, may inspire one with lofty ideals and stimulate one to strive to be a more worthy person. And though the foundations of inductive science are matters of faith, and Science's verification of them is also merely pragmatic, it is of a different kind from that which is illustrated in the Epistle. Verification of a scientific postulate or theory does not consist in disciplining the scientific researcher, either as a lover of truth or as a moral citizen, and consequently cannot be likened to the pragmatic verification of religious faith. It consists in finding that the postulate or theory is borne out by appeal to external facts and tallies with them. It is true that this latter kind of verification also falls short of being logical certification; for to be *the* explanation of facts, a theory must not only fit and be exemplified by the facts, but must be the *only one* that does so; and that scarcely admits of proof. Still, such verification has probability of a higher order than the other. Nevertheless, verification such as religion claims for its faith will satisfy most men. "Nothing that science can say," wrote the late Professor J. Ward, "will ever quench men's faith in God if they find that on the whole they make the best of the world by it: . . . however much in theory men consider premises, in practice, which ever precedes theory, they consider only results. But the practice which justifies itself by results is also in the end at one with the theory it has helped to complete."[4]

It has been pointed out that there is nothing unique in *religious* faith if it be such as is described in the Epistle to the Hebrews: religious faith is psychologically of the same nature as that which underlies inductive science, and the only difference lies in the objects to which the faith refers. For all his exclusively religious concern, the writer would doubtless have sanctioned an application of his definition of faith to other departments of thought. Had he lived now he might extend his list of the faithful and say, for instance, that by faith Newton founded modern physics on his few and simple laws of motion, or that more recent physical theory was the outcome of the faith-creation of the electron. There is a close similarity between his teaching and that contained in the lines of Hartley Coleridge:

> Think not faith by which the just shall live
> Is a dead creed, a map correct of heaven,
> Far less a feeling fond and fugitive,
> A thoughtless gift, withdrawn as soon as given;
> It is an affirmation and an act
> That binds eternal truth to present fact.

It has been already remarked that this conception of faith is very rarely to be met with in literature dealing with faith, since faith has almost universally been regarded as identical with belief. There is, however, one ancient father whose teaching has some resemblance to that of the unknown sacred writer, namely, Clement of Alexandria. The resemblance is but superficial, and Clement's meaning is not easy to

---

[4]*Essays in Philosophy*, 1927, pp. 107–8.

ascertain, as the following quotations will show. "But faith, which the Greeks disparage, deeming it futile and barbarous, is a voluntary preconception [or anticipation], the assent of piety." After citing Heb. xi 1, Clement continues: "Others have defined faith to be a uniting assent to an unseen object, as certainly the proof of an unknown thing is an evident assent. If then it be choice, being desirous of something, desire is in this instance intellectual. And since choice is the beginning of action, faith is discovered to be the beginning of action, being the foundation of rational choice in the case of anyone who exhibits to himself the previous demonstration through faith. Unswerving choice, then, gives considerable momentum in the direction of knowledge. The exercise of faith directly becomes knowledge, reposing on a sure foundation."[5] In this passage the description of faith as "the assent of piety" shows that the writer is contemplating Christian belief, not faith in general; and other passages give the impression that this particular kind of "faith" is the only one that he ever has in mind. Assent to [i.e., belief in] an unknown object is certainly not a "proof" of the unknown thing's existence; what choice, which presupposes reference to alternatives, has to do with actions in general and faith in particular, is difficult to see; as is also how or why the exercise of faith, through its supposed connexion with choice, reposes on a sure foundation and passes directly into knowledge: a passage could hardly be more dogmatic and obscure. A little further on in the same work, Clement, again contemplating Christian "faith" [i.e., belief] founded on the Scriptures, etc., speaks of "the infallible criterion of faith" and of faith's advancing over the pathway of the objects of sense to things free of deception, and reposing in the truth. Here again he cannot be speaking of faith such as is described in Heb. xi 1, which is verified only by the kind of conduct which it inspires, or of faith such as may issue in denial of the reality of its objects as well as in discovery of their actuality. In a later chapter (Ch. xi.) he speaks of intelligent faith as produced by the opening up of the Scriptures, the result of which is knowledge; and though in more than one passage he asserts that "faith" is the foundation of knowledge, he speaks of knowledge other than that acquired by the inductive method — the only kind of knowledge of which faith is known to be the foundation. Instead of being a venture beginning in unfounded supposition, Clement's faith is the direct leap to certainty, and is explicitly contrasted with supposition. And though he makes the sound assertion that the faith of the simple believer may be transformed by education into knowledge, the faith which he has in view seems always to be identical with that of Anselm, whose *credo*, in *credo ut intelligam* (I believe in order to understand), expresses belief (not faith) founded on

---

[5]The quotations of Clement are from Vol. XII of the *Ante-Nicene Christian Library*, containing his *Stromateis*. See pp. 5–6, 8.

the authority of the Church. Thus, though Clement now and again uses words which suggest that he *might* be aware of the nature of faith, as distinct from Christian belief, the contexts in which such words occur preclude the crediting him with the psychological insight of the writer of the Epistle to the Hebrews. He does not anticipate the discovery that faith is the origin of much secular as well as religious knowledge, but rather starts in the Church the tradition which is handed on by Augustine to Anselm and others, that the belief in doctrines having the authority of the Church and Scripture may be explicated and made clear in the light of reason, so that the simple Christian who begins with believing may go on to understand what he believes, and become what Clement calls "the true gnostic."

There remains one other philosophical writer to be mentioned who has made use of the conception of faith described in this chapter, though it is sometimes given a different name by him. Kant drew a distinction between understanding and reason, involving the use of the latter word in a restricted sense, narrower than that in which he elsewhere employs it.[6] By "understanding" he means the operation of applying to the impressions of sense ideas ("categories") such as those of substance and cause, likeness and difference, and thereby *constituting* the things or objects of social experience. These are the objects of which science treats, and of which we have knowledge, in the stricter sense of the word. Such knowledge, however, is but of particular laws, etc., as separate items; it is not unified knowledge of the world as one whole, nor does it embrace the realm of the moral. Thus knowledge has its bounds and limits; and if we would unify scientific knowledge and envisage the world as a totality, we must employ some faculty other than understanding. It is here where Kant finds use for what he technically calls "reason," and what equally well might be called "faith." The objective validity of knowledge fashioned by the supposedly *a priori* categories was regarded by Kant as complete, since the experience we actually have would be impossible without the principles based on those categories. But the ideas supplied by reason, as distinct from understanding, for the purpose of answering the wider questions which science raises but cannot solve, are not, he taught, of the same kind as the categories which constitute knowledge: they are not indispensable to scientific experience *as such,* since they presuppose that experience and it does not presuppose them. The ideas of reason do not yield knowledge, they do but unify knowledge. They satisfy desire rather than the rational understanding. Thus, he wrote, "all human knowledge begins with intuitions, advances to concepts, and ends with Ideas." Reason begins where understanding ends. The three ideas which it

---

[6]As in the title of one of his chief works, *The Critique of Pure Reason,* where reason includes understanding.

supplies for the transcending and unifying knowledge are those of the soul (the unity underlying all mental operations), the world (the unity of the whole series of the conditions of natural phenomena) and God (the unity of all objects of thought). The soul, the world as a whole, and God are not entities that can be rigidly demonstrated or be known; they are regulative, but not constitutive, of knowledge. The ideas of them are suggested by knowledge, and in order to unify our knowledge reason [or faith] postulates them. They belong to the realm of things hoped for and unseen: they are possibilities.

So Kant taught: and he thus finds room for faith left by the limitations of knowledge. His hard line drawn between "constitutive" understanding and "regulative" reason [or faith] is psychologically without warrant, and we are now able to see continuity where he was inclined to see or create gaps. He drew his hard line, indeed, in the wrong place; for the categories of substance and cause, which are indispensable for scientific knowledge, have turned out to be as "regulative" as his ideas of reason, and to be of anthropomorphic rather than of "logomorphic" *i.e.*, logical origin. But his contribution to our knowledge concerning faith, or reason as he called it, with its delimitation of the spheres of faith and knowledge, is nevertheless important and suggestive. The idea of God as the world-ground, he declared to be "a flawless ideal," and "a conception which completes and crowns the whole of human knowledge." The idea of the soul includes that of its freedom, and Kant says of it that this is consequently the only one of the three ideas of reason whose object is matter of fact and can be counted among things known. And it is in virtue of this fact of human freedom that Kant was led to find a further use than that of unifying knowledge for postulating by faith the existence of the Deity.

He was shrewd enough to see — what so many others have not been able to see — that doctrine as to theological matter of fact cannot logically be extracted from pure judgments of value. Even if ethical principles and ideals were absolute, or independent of all cognition and human interests, we should need to be assured that the universe respects our ideals and aspirations before we could argue from their present existence to their perpetuation beyond this life and their fulfilment hereafter. The value of goodness is one thing: the permanent existence of the good is another thing. So far as ethics can know, the moral life of human beings may be but a transient episode in a cosmic process which has blindly stumbled on man. There is thus no direct implication, in man's possession of the moral status and categorical imperatives of conscience, of the existence of a Deity or a supersensible world. Knowing all this, Kant did not profess to provide a moral demonstration of theism; he merely argued that the idea of God is a postulate — a venture of faith — required by the practical reason (*i.e.*, will and conscience) as well as a regulative idea for the theoretical reason which supplements the understanding. He taught that *if* the moral order is to stand permanently, and *if* the highest good, which ought to be realised, is to be realised, then God must exist in order to secure the requisite conditions. God and immortality are apprehended by faith. They are postulates which justify themselves because they are bound up with the facts of moral life, which cannot be unified into knowledge of a meaningful or reasonable world without them. They can produce conviction or certitude — indeed for Kant they were the only legitimate ground of religious belief — but they are not demonstrated certainties.

In these ways Kant insisted on man's right to believe or to exercise faith. Belief and faith cannot be entertained if they are in opposition to known truths; but science knows of no truths to which the fundamental articles of religion are in contradiction. The assertion of faith, that there is a God and a supersensible world, can no more be disproved than it can be proved, he might say; for the things that are seen and are temporal depend for their existence on real but unseen conditions which are beyond the ken of all the sciences.

The limitations of knowledge will now be seen to have an important bearing on the scope and the rights of faith. A century or so ago it was often maintained that the scientific method is the sole means of approach to the whole realm of possible knowledge; that there are no reasonably propounded questions that science cannot hope to answer, and no problems worth discussing to which its method is inapplicable. But since men of science have scrutinised their method they have become more modest. They no longer speak, for instance, of a natural law as an assertion of what always was, will be, and must be, but of what has been up to date and may be expected to be in the future. They acknowledge that science can only deal with the repeatable — *i.e.*, with phenomena and events sufficiently alike to be accounted the same, and that it is inapplicable to the once-occurring, *i.e.*, to history, which never can repeat itself. Science needs to abstract and select from experience in its fullness and concreteness, and therefore to leave out: but what it is compelled to leave out is nevertheless still there. The intelligibility which it seeks and finds in the world is but intelligibility of one kind, namely causal connectedness and calculability. With the world's possibility of being "rational" in the teleological sense, that is reasonable, in virtue of being the outcome of purposeful intelligence and achieving an end, science has nothing to do. Hence Ward's saying, that "science might have furnished its work and yet be a fool."

There is another line of thought by which the claim that knowledge leaves room for faith may be justified. It has been represented in an earlier context that the view of the world which has been made accessible to us through intercommunication cannot be shared by the individual until he has been socialised. Still less can the world as seen from the intellectual level be viewed by the lower animals; for the lowest level of experience, *i.e.*, the merely sensory, gives no hint of it. And yet it is there.[7] There *may*, then, be a higher world which intelligence, in turn, is incapable of discerning. In the beautiful and the good we get hints suggestive of such a world. Faith is thus moved to create its belief in God whom "no eye hath seen" and who is not found by intellectual searching. In the case of Kant it is suggestions caused by the existence and the conditions of man's moral status that beget the assurance of the hoped for and the evidencing of the unseen. And faith thus caused is continuous with the faith of science and is "foreshadowed in the upward striving that is the essence of life."

It will now be seen that faith, as distinct from either objectively evoked belief or authoritatively dictated belief, is essentially conative and creative. It is creative in supposing and postulating its unknown objects, and is conative in that it is an impulse fraught with desire, but not, as some would say of religious belief, the outcome of deliberate willing. It is rather an incentive to such volition than the result of it. It will also have become plain that faith is no one of any of the following things with which various writers have identified what they call faith: feeling, emotion, instinct, immediate intuition of objects, immediate apprehension of eternal values, certified knowledge. Moreover, it is not a supernatural gift, or a bestowal of divine grace, or the outcome of volition guided by God. What is commonly called faith, but is rather religious belief, has been asserted by theologians of different schools, *e.g.*, Aquinas and Luther, to be of this nature. It would be difficult to reconcile this doctrine with that according to which belief is caused by the authority of the Church, and also to account for the apparently promiscuous and parsimonious distribution of "faith" among the sons of men. Psychologically speaking, the emergence of religious belief calls no more for supernatural causation than any other kind of belief: belief is always the same attitude, however different its objects may be. Still less reason would there be for assigning faith a supernatural origin, since religious faith is continuous in nature with faith in non-religious objects. Faith is an outcome of the inborn propensity to self-conservation and self-betterment which is a part of human nature, and is no more a miraculously superadded endowment than is sensation or understanding.

Faith, in the sense of Christian belief or trust, is often associated with hope, as in St. Paul's trio of faith, hope and charity. Naturally hope was highly esteemed at the time when the second coming of Christ was eagerly looked for, else it would seem difficult to account for the selection of hope, out of so many possible candidates, as one of the

[7] J. Ward, *op. cit.*, p. 354.

highest virtues. Faith which is neither belief nor trust, but venturesome supposition, also has a natural kinship with hope, but is not to be identified with it. Hope is a species of expectation fraught with pleasant feeling and desire. It is relatively passive, whereas faith is a creative activity provocative of effort. The opposite of hope is fear or despair: the opposite of faith is mental inertia or indifference as to any spiritual Beyond. Hope involves a slight degree of assurance: faith is assurance sanguine enough to be called certitude.

TERENCE PENELHUM

The Analysis of Faith
in St. Thomas Aquinas*

My intent in this paper is to give an account of Aquinas' analysis of
the nature of Christian faith, to indicate some difficulties to which it
seems to me, and has seemed to others, to give rise, to try to evaluate
the degree to which his analysis can suggest answers to those difficulties, and then to conclude with some general comments about the
sources of those perplexities that still remain.[1]

I must preface my argument with some remarks about the manner in
which I shall approach this topic, since it differs radically from the
manner in which St. Thomas approaches it. My inquiry, like most
analytical philosophy of religion, is a second-order conceptual exercise.
As such it is intended to be religiously neutral. Aquinas' account of faith
is nothing of the sort. For him it is an enterprise undertaken within the
faith, not in artificial detachment from it; it is theology, not philosophy.

At first sight this will not seem to present a problem. Theologians,
one might say, engage in second-order examination of religious concepts in much the same way that philosophers do, and the fact that the
neutrality the philosopher assumes is not assumed by the theologian
does not prevent the philosopher asking whether the theologian's in-

[1]This is a revised version of a paper originally presented at an Aquinas Septcentennial
conference at the University of Calgary in October 1974. My subsequent reflections
have benefited greatly from the comments of Dr Anthony Kenny on that occasion;
although he would not, I am sure, agree with all the arguments as they now stand.

*From *Religious Studies*, Vol. 13, 1977. Copyright © 1977 Cambridge University
Press, pp. 133–154. Reprinted, with abridgments, by permission of the publisher.

terpretations are accurate analyses of their first-order use. For example, if the philosopher is interested in elucidating the concepts of revelation or miracle, the fact that theological analyses of those notions presuppose that they have real application (that there *is* revelation or *are* miracles) makes it no harder for a philosopher, who does not presuppose these things, to ask whether the theologian's analysis reflects a correct understanding of the first-order use of them by Christians. It is just a matter of distinguishing between understanding a tradition and accepting it.

In the case of faith, however, this answer will not serve. For a neutral analysis of the concepts of revelation or miracle is one which tells us what those who believe in these things understand them to be, without thereby committing the author of the analysis on the question of whether anything *is* a revelation or a miracle. But to say this about the analysis of the notion of faith is to imply that one is neutral on the question of whether anyone *has* faith or not. And this seems absurd. Surely faith, like virtue, is common and recognizable, and the problem is that of deciding what sort of a state it is? But this will not serve either; for it is integral to some accounts of what it is, and Aquinas' is one of these, that faith only occurs in consequence of an infusion of divine grace, that it can only have as its object the entire set of Articles proposed for acceptance in the Creeds of the Church, and that faith in anything false is impossible. It looks as though these are propositions on which no neutrality is possible; in particular, it looks as though on this account no one who assumes professional neutrality about the truth of the Articles of the faith is in a position to say that there are instances of it.

I cannot produce a satisfactory resolution of this methodological impasse without taking the whole paper to deal with it. I shall content myself with a short and unargued statement of how I shall proceed.[2] I shall assume that there is a phenomenon, or group of similar phenomena, of which the world 'faith' is the name, and which is characteristic of Christians. I shall assume that a major part of the purpose of the theological debates to which St. Thomas's discussions of faith are a contribution is the kind of understanding of the nature of that phenomenon that philosophers also wish to attain. I shall further assume that some of the claims St. Thomas makes about faith are additional claims about the cause, appropriate object, and salvific significance of the phenomenon, and that although one must outline these claims in the course of the philosophical analysis of faith, the uncommitted nature of that analysis prevents a direct evaluation of them. But I shall proceed on the assumption that this does not preclude us from identifying

[2]For an extended discussion of this question, see Chapter 6 of my *Problems of Religious Knowledge* (Macmillan, London, 1971).

instances of faith, or from obtaining a substantial degree of understanding of the distinctive features of the phenomenon. More simply, I shall take it for granted that some men have faith, and that it is possible, without theological commitment, to come to an understanding of what it means to say this of them.

I

In Aquinas' theology faith, hope, and charity are the three *theological virtues*. As virtues they conform to the definition that applies to all virtues, namely 'a good habit (or disposition) of the mind, by which we live righteously, of which no one can make bad use'.[3] They differ from the natural virtues, both moral and intellectual, in several key respects.

1. They are due to a special infusion of grace, and do not derive from any natural aptitude in us in the way that the natural virtues do. They come, as Thomas puts it, 'entirely from the outside.'[4] The need for grace is not, here, a consequence of the fact that our natures are corrupted. The happiness for which the theological virtues prepare man surpasses the powers even of uncorrupted human nature; hence it is mistaken to think that man before the fall, or the angels before lapse or confirmation, had no need of faith, hope, or charity, or could acquire them without special grace.[5] Accordingly the definition above is incomplete in the case of the theological virtues. Theological virtue is 'a good disposition of the mind, by which we live righteously, of which no one can make bad use, and *which God works in us without us*'.

2. It follows from this that we cannot acquire the theological virtues in the manner we can acquire the natural virtues. In particular, we cannot acquire them by the repetition of suitable actions.[6] We can, however, lose them by a single contrary action: a brittleness which is not a feature of the natural virtues either.[7] This means, for example, that if someone denies one article of faith, he no longer can be said to have faith even with respect to the other articles which he still accepts; similarly if he hopes for some of what is promised but despairs of the rest, the virtue of hope is lost to him.

3. Aquinas follows Aristotle in holding that the natural virtues are characterized by the observance of the Mean between extremes. (He has to strain a little to make this fit the intellectual virtues, but holds that it does.)[8] It looks as though faith, which holds a *via media* between

---

[3]*Summa Theologiae* 1a2ae.55,4. In the case of long quotations I have used the new Blackfriars edition of the *Summa*, published by Eyre and Spottiswoode, London.

[4]*S.T.* 1a2ae.63,1; see also 51,4.

[5]See *De Veritate* 14,10, reply to second difficulty; also *S.T.* 2a2ae.5,1.

[6]*S.T.* 1a2ae.63,2.

[7]*De Veritate* 14,10, reply to tenth difficulty.

[8]*S.T.* 1a2ae.64,3.

competing heresies, does observe a Mean; the same seems to be true of hope, which steers a middle course between despair and presumption. But in spite of these considerations he denies that the doctrine of the Mean applies to the theological virtues. His reason is that

> . . . we can never love God as much as He ought to be loved, nor believe and hope in him as much as we should. Much less, therefore, can there be excess in such things.[9]

4. Dispositions can be distinguished from one another by the nature of the objects which they have; beliefs are classified as mathematical or historical, for example, because of the formal differences in the objects (in this case propositions) with which they are concerned. The theological virtues are distinguished from other dispositions by the fact that it is God himself who is their object. It is he whom we believe in in faith, have confidence in in hope, and love in charity.[10]

5. Not only do we have need of grace to acquire the theological virtues, but we need to learn of their very existence and availability to us through revelation. This distinguishes them sharply from the natural virtues, which were known and described in the pagan world.[11]

In spite of these differences, the theological virtues share many key features with the natural ones.

1. Each is a disposition (habitus).[12]

2. Although there are detailed problems in interpreting this, virtues can be had by individuals in varying degrees: two individuals can have the same virtue at the same time in differing degrees, and one and the same person can have a particular virtue in differing degrees at different times.[13] In the case of the theological virtues, of course, this will be due to greater or lesser gifts of grace. In 1a2ae.66,1 he considers the objection that since infused virtues are from God, whose powers are infinite, they cannot be greater or less than one another, and answers:

> God does not work by necessity of nature, but according to the order of His wisdom, by which he bestows on men various measures of virtue, according to Ephesians iv 7: 'To every one of you is given grace according to the measure of the giving of Christ.'[14]

3. Like the natural virtues, the theological virtues are interconnected. The nature of their interconnection is important, and not altogether easy to outline. Just as moral virtues can only exist imperfectly

[9] 1a2ae.64.3.
[10] 1a2ae.62.2.
[11] 1a2ae.62,1.
[12] On the unsuitability of 'habit' as a translation of *habitus*, see Anthony Kenny's introduction to his translation of 1a2ae.49–54 in Vol. 22 of the Blackfriars edition of the *Summa*, 1964.
[13] 1a2ae.52,1.
[14] 1a2ae.66,1 ad 3.

in a man if isolated from one another, or in the absence of prudence,[15] so faith and hope can exist without charity, but do not have 'the perfect character of virtue' without it.[16] Charity, on the other hand, is 'quite impossible' without faith and hope.[17] Charity, which is a friendship of man with God,[18] cannot exist unless men believe in God and aspire to such fellowship with him. What is presupposed in this way cannot have the charity to which it naturally leads as part of its own essence, but if it is found without that to which it properly leads, we will have to regard it as frustrated, lifeless, or unfulfilled. This is turn will make us qualify the ascription of the virtue and cause us to doubt the perfection or completeness of the acts which manifest it; which would force us, Thomas thinks, to deny that the disposition they manifest is a virtue after all[19] — just as we would have reservations about calling a man's habitual moderation 'temperance' when it is not due to a conscious perception of the good, even though the man who manifests it might make exactly the same choices if he did perceive the good. It is clear that the relationships between faith and hope on the one hand, and their characteristic manifestations in a mode of life that is characterized by charity on the other, have to be articulated without making these manifestations logically necessary (so that faith and hope could not exist without them) but cannot be articulated in a fashion which makes it merely accidental, or contingent, that these *are* the manifestations. Insofar as faith is concerned, the question is one that requires us to steer a middle course between the competing theological claims of St James and St Paul. The briefest reflection on the structure of the problem, and its likeness to the notoriously difficult question of the criteria of moral assent in secular contexts, can show that we are not dealing here with a difficulty that is purely theological. It should also make us take proper note of Thomas's discussions of issues that would otherwise seem of purely domestic interest, namely his discussions of the status of unformed faith, and the nature of the belief in God which is found in the devils or in heretics.

II

With these preliminaries behind us, let us turn to what Thomas says about faith itself. The very fact that faith is merely the first of the theological virtues is enough to make it clear that faith will not, in itself, comprehend all the distinctive features of the character of the man infused by grace. However closely connected the three theological

[15]1a2ae.65,1.
[16]1a2ae.65,4.
[17]1a2ae.65,5.
[18]2a2ae.23,1.
[19]*De Veritate* 14,6.

virtues may be, if they are clearly distinguishable at all, no one of them can embody, within itself, all the salient and distinctive features of the Christian life.

For Aquinas faith is the cognitive or epistemic element in the Christian life, and hope and charity are, respectively, the dispositions toward trust and fellowship which follow naturally, but not necessarily, from it. Since virtues are dispositions which issue in characteristic voluntary actions, faith, as one of them, will have to issue in voluntary acts in which its possessor will acquire, or use, that form of knowledge of God and his dealings with men which we must have for salvation. There are, in his view, two such acts. The first is the assent to those propositions about God and his dealings with men which constitute the articles of faith as expressed in the Creeds; this act of assent he refers to as the inner act of faith (actus interior fidei).[20] The second is confession, the outward act of faith (actus exterior fidei).[21] Confession he holds to be a direct expression of faith in a way in which good works are not, since although faith may command good works it does not compel them, yet in confession, 'faith is causing its own act, without the mediation of any other virtue'.[22] This act is a consequence of the inner act, since 'the aim of outward speech is to indicate what is conceived in one's heart'.[23] It is not surprising, therefore, that it is the inner act, and not the outward act, that occupies the greater share of attention.

In the context of the analysis of faith, therefore, Thomas speaks throughout of belief (credere) as though it is an internal act of assent. There is evidence elsewhere that he also thinks of belief as a disposition.[24] The passages that suggest this, however, refer to what he calls the *habitus opinionis*. In discussing faith, he contrasts it with opinion, so although there may be in Thomas a dispositional theory of belief, he is committed in his account of the interior act of faith to the view that it is a mental performance in which the subject assents to propositions, or, as philosophers have become used to saying, in which the subject makes a judgement. Since to most contemporary philosophers the language of belief is more likely to carry dispositional connotations than the language of assent or judgement, I will try to use the latter as far as possible in what follows.[25]

[20]S.T. 2a2ae.2.
[21]2a2ae.3.
[22]2a2ae.3,1 ad 3.
[23]2a2ae.3,1.
[24]See the discussion of cognitive dispositions in 1a2ae.50,4 and 53,1 and 2. See also Appendix 10 to Kenny's Vol. 22 of the Blackfriars *Summa*.
[25]Dr Kenny's comments on the conference version of this essay have made it clear to me that *credere* is used by Aquinas as a success-term—so that, in contrast to *opinio*, it can only have truth as its object. This restriction, required by his theological understanding of faith as excluding the acceptance of falsehoods, is obviously not a feature of the English 'belief', which is an additional reason for treating it with caution as a translation, though of course in this last respect 'assent' does not carry this restriction either.

It is essential to faith, then, that its possessor performs the mental act of assent to the articles of faith. Since faith is a virtue this essential act has to be 'meritorious'. To be meritorious it has to be voluntary. Since it is concerned primarily with assent to propositions, it is an epistemic act. It is therefore an act which requires the operation both of the intellect and of the will.

The examination of faith is not the only place in the *Summa* where the act of interior assent is discussed. The most directly relevant treatment is Article 6 of Question 17 of the *Prima Secundae*. In this article Aquinas discusses the question 'Whether the activity of reason is commanded?' His answer is as follows:

> Because reason reflects on itself it can command its own activity, as it does that of other powers. Consequently its own activity can be commanded.
>
> Remember, however, that an act of reason can be looked at in two ways, first, as to its exercise, and second, as to its object. As to its exercise it can be commanded, as when one is told to be attentive or use his wits. As to its object, two acts of mind come into play. The first is that of simply perceiving the truth about something, which is in virtue of some light, natural or supernatural. As such it is not of our making or controlling, and is not to be commanded. The second act is when the mind commits itself to what it perceives.
>
> Now if the objects are such that the mind assents to them of its nature, thus first principles, the giving or withholding of assent does not lie within its power but arises from the nature of things, and is therefore not subject to command in the proper sense of the term. However there are some objects perceived which for some cause or another do not so convince the mind but that it is left open either to assent or dissent, or at least to suspend judgment. Assent or dissent in these cases lies within our power, and comes under the act of command.[26]

This passage shows that what Aquinas subsequently says about the interior act of faith in the *Secunda Secundae* is a special application of a more general view about the nature of judgement. He distinguishes between acts of assent, or judgements, and other intellectual activities to which the term 'thinking' is applied, such as the operation by which the intellect 'forms the simple quiddities of things', i.e. forms concepts.[27] The fact that he speaks of our ability to withhold assent or dissent implies (although it is not here explicit) that we also have the capacity to entertain propositions without committing ourselves to their truth of falsity. He defines *credere* following Augustine, as *thinking with assent* (cum assensione cogitare).[28]

Assent to propositions is sometimes subject to our voluntary control and sometimes not. We cannot withhold assent to a proposition we are considering when it expresses a self-evident truth. Nor can we fail to

[26]Trans. Gilby, Blackfriars Vol. 17, page 197.   [28]S.T. 2a2ae.2,1.
[27]De Ver. 14,1.

assent when we consider the conclusions of demonstrative arguments that begin with such self-evident principles (when, as St. Thomas sees the matter, we acquire scientific knowledge). The occasions when we can choose to give our assent or choose to withhold it are cases where we have neither self-evidence nor proof. Here, and only here, the intellect can be commanded by the will; and here, and only here, is it possible for assent, in consequence, to be meritorious.[29]

Of the voluntary intellectual states that can emerge from such occasions, St Thomas distinguishes four. (i) First, there is *doubt*, when the subject is not clearly inclined either to affirmation or denial. (ii) Then there is *suspicion*, where the evidence inclines him in one of the two possible directions, but only slightly. (iii) Next is the form of assent given by someone who has *opinion*: such a person does choose to affirm the proposition, but does so 'with fear of the opposite' (tamen cum formidine alterius). (iv) But the act in which *credere* consists differs from all these three, because it represents 'firm adherence to one side rather than the other' with none of the reservations characteristic of doubt, suspicion, or even opinion. In *this* respect it resembles the assent to first principles or assent to the conclusions of demonstrations. It differs from them, of course, in respect of the epistemic status of the proposition assented to. The very inconclusiveness of the evidence available for the proposition is what frees the intellect to choose whether to assent or not; but when it does assent in the manner required by faith it does so with a firmness found nowhere else in the range of voluntary epistemic acts.

Since the source of this firmness cannot lie in the epistemic disposition of the intellect, it has to lie in the will which commands it. For the will so to command it it has to be infused with divine grace. Left to themselves, neither the intellect nor the will can so combine freedom with wholeheartedness.

Faith, then, is a virtue whose primary act is the assent to propositions at the command of the will. Thomas asserts a necessary connection between the freedom of the assent and the inconclusiveness of the reasons available in support of the propositions to which assent is given. Faith and knowledge, therefore, are exclusive of one another. It is noteworthy that this insistence is one which Thomas shares with theologians who otherwise differ profoundly from him in their understanding of what faith is. It is common for Protestant, as well as Catholic, thinkers to say that there cannot be conclusive reasons for the commitment that faith involves, since if there were such reasons, there would be no freedom in the commitment and hence no merit in making it.

---

[29] 2a2ae.2,1.

III

I shall begin discussion by attempting to outline ways in which Thomas responds, or could respond, to three questions. (1) First, does not his understanding of faith overemphasize the assent to propositions *about* God and his dealings with men, and ignore the essential character of faith as *trust* in God and in his dealings? (2) Second, can the representation of faith as assent to propositions which are not conclusively established be reconciled with St Thomas's fundamental commitment to the rationality of faith? (3) Third, how is the non-cognitive, or volitional, element in faith to be understood, and how does it differ from the commitment that we find in men who seem to adhere in similar ways to false propositions, and cannot be said to have faith at all?

1. St Thomas's answer to the first question can be divided, I think, into a direct and an indirect part.

a. The direct reply is found in Articles 1 and 2 of Question 1 of the *Secunda Secundae* and in Article 8 of Question 14 in the *De Veritate.* It consists in denying the sharp distinction between believing *in* God and believing propositions *about* him. We can begin with the eminently sensible reply to the second objection in Article 2 of the *Summa* discussion. The objection is that in the confession of faith one says that one believes in God Almighty, not that one believes that God is Almighty, hence the object of faith is 'not the proposition, but the reality', i.e. God himself. The reply is as follows:

> As is clear from its language, the Creed expresses the things of faith as they are the term of the believer's act. Such an act does not have a proposition as its term, but a reality, since just as with scientific knowledge, so also with faith, the only reason for formulating a proposition is that we may have knowledge about the real.

So not only is the point of formulating propositions that of knowing the realities they are about, but it is by assenting to propositions in judgement that the human intellect has to come by its knowledge. In the main body of the Article Thomas has gone deeper. Even though God, the First Truth, is simple, he is known to us only through a multiplicity of distinct propositions: 'The human mind knows in a composite way things that are themselves simple; this is quite the opposite of the divine mind, which in a non-composite manner knows things which are themselves composite.' This argument concentrates upon the unique unity of the object of faith, a unity which is the source of the inner coherence of the articles of the Creed to which the believer assents. It is not just that the judgements the believer makes are directed towards the realities they are about, as all epistemic judgements are; it is that they are, in this case, inevitably, approximations to an understanding of an object which unites, indissolubly, those acts and characteristics of which they speak.[30] Finally, and most fundamentally, we must turn to the main body of Article 1. Here Thomas tells us that although what one assents to in faith includes many items not ostensibly about God himself, one assents to them, in faith, because they are revealed by God, and because they 'help man in his striving towards joyous rest in God'. It is because they come from him and because they lead to him that the will disposes the intellect to accept them.

So even though the act of faith is an act of assent to propositions, assent to *these* propositions in *this* manner is a response to God and a movement *towards* God, because of grace *from* God. But all this is only a partial answer to our question. It is also an answer that leaves a puzzle behind it. The puzzle is this. Thomas seems to be telling us both that one cannot believe in God unless one believes certain propositions about him, and that when one believes these propositions in faith, one accepts them as coming from him. But there is an obvious circularity about holding both together. One cannot accept a given proposition as coming from God unless one believes that God exists and has spoken; but one cannot (can one?) believe that God exists and has spoken because *these* propositions come from God. Surely at some stage one's assent has to be based on something less explicitly part of the faith than this, or how could it all begin?

b. Next, the indirect answer. To Aquinas faith is the first, but only the first, of the theological virtues. It is an indispensable prerequisite for hope and charity, and they complete it. If a critic complains that Thomas's account of faith concentrates too much upon the acceptance of propositions and neglects the fact that faith is trust in God, it seems to me that a Thomist must reply that the critic has made two mistakes. (i) First, he has so extended his own understanding of what faith is that he has stretched the title to cover the virtues of hope and charity as well. (ii) Second, he has forgotten that the attitudes characteristic of these two virtues can only exist in us if we are already committed to the truth of the Credal propositions which St Thomas considers it is the essence of faith proper to accept: so that faith has to be definable independently of these attitudes. Those to whom faith is trust, or *fiducia*, regard it as a state in which a man has confidence that God's promises for him will be fulfilled, and is sustained in that confidence, through his sacramental and devotional experience, by a conviction that his life *in via* is one of fellowship with God. But these are the characteristic attitudes of one who has hope and charity, as Thomas describes them. And one cannot have hope and charity without having faith first.[31]

---

[30]He uses this argument in Article 12 of the *De Veritate* discussion to establish the indivisibility of the articles of faith themselves. I am indebted here to a valuable essay by Tad W. Guzie, S.J., 'The Act of Faith According to St. Thomas: a Study in Theological Methodology', *The Thomist,* xxix (1965), 239–80.

[31]*S.T.* 1a2ae.65,5.

There is an appealing obviousness about this answer. But it leads to a puzzle very like the one to which the direct answer led us. It seems clear enough that there has to be acceptance of the propositions of faith, or at least some of them, before one can properly speak of anyone's manifesting the attitudes that derive from hope or charity. But then how can it be maintained, as Thomas certainly does maintain, that the interior act of assent, and the exterior act of confession, are themselves signs that the will is disposed by charity? Surely this suggests that one of the consequences of faith is a necessary condition of it? We do find it natural to say that a man's beliefs are due to his attitudes as well as saying that his attitudes are due to his beliefs — it is just as common to think of a man's economic conservatism as a fruit of his parsimony as to think of his parsimony as a fruit of his conservatism. There is nothing odd about suggesting that a man's faith may reflect his charity, just as his charity may be a consequence of his faith. But do we not, in a given case, have to choose which is the consequence of which?

St Thomas's answer is not hard to find. It is partially satisfactory, but not wholly so. I shall defer saying what I think is wrong with it, and attempt at this point merely to outline it. It is a development of his claim that while hope and charity complete, or fulfil, faith, neither is of its essence. He considers this matter in some detail in his discussions of the differences between formed and formless faith. I take the difference between them to be this. Formed faith is the living faith that is found in the ongoing, sustained Christian life. Formless faith is a mere intellectual assent which is not, because of sin, pervaded by charity and does not bear fruit in the Christian life. Formed faith is living faith, formless faith is dead faith. They are one and the same disposition,[32] but only formed faith is a virtue:

> Since, therefore, the act of believing depends on the understanding and the will . . . such an act cannot be perfect unless the will is made perfect by charity and the understanding by faith. Thus, formless faith cannot be a virtue.[33]

Nevertheless, formless faith is still a gift of God, for although it is 'not perfect in the unqualified sense of completeness as virtue, (it) is perfect with the kind of completeness sufficient to preserve the meaning of faith.'[34] Sin can take away the virtuousness of faith, but faith can still remain, thus making it possible for its virtuousness to be restored through penance. In less technical terms, I take St Thomas to hold that a man who has a living faith is a man who assents inwardly and outwardly to the articles of the faith out of love for God and out of a live trust in him; but it is possible for someone who has sundered himself from God still to retain his belief in those articles, although such a

---

[32]De Ver. 14,7.
[33]14,6. Translation by James V. McGlynn in vol. II of Truth (Chicago, 1953), p. 237.
[34]S.T. 2a2ae.6,2 ad 1.

person, if he affirms them, will do so from a lesser motive. He will have faith, but no merit will accrue to him from it because his sinful behaviour has frustrated its natural expression.

This would imply the following answer to our puzzle. Whenever someone has faith at all, he assents to certain required propositions. He cannot do this in faith unless his will is properly disposed towards the truths expressed in them, and no one can achieve this state without the grace of God. But to be willing to assent to those propositions is not necessarily to be at the level of spiritual development to which faith will naturally lead if sin does not prevent it. When a man does attain to this level, however, this will not only be a consequence of the faith he has, but will then be reflected in the character of his faith in itself. The acts of faith (assent and proclamation) will themselves reflect the trust and love to which his initial commitment has led him. He will not merely have confidence and love because he has believed; he will also assent from a richer motive, and deepen his understanding of what it is that he assents to. If he does not attain to this level, or falls from it, however, he will still have faith, albeit in an incomplete and undeveloped manner. One can begin in faith at this level, and may perhaps not progress beyond it.

2. For the present I will leave my first question, and proceed to the second, concerning the rationality of faith. I suggest that there is an unresolved tension between Aquinas' insistence that the propositions of faith are not established conclusively, and his insistence that the assent to those propositions is a rational assent.[35]

It is well known that he held that some of the propositions that it is necessary to assent to for salvation can be established by natural reason — such as the propositions that God is, or that he is one. These form the subject matter of natural theology, and for those who can comprehend the arguments of that science, these propositions are established. For them, assent is rational in the strong sense that it is irrational *not* to believe them. But for them, also, such assent is not meritorious and not a sign of faith. It is only a sign of faith for those who do not have access to the demonstrations of natural theology and believe these propositions on authority.[36] All believers, however, have faith in regard to those articles which it is not possible for reason to demonstrate. Faith in these articles is rational in a less strong, or ostensibly less strong, manner. In the first instance, there is nothing in these articles which is contrary to reason, and it is the task of the Christian philosopher to remove spurious obstacles to the acceptance of them. In the second instance, when a man accepts these articles in faith, he accepts them *on*

---

[35]I am indebted here to John Hick's treatment of this theme in chapter 1 of *Faith and Knowledge*, 2nd edition (Cornell, Ithaca, N.Y., 1966).

[36]See, for example, *Summa Contra Gentiles* Book One, chapters 1–8; *S.T.* 1a.1,1; 2a2ae.2,4.

the man who has it as something with which he should contend, then he sees the onus upon him as being primarily that of retaining his commitment to the propositions that the doubt puts in question. His obligation is to the commitment. In this respect, as has often been said, adherence to the propositions of faith is quite different from the provisional commitment appropriate to scientific hypotheses. The latter can and should be abandoned if the counter-evidence mounts.[48] The man of faith who faces contrary considerations perceives his obligation differently. But this obligation makes moral sense only in a context where the impact of the apparent counter-evidence is a test of *trust*—or if it could make moral sense otherwise, I would suggest that it is this sort of moral sense it makes in the context of faith.

I would suggest, therefore, that although the necessary priority of belief makes the conceptual separation of faith from the other theological virtues plausible at first sight, this separation prevents Aquinas from incorporating any recognition of the manner in which the man of faith contends with doubts—a contest which is a common characteristic of actual, as opposed to ideal, faith.

This is especially surprising when one considers how clear Thomas is on the fact that although faith resides in the intellect it depends upon the will. There are many signs, however, that he misdescribes their actual relationship in faith. Aquinas is clearly on the side of Descartes and the Pyrrhonian sceptics, and on the other side from Spinoza and Hume, in his contention that when the grounds for a proposition are less than conclusive, one has a degree of choice whether or not to give assent to it. We have seen an apparent ambiguity over how conclusive the grounds for the articles of faith really are, but I would like to comment now upon the central claim that the assent to them is a voluntary act.

I must begin by confessing that I am one of those who find it difficult to understand the contention that one can choose to believe wholeheartedly a proposition for which one does not consider the grounds one has to be conclusive—unless such a choice is a choice to induce belief indirectly by putting oneself into situations where one will *come* to believe it. I have no difficulty in understanding the suggestion that one might wish that the proposition were true, or that one might, since one would like it to be true, wish that one believed it. The difficulty I encounter is with the contention that when I have a wish of either kind, I can then command the belief I wish I had. I do not think the problem, if it is a real one, can be met by saying that grace is needed for the will to command the intellect; for this merely relates to the disposition of the will, to our capacity to wish for the salvation that is promised and to

[48]See, for example, Alasdair MacIntyre, 'The Logical Status of Religious Belief' in *Metaphysical Beliefs* (SCM Press, London, 1957), esp. pp. 195–205.

command the intellect to believe; and the problem I have is with the efficacy of such a command. I can only report this difficulty, in the full recognition that there are famous writers who do not have it, or say that they do not.

The difficulty prompts me to suggest again that Aquinas, and a great many other thinkers who follow him, are mistaken in holding that the voluntariness, and hence the merit, of faith depends upon the inconclusiveness of the grounds for it. Perhaps acceptance can be given voluntarily even though the grounds are conclusive. If this seems absurd, let us reflect first that there are two ways in which one can accept what is proved to one: one can be reluctant to accept it, as Thomas's devils are, or one can be glad to accept it. Perhaps the man of faith has merit because he is glad to accept the truths of faith when the devil is not. The natural objection to this is that whether it is glad or whether it is reluctant, such acceptance is not to one's credit either way, because it is not free. But this may be to locate freedom in the wrong place, to be too dominated by the picture of free action as action explicitly commanded. It is probably true that when someone recognizes that the grounds for a proposition are enough to establish it conclusively he cannot *not* accept it; but it is also true that as he sees such a recognition approaching, he can fend it off through fear or pride or sophistry. Perhaps what makes faith voluntary is not that its grounds are inconclusive, but that even if they are conclusive, men are free to deceive themselves and refuse to admit that they are. Faith would be the outcome of a willingness to admit this, and faith and knowledge need not then be exclusive at all. It should be added that faith thus understood could perfectly well have subsequent doubts to contend with. It is just false that we cannot feel doubtful about things that we already know to be true. Even if we knew the propositions of faith, it is surely not impossible that the exigencies and distractions of worldly existence constantly made us liable to doubt them, and that one had to seek prophetic or sacramental reminders of them at regular intervals to contend with these doubts.

I am not arguing that the grounds for faith *are* conclusive; only that it is not impossible that the man of faith derives the wholeheartedness of his belief from the conviction that they are. Faith might be, or include, supposed knowledge. Both the wholeheartedness of faith, and its relation to lingering doubt, would be intelligible, I think, on such an analysis.[49]

There are examples of faith, especially examples of vivid and intense faith, that such an analysis would seem to me to fit, and that may indeed require it. But it may also be true that there are other cases of faith that

---

[49]I have attempted to outline such an analysis in *Problems of Religious Knowledge*, esp. chapter 6.

it would not fit. Some believers speak of themselves with the language of knowledge, and some do not, and it needs to be demonstrated that they cannot both be right. Perhaps it is possible to have faith when it is recognized that for all the subject knows what is proclaimed to him *may* be false, but he is still unreservedly willing to live and act upon it. Such a decision, based upon a sense of likelihood rather than certainty, could issue in a developed state where the subject's subsequent experience may remove his intellectual hesitations. This sort of decision can be commanded to oneself directly, or urged upon one quite intelligibly by others, and I think often is. To apply the word 'faith' to a subject who has made this sort of decision would be to admit that faith is possible without unreserved intellectual assent, provided personal commitment accompanies the assent that there is. Such a state could also be one in which the subject had, and felt obliged to contend with, subsequent doubts.[50]

It is not my purpose here to develop these brief comments into an analysis of faith, even if I had a satisfactory one to offer. Their purpose has been merely to suggest that if we wish to escape the perplexities which Aquinas' analysis leaves with us, while doing some justice to the complexities of the phenomenon itself, we have to recognize not only that faith has to include within its essence factors which he is obliged to exclude, but also that some of the assumptions about freedom and conviction that his opponents have shared with him need to be re-examined also.

---

[50]It is this understanding of faith that is developed in Basil Mitchell's *The Justification of Religious Belief* (Macmillan, London, 1973).

R.T. HERBERT

Two of Kierkegaard's Uses of "Paradox"*

In the span of a few pages of his *Concluding Unscientific Postscript*[†]
Soren Kierkegaard makes important use of the notion of paradox to
distinguish two sorts of religiousness. I propose to study this notion as
he employs it in characterizing the two.

The first sort he discusses is exemplified by the religiousness of
Socrates and is what in other places he calls religiousness *A*. Regarding
religiousness in this sense, Kierkegaard writes, "the eternal and essential truth, the truth which has an essential relation to an existing individual because it pertains essentially to existence . . . is a paradox.
But the eternal essential truth is by no means in itself a paradox; but it
becomes paradoxical by virtue of its relation to an existing individual"
(*PS*, p. 183).

The second sort of religiousness is exemplified by Christianity and is
what Kierkegaard elsewhere calls religiousness *B*. He distinguishes the
two sorts in the following passage:

---

*This essay is Chapter 3 of the author's *Paradox and Identity in Theology* (Cornell
University Press, 1979). It appeared originally in *The Philosophical Review*, Vol. 70,
1961, and is reprinted here by permission of the Department of Philosophy, Cornell
University.

†Translated by David F. Swenson and Walter Lowrie (Princeton: Princeton University Press, 1941), pp. 177–188. All subsequent references in this chapter to *Concluding
Unscientific Postscript* will be abbreviated to *PS*, followed by the page number. [The
passages discussed are included in the selection from Kierkegaard on pp. 87–95 of this
volume — ed.]

Subjectivity is truth. By virtue of the relationship subsisting between the eternal truth and the existing individual, the paradox came into being. Let us now go further, let us suppose that the eternal essential truth is itself a paradox. How does the paradox come into being? By putting the eternal essential truth into juxtaposition with existence. Hence when we posit such a conjunction within the truth itself, the truth becomes a paradox. [PS, p. 187]

So far then we have the following picture. There is a paradox involved in the first sort of religiousness, a paradox that arises from the fact that the existing individual, the believer, is related essentially to the eternal essential truth. The second sort of religiousness is distinguished by the presence of a second paradox in addition to the first: "the eternal essential truth is itself a paradox."

I

The paradox in the first sort of religiousness involves the concepts *truth* and *objective uncertainty*. We may show what these concepts involve by making use of one of Kierkegaard's illustrations.

When one man investigates objectively the problem of immortality, and another embraces an uncertainty with the passion of the infinite: where is there most truth, and who has the greater certainty? The one has entered upon a never-ending approximation, for the certainty of immortality lies precisely in the subjectivity of the individual; the other is immortal, and fights for his immortality by struggling with the uncertainty. [PS, p. 180]

Here two sorts of people are contrasted: one who seeks objective certainty or proof of the soul's immortality but is necessarily embarked "upon a never-ending approximation" and the other who is certain, for he has embraced the uncertainty with the passion of the infinite, and "the certainty of immortality lies precisely in the subjectivity of the individual." Kierkegaard continues thus:

Let us consider Socrates. Nowadays everyone dabbles in a few proofs; some have several such proofs, others fewer. But Socrates! He puts the question objectively in a problematic manner: *if* there is an immortality. He must therefore be accounted a doubter in comparison with one of our modern thinkers with the three proofs? By no means. On this "if" he risks his entire life, he has the courage to meet death, and he has with the passion of the infinite so determined the pattern of his life that it must be found acceptable — *if* there is an immortality. Is any better proof capable of being given for the immortality of the soul? But those who have the three proofs do not at all determine their lives in conformity therewith; if there is an immortality it must feel disgust over their manner of life: can any better refutation be given of the three proofs? The bit of uncertainty Socrates had, helped him because he himself contributed the passion of the infinite; the three proofs that the others have do not profit them at all, because they are dead to spirit and enthusiasm, and their three proofs, in lieu of proving anything else, prove just this. . . . The Socratic ignorance, which Socrates held fast with the entire passion of his inwardness, was thus an expression for the principle that the eternal truth is related to an existing individual, and that this truth must therefore be a paradox for him as long as he exists. [*PS*, p. 180].

In the above passage one can see what the concepts of objective uncertainty and truth are. Objective uncertainty is the *if* of Socrates. He does not *know* whether his soul is immortal, but *if* it is . . . On the other hand, truth — the certainty of Socrates — is shown in this: that "he has with the passion of the infinite so determined the pattern of his life that it must be found acceptable."

Second, the above passage shows, though not very clearly, the way in which the notion of paradox is involved with the concepts of objective uncertainty and truth. As Kierkegaard puts it here, "The Socratic ignorance [that is, Socrates' objective uncertainty], which Socrates held fast with the entire passion of his inwardness, was thus an expression for the principle that the eternal truth is related to an existing individual, and that this truth must therefore be a paradox for him as long as he exists." Another passage makes clearer the relation between the notion of paradox and the concepts of objective uncertainty and truth: "When subjectivity, inwardness, is the truth, the truth becomes objectively a paradox; . . . The paradoxical character of the [subjective, inward] truth is its objective uncertainty" (*PS*, p. 183). Thus in the case of Socrates the paradox enters in this way: whereas Socrates is subjectively *certain* that he is immortal (and this is shown in "the pattern of his life"), still he is objectively *uncertain* that he is immortal. To paraphrase the second of the two sentences quoted above: the paradoxical character of Socrates' "certainty," his "subjective truth," is its objective uncertainty, or his objective uncertainty of it. The paradox is that he is at once certain and uncertain — certain subjectively and uncertain objectively. What might be called the logic of this notion of paradox is perhaps made clearer in the following.

Suppose a woman and her child live in a house in one room of which there is possibly a poisonous snake. The snake has never been seen *in* the room, but the woman once saw it outside the house, apparently about to crawl through a hole into the room. She did not, however, see it actually enter. Further, though she has never seen the snake in the room, there are many places where it might hide there, and at night she has heard queer noises that come, perhaps, from the room.

Now the woman does nothing. Yet she fears snakes terribly, and it is not as though she is embarrassed to ask someone to search the room — anyone would understand her fear of snakes and her wanting to make certain in this case. But she does nothing. Moreover, she conducts her life as though there were no possibility of a poisonous snake's being in the room. She sends her child to the room to get thread; she goes there herself and rummages in the closets for extra blankets when the night turns cold.

Noticing how she conducts herself, someone asks her, "What makes you so sure that there is no snake in that room?" She replies, "Oh, but I'm *not* sure. Would you be sure? For, as you know, I saw the snake outside near the hole, and at night I've heard noises." "But then," responds the other, amazed, "if you're *not* sure, how can you *live* in such assurance!" "But don't you see," comes the reply, "I believe that the snake is not there."

This case exhibits the logic of "paradox" as Kierkegaard brings that word into his discussion of Socrates and immortality.[1] The woman is "objectively uncertain"; that is, she is not sure whether or not the snake is in the room and can give reasons that would lead anyone to be unsure and to want to make sure. Yet she is subjectively certain; that is, she lives just as though she had made sure there was no snake in the room.

It is safe to say that one would meet such a woman only in fiction, and not even there if the fiction was worth reading. For if one tried to imagine her life in detail, insurmountable problems would arise. What, for instance, does she do when in bed at night she hears the strange noises that *might* be those of the snake? If she believes, as she says, that the snake is not in the room, that is, if she *lives* in the assurance that the snake is not there, then her reaction to the noise also must express this assurance. And so when she cites as a reason for being uncertain the fact that she has heard the strange noise, one can only suppose that she is not taking her "reason" seriously as a reason and so she is not really uncertain. Or if she does take her reason seriously as a reason, then when she hears the noise she shudders in fear and repulsion, or she frets, "I wonder if that's that snake"—in which case she does not believe, she does not live in assurance.

Now to say that insurmountable problems arise if one tries to imagine in detail the life of this woman is to say that no such life can be imagined, let alone lived—not because even the geniuses of fiction are not equal to the task, but because it makes no sense to say of a person, real or fictional, that he is objectively uncertain and also subjectively certain. The facts which would justify our saying that a person is

---

[1] There is this difference in the logic of the two cases; the woman's "objective uncertainty" is due to insufficient evidence, whereas Socrates' is due to his continuing dissatisfaction with the rational proofs for immortality which he offers in the *Phaedo* (at least this seems likeliest to be what Kierkegaard has in mind). Kierkegaard himself, however, is not consistent on this point, for, as a passage I will quote later shows, he connects "objective uncertainty" with *evidence for* and *evidence against*. In any case, these differences are not important for the purpose at hand.

objectively uncertain are the very facts which would justify our saying that he is not subjectively certain, and vice versa.

What I wish to argue is this: there is nothing in the case of the person in religiousness A that can be called a paradox in the sense in which there is one in the case of woman, even though Kierkegaard supposes that there is.

"The paradoxical character of the truth is its objective uncertainty." So says Kierkegaard. And to the case of the woman this sentence applies perfectly. For without the "objective uncertainty," that is, with objective certainty, there is no paradox — and then we can make sense of her case. In religiousness A, however, there is nothing like a woman's "objective uncertainty," nothing like what we might naturally understand by that phrase, nothing like what Kierkegaard himself, at least sometimes, understands by it.

How then does Kierkegaard understand the phrase "objective uncertainty"? He understands it as involving the concept of evidence, as it does in the case of the woman. The following passage indicates this: "I contemplate the order of nature in the hope of finding God, and I see omnipotence and wisdom; but I also see much else that disturbs my mind and excites anxiety. The sum of all this is objective uncertainty" (PS, p. 182). This is like: "I contemplate the evidence in the hope of finding him innocent, and I see that he can pretty well account for his time on the day of the crime and that he has little motive; but I also see much else that disturbs my mind and excites anxiety. The sum of all this is objective uncertainty." Thus we see that here for Kierkegaard the concept of objective uncertainty is connected with the notion of evidence for and evidence against.[2] And of course when one has both kinds of evidence, then the evidence is said to be inconclusive and one is uncertain.

One can now see pretty clearly how Kierkegaard comes to think that a paradox is involved in religiousness A. One contemplates the order of nature, finds evidence both for and against saying there is a God, sees the evidence to be inconclusive, becomes (objectively) uncertain, and then — despite his uncertainty — is (subjectively) certain there is a God. But, as in the case of the woman and the snake, when this is considered in detail the nonsense involved becomes evident. For if one is subjectively certain, that is, if he lives assured that he is in God's hands, then when he is confronted with what he regards as evidence for the nonexistence of God, he must either be disturbed and so not be in assurance, or remain in assurance and so not be taking the "evidence" seriously as evidence.

It is perhaps surprising that Kierkegaard should have introduced the

---

[2] Cf. PS p. 173: "The way of objective reflection leads . . . to historical knowledge of different kinds." But see note 1 above.

concept of objective uncertainty in this way at all. For in other places he insists that "Christianity is not a matter of knowledge, so that increased knowledge is of no avail, except to make it easier to fall into the confusion of considering Christianity as a matter of knowledge."[3] I take it that this goes for religiousness A as well as for Christianity. Now if Christianity or religiousness A "is not a matter of knowledge, so that increased knowledge is of no avail," then *it is not a matter of objective uncertainty either.* For saying that it is not a matter of knowledge, and so on, is not to say that we do not as a matter of fact know something or other and so are uncertain; it is to say that knowing *and* not knowing (hence, being uncertain) are irrelevant.

Thus for Kierkegaard (at this place in the *Postscript*) the concept *knowledge* is irrelevant to the faith relationship; that is, such a sentence as "I know that God exists," where knowing involves finding out or making proofs, brings together concepts which on coming together curdle into nonsense. But he is not clear that the irrelevancy he is claiming involves also the irrelevancy of the concept of objective uncertainty; that is, that such a sentence as "I am (objectively) uncertain that God exists" likewise brings together concepts that curdle on contact into nonsense.[4]

My argument here is this: religion, Kierkegaard claims, is not a matter of knowledge. If this is true, then religion is not a matter of objective uncertainty either. And if it is not a matter of objective uncertainty, then there is no paradox, since there being a paradox depends on religion's being a matter of objective uncertainty.

II

Before turning to the paradox distinguishing religiousness B from religiousness A, we must consider an objection to the foregoing critique. The objection is this. "It is a mistake to take the claim that religiousness A is not a matter of knowledge such that it is also not a matter of objective uncertainty. Whatever Kierkegaard's claim may come to, his reliance on the notion of objective uncertainty is too important to his position to be dismissed in this way. What he means by 'objective uncertainty' is made quite clear in the passage, already cited, in which he speaks of contemplating the order of nature and seeing omnipotence and wisdom but also much else that disturbs the mind and excites anxiety. 'The sum of all this,' he says, 'is objective uncertainty.'

---

[3] *PS*, p. 192. Also one *confuses* faith with knowledge; cf. ibid., p. 30.
[4] Cf. "The sum of all this is objective uncertainty" as it occurs in the passage quoted above.

"Objective uncertainty, so understood [the objection continues], is integral to religiousness A, to man's relationship to God. So long as a man lives he cannot be objectively certain of God's existence. Contemplating the order of nature can never resolve the uncertainty; what disturbs his mind and excites anxiety will always be there. Moreover, it is this objective uncertainty that produces or constitutes the risk that Kierkegaard rightly considers the *sine qua non* of faith (*PS*, p. 182). Thus in a man's proper relationship to God both subjective certainty (faith) and objective uncertainty, with its disturbance of mind and anxiety, must be present. It is this that constitutes the paradox of religiousness A."

If this presentation of Kierkegaard's position is not to be vulnerable, as the earlier presentation is, to reduction to absurdity by means of the woman and snake case, we must understand subjective certainty and objective uncertainty in one of three ways.

1. Objective uncertainty with its disturbance and anxiety interrupts one's subjective certainty each time one honestly considers the order of nature, which is impenetrably ambiguous.

2. Objective uncertainty describes only the situation's, not the believer's, condition. The order of nature is ambiguous, yielding no conclusive evidence either for or against, but yielding partial evidence both for and against, the proposition that God exists. Objective uncertainty's psychological aspect, the disturbance of mind and anxiety, is here absent. Thus in the face of nature's ambiguousness it is possible for the believer to maintain an uninterrupted subjective certainty.

3. Objective uncertainty, including its psychological aspect, is a constant conditioner of subjective certainty with the result that subjective certainty is not after all the conviction, but is instead the hope, that God exists.[5]

Interpretation (1) seems to make the believer remarkably slack-souled and self-deceived. Whenever he considers the ambiguous order of nature, he is assailed by disturbing and anxious doubts about God's existence, but when this ambiguity is out of sight his doubts are out of mind and certainty floods in again, allowing him to pray to God in perfect confidence that God is there to hear—until of course it is time for another assessment of the evidence. He must, it seems, make frequent reassessments of the evidence, for he must "constantly be intent on holding fast the objective uncertainty" (*PS*, p. 182). But despite

[5] Cf. James L. Muyskens' "James' Defense of a Believing Attitude in Religion," *Transactions of the Charles S. Pierce Society*, 10 (Winter 1974), esp. 52–53.

these efforts doubt falls asleep, certainty returns, and the believer can again live, unconscionably, beyond his evidential means.

Can this be Kierkegaard's portrait of the believer? Surely not. For one thing Kierkegaard's believer does not oscillate between subjective certainty and the anxious doubts of objective uncertainty. Instead, both the subjective and the objective elements are somehow constantly present. The believer is in fact to intensify his subjective certainty by vigilantly maintaining a constant objective uncertainty. Kierkegaard would not promote the ideal of an oscillating belief, which to call it by its right name is nothing but inconstancy.

But if in Kierkegaard's portrait both subjective and objective elements are constantly present, is that portrait not again vulnerable to the *reductio* of the woman and snake case? Is it not correct to say of the believer's as well as the woman's case that the facts that would justify saying that a person is objectively uncertain are the very facts that would justify saying that he is *not* subjectively certain, and vice versa?

Interpretation (2) avoids this *reductio* as well as the objectionable oscillation in interpretation (1). In the second interpretation the psychological aspect (the anxieties and doubt) of objective uncertainty is absent. It is the situation, not the believer, that is uncertain. He maintains a subjective certainty uninterrupted by doubts fostered by nature's ambiguity. Presumably he manages to do this by simply ignoring the ambiguity.

This interpretation of Kierkegaard's portrait of the believer seems as objectionable as our first one. It invites invidious but apparently unavoidable comparisons: the believer is like a police detective who remains convinced that Mrs. B is guilty of murdering her sister only because he ignores evidence that makes this doubtful; or the believer is like a cancer sufferer who remains convinced that Laetrile cures cancer because he ignores evidence that makes this doubtful; or (to adapt our woman and snake case) the believer is like the woman who remains free of all doubt that the room is safe just because she ignores two important facts: first, that though she did not see the snake actually enter the room, she saw it outside the house, apparently about to crawl through a hole into the room, and, second, that at night, when the house is quiet, she hears strange noises coming, perhaps, from the room, noises that might be made by the snake.

Under our first interpretation Kierkegaard's believer is slack and inconstant. Under our second he is intellectually irresponsible, and the fact that nature's impenetrable ambiguity renders conclusive evidence unattainable constitutes no mitigation of this irresponsibility. A freedom from doubt maintained by ignoring contrary evidence is despicable whether or not conclusive evidence can be attained.

Interpretation (3) escapes both difficulties. Here the believer is neither inconstant nor irresponsible. His objective uncertainty is such that he understands the risk involved in being subjectively certain of God's existence. He understands that certainty is not justified by the evidence. He is not intellectually irresponsible, he does not live beyond his evidential means. His subjective certainty, then, is not the conviction, but is instead the hope, that God exists. And since contrary evidence need touch only the conviction, the hope may remain steady, the believer thereby avoiding inconstancy.

One this interpretation are there other difficulties? The believer understands that nature's ambiguous face does not afford conclusive evidence of God's existence, that it affords some evidence to the contrary. Thus he is not convinced that God exists, but he hopes so and on the basis of this hope lives *as though* it is true that God exists.

To examine this interpretation let us again adapt the woman and snake case. The woman is not convinced that the room is safe, yet she hopes that it is and on the basis of this hope lives her life as though it is true that it is. Hoping that the snake has not entered, she goes into the room and rummages in the closet for household items and sends her child there for the shoes she has left under the bed. Is her search for blankets a bit rushed and perfunctory? Does she glance anxiously about? Does she step gingerly? Is she apprehensive about her child's safety? No. She lives as though it is true that the snake is not in the room. To a neighbor who knows what the woman has seen outside the house and what she hears in the dead of night and who consequently is puzzled at her lack of fear and concern, she explains that her equanimity is due to her hope that the snake is not in the room.

Clearly, hope is no explanation of the woman's behavior. The arithmetic is bad. Realization of the grave risk plus hope that the snake is not in the room does not add up to perfect equanimity. But though bad in the woman's case, perhaps the same arithmetic is correct in the believer's. The risk may seem far less grave here. The believer realizes only that God may not exist—a realization not nearly as disturbing, one may think, as that a poisonous snake may lie hidden in a bedroom of one's house. Does this realization plus the hope that God exists equal the analogue of the woman's equanimity? Do we understand a life of faith that is lived on the basis of the hope, not the conviction, that God exists?

The life of faith is a life lived to fulfill the Commandments, the chief of which, believers are taught, is to love the Lord your God with all your heart, with all your soul, and with all your mind. One important expression of this love is understood to be prayer: for example praise and declarations of love like these:

I love thee, O Lord, my strength.
The Lord is my rock and my fortress, and my deliverer, . . .
[Ps. 18:1–2]

O my Strength, I will sing praises to thee,
for thou, O God, art my fortress,
the God who shows me steadfast love. [Ps. 59:17]

Surely in reading these verses it will not do to imagine in the psalmist only the hope and not the conviction that God exists! Surely the serious believer, who tries to conform his life to the Commandments, cannot be thought merely to hope that God exists. Kierkegaard himself seems to agree. He writes: "Do away with the terrors of eternity (either eternal happiness or eternal perdition) and the idea of an imitation of Christ is fantastic. Only the seriousness of eternity can compel and move a man to take such a daring decision and answer for his so doing. . . . It must be a question of heaven or hell — and of imitating him for that reason *i.e.* to be saved: that is seriousness" (*Journals*, X[1] A452). What are the terrors of eternity to one who is not even convinced of their existence?

Furthermore, believers are instructed that they must believe, not that they must hope, that God exists: "For whoever would draw near to God must believe [the word is not "hope"] that he exists and that he rewards those who seek him" (Heb. 11:6).

The arithmetic seems no better in the believer's case than it is in the woman's. The realization that God may not exist plus the hope that He does exist cannot add up to a life of faith. To think that it does is to be prepared to think that when Simone Weil penned her account of her mystical experience, after finishing its culminating sentence — "And it happened that as I was saying this poem . . . Christ himself came down, and He took me" — she ought really to have added self-reprovingly, "Of course I ought only to have *hoped* it was He!"

In any attempt to repel the supposed encroachment of nature's ambiguity on the intelligibility or intellectual respectability of religious belief, it is a strategic error to establish the battle line at the hope that God exists. If that is done the battle is lost. It seems that the line must be established farther forward at the conviction or belief that he exists. But is the battle not lost if fought here as well? Haven't we already seen it lost here to the charges of logical absurdity, inconstancy, or intellectual irresponsibility? If the life of faith requires the conviction that God exists, there seems no way the believer can avoid the charge of irresponsibility at least. For the evidence that nature affords simply does not justify that conviction.

At this point one may feel that the battle is lost: that the life of faith is really intellectually irresponsible because evidentially underfunded and that Kierkegaard's claim of "paradox" is the Grand Mystifier's way of alluding to that irresponsibility while at the same time trying to keep us, and no doubt himself as well, from seeing the irresponsibility for what it is.

On the other hand, one may feel that Kierkegaard's portrait of the believer has somehow placed us in that notorious Wittgensteinian room on one wall of which is painted a series of dummy doors and that we have all this while been fumbling at one after another of those doors trying to find an exit and have only to turn around to see the real way out.

Let us try turning around. To do this we must reject the notion that the believer irresponsibly ignores the insufficiency of the evidence nature affords. Of course we must not do this by claiming that the evidence is after all sufficient. Instead, we must do it by understanding that the believer does not come to the conviction that God exists by *concluding* to it—either responsibly or irresponsibly. The psalmist who declares the heavens to be the work of God's fingers is not "announcing his findings." He is not, then, irresponsibly ignoring contrary evidence in nature, for nature is not evidence in his enterprise. His conviction arises quite otherwise.[6]

If the conviction that God exists does not arise in the serious man of faith through an assessment, or misassessment, of the order of nature, then how does it arise? What Hume once wrote, though hostile to belief and ironic in intention, actually comes very close to Belief's own answer to this question. At the end of the discussion of miracles in his *Inquiry Concerning Human Understanding* he wrote:

> So that upon the whole we may conclude, that the *Christian Religion* not only was at first attended with miracles, but even to this day cannot be believed by any reasonable person without one. Mere reason is not sufficient to convince us of its veracity: and whoever is moved by *Faith* to assent to it, is conscious of a continued miracle in his own person.

Does Hume's remark indicate a way out of the Wittgensteinian room? If we ignore its irony the remark suggests that in the serious man of faith the conviction that God exists is established by God, by miracle.

Saint Paul, in his first letter to the Corinthians (2:14) suggests the same thing when he says that "an unspiritual person," that is, one "left to his own natural resources,"[7] "does not accept anything of the Spirit of God" and that such a person "sees it all as nonsense." Understanding and acceptance come only "by means of the Spirit." Paul is suggesting that the "message of the Kingdom," in which with much else is revealed the King's existence, can be believed only by one who is prepared by God's Spirit to do so. This preparation, this spiritualizing of

---

[6]Cf. *The Interpreter's Dictionary of the Bible,* vol. 2, p. 420, col. a, first paragraph.
[7]See *The Jerusalem Bible* 1 Cor. 2:14, fn.h.

the natural man that enables him to believe, is the miracle that Hume, himself unbelieving, ironically spoke of.

It seems that at this point it is not open to the unbeliever to speak otherwise than ironically. An unbeliever cannot accept the believer's account of how the conviction of God's existence arises. If he did, he would not be an unbeliever. Is the unbeliever then forced to accept the account we have already rejected—that the conviction is concluded to from (insufficient) evidence found in the order of nature? No; one need not be a believer in order to see that no concluding, no announcing one's findings, is involved. But are not "miracle" and "insufficient evidence with intellectual irresponsibility" the only alternatives available? Again, no; there is at least the additional alternative of silence, of having no account to give. In fact it seems to be to Hume's credit that in the passage quoted he gives no account and instead contents himself with scoffing.[8]

We have now examined Kierkegaard's portrait of the believer. The puzzling aspect of that portrait is the claim that the believer is both objectively uncertain and subjectively certain that God exists. We first argued by means of the woman and snake case that this claim involved logical absurdity, for the facts justifying an affirmation of objective uncertainty are the very ones that justify a denial of subjective certainty, and vice versa. We then considered three "interpretations" of Kierkegaard's portrait, finding each to sustain a different serious objection: the first, inconstancy; the second, intellectual irresponsibility; the third, the absence of the conviction that God exists.

We then presented a portrait of the believer that avoids all of the above objections. But in our portrait he is not "objectively uncertain" of God's existence. He does not harbor that "bit of uncertainty" that Kierkegaard finds in Socrates and gives to his believer. Nor does the ambiguity of nature's face leave our believer's conviction that God exists evidentially underfunded. The situation's "objective uncertainty" is irrelevant. In his enterprise nature is not evidence.

What then becomes of Kierkegaard's claim that a paradox is involved in religiousness A? It seems that since there is no place for a Kierkegaardian objective uncertainty, there is none for a paradox, because paradox arises only out of a conjunction of subjective certainty with that objective uncertainty.

Before concluding this section, we must consider briefly how our disposition of the difficulty in Kierkegaard's portrait of the believer bears on a well-known fact of religious life: the vicissitudes, the infirmity, of faith. This infirmity I will here refer to as doubt.

Doubt admits of degrees of seriousness, ranging from double-mind-

---

[8]Another alternative open to the unbeliever is to advance a Freudian account of belief. I omit discussion of it here. [It is discussed in Chapters 1 and 2 of the author's *Paradox and Identity in Theology*—ed.]

edness to apostasy. There is the occasional visitation of profane thoughts, such perhaps as those evil thoughts against whose violent incursions Dr. Johnson petitioned God's defense. There is also that condition of religious melancholia, called *accidia* or sloth, in which, as Evelyn Waugh describes it in *The Seven Deadly Sins*, "a man is fully aware of the proper means of his salvation and refuses to take them because the whole apparatus of salvation fills him with tedium and disgust." This seems close to the condition Graham Greene describes in his autobiography, *A Sort of Life:* "we may become hardened to the formulas of Confession and skeptical about ourselves; we may only half intend to keep the promises we make, until continual failure or the circumstances of our private life finally make it impossible to make any promises at all and many of us abandon Confession and Communion to join the Foreign Legion of the Church and fight for a city of which we are no longer full citizens."

But of course doubt can take a more deadly form, that of perfect indifference of the heart. This is the doubt of the *pococurante*, whose attitude H. H. Price characterizes in "Faith and Belief"[9] by letting him speak out: "Oh, yes, of course there is a God and of course he loves every one of us, and no doubt he asks each one of us to love him. But what of it?" The *pococurante* approaches but does not quite reach apostasy, for though he cares nothing about it, he refrains from denying or questioning God's existence.

The apostate passes Dr. Johnson's evil thoughts, Waugh's *accidia*, Green's foreign legionnaire, and Price's *pococurante;* he does not stop at tedium or indifference to God. He scoffs at the notion of God's existence.

This sampling of religious doubting, or defection, can at best only suggest its many forms. Indeed, it may not be amiss here to adapt a famous sentence of Tolstoy's: Firm believers are all alike; every doubter doubts in his own way. Yet one may wonder too whether firm believers can be separated in this way from doubters. Perhaps to apostasy's deepest doubt even the firmest believer is not always immune. Perhaps some of those evil thoughts that so appalled Dr. Johnson were, in whatever form, doubts of God's existence, doubts against which, like a man trying to hang on, Johnson appealed to God for protection.

Suppose, then, that no believer-doubter completely escapes the apostate's doubt; suppose that even the psalmist's firm and abiding conviction of God's existence is sometimes, however fleetingly, clouded by what the fool says in his heart.

Despite one plausible reading of Kierkegaard, such doubt, however unavoidable, is the believer's shame, not his glory. If that doubt is what Kierkegaard was calling objective uncertainty, it is emphatically not

---

[9] *Faith and the Philosophers* (London: Macmillan, 1964), John Hick, ed., p. 9.

something the believer thinks he must "constantly be intent on holding fast."

More importantly, this doubt is not something he should think he finds evidence in nature to support. Just as in declaring the heavens to be the work of God's fingers the psalmist is not announcing his findings, so the doubt that God exists and created the heavens is not the product of further research. Instead, as Kierkegaard observes in a *Journal* entry (VIII A 7) that is at once a piece of profound religious psychology and an important delimiting conceptual remark, the doubts of a faltering faith are really objections that "spring from insubordination, the dislike of obedience, rebellion against all authority"—not, then, the intellect, dissuaded by counterevidence, weakening or abandoning its "God-hypothesis"; but the will or spirit enfeebled, perhaps in circumstances too hard, or not hard enough, failing like five foolish virgins.

III

Let us now turn to the paradox which distinguishes religiousness *B* from religiousness *A*. To study this paradox, let us focus on Kierkegaard's discussion of the story of Abraham and Isaac. Though I know of no place in Kierkegaard's writings where he explicitly says that Abraham is in religiousness *B*, there is much in his work that naturally leads one to think that he *would* have said so. The category of the absurd, for example, has office in religiousness *B* but not in religiousness *A*; also faith in its highest sense pertains to religiousness *B* but not in its highest sense to religiousness *A* (*PS*, pp. 183–184 and 187–188). Now the category of the absurd plays a major role in Kierkegaard's characterization of the religion of Abraham, and also Kierkegaard's passionate interest in the Abraham story results from his regarding it as exhibiting the archetype of the faithful man. In addition to these considerations, there is also the authority of Walter Lowrie, the scholar–translator of Kierkegaard's works. In one of his "translator's notes" to his translation of *Fear and Trembling*, he writes: "It is Johannes de silentio who says [that he cannot understand Abraham] and the purpose of [saying this] is to emphasize the fact that the paradoxical religiousness (religiousness *B*) is and remains a paradox to everyone who stands on a lower plane."[10]

This note, in addition to the considerations concerning faith and the absurd, seems sufficient warrant for regarding Abraham as one who, for Kierkegaard, is in "the paradoxical religion" and for allowing our analysis of the paradox in Abraham's case to stand as an analysis of the paradox that distinguishes religiousness *B* from religiousness *A*.

---

[10]*Fear and Trembling* (Garden City, N.Y.: Anchor Books, 1954), p. 265.

It has been contended that by "paradox" in the case of religiousness *B* Kierkegaard means "logical contradiction" or "logical impossibility," and there is much in Kierkegaard's writing that might easily be taken to support this view. In fact Kierkegaard does use the word "contradiction" to refer to the paradox.[11] The remainder of this chapter will be devoted to a consideration of this question: does the paradox of religiousness *B*, as it is exemplified in the case of Abraham, involve a logical contradiction or impossibility? Is there, in other words, a logical impossibility involved in this paradox: that Abraham intended to obey God's command to *sacrifice* Isaac while at the same time believing that God's promise to him would be fulfilled — the promise that *through Isaac* his seed should be multiplied as the stars of the heaven? In examining this paradox I shall bear in mind Kierkegaard's warning that the paradox cannot be understood (*PS*, pp. 196 – 197). I will not try to explain away the paradox, to resolve it, but only to make clear what Kierkegaard is calling a paradox.

To help us in characterizing what Kierkegaard calls a paradox we shall consider the following case, which is similar in some respects to Abraham's. An army private has received his company commander's promise of a pass for the following weekend. He will spend the weekend in a nearby town. The day after receiving the promise he is informed that the company commander has chosen him to do guard duty on the weekend covered by the promise. The private casually mentions this state of affairs to a friend. His friend notices, however, that the private shows no concern — he is not resentful or upset at having his plans spoiled, nor does he give evidence of thinking that the commander has forgotten his promise and ought to be reminded. Nor does he have the grim appearance of one who is resigned. Rather, he almost appears not to understand his situation. The surprised friend asks, "Well, aren't you going to do anything about it? You certainly have a legitimate gripe — or if you think the old man has forgotten his promise why don't you go and remind him?"

Now the private looks surprised. "Legitimate gripe? About what? Of course he hasn't forgotten his promise. I'll have my pass."

"Oh, you think that your name being on the guard roster for the weekend is a mistake. Well, you'd better get it straightened out."

"No, there's no mistake. I'm on guard duty all right."

"Well, then, who've you decided to ask to take your place? Not me, I've got a pass, too."

"Nobody's going to take my place. I'm going to stand guard myself."

"What do you mean, you're going to stand guard yourself? You said you were going on pass!"

There is no need to continue this dialogue. The similarity to Abra-

---

[11]*Training in Christianity* (Princeton: Princeton University Press, 1944), p. 125.

ham's situation should now be apparent: just as Abraham believed that God's promise to him would be fulfilled, while at the same time intending to obey God's command, so the private believes that his commander's promise to him will be fulfilled, while at the same time intending to obey his command. About either case we might shake our heads and exclaim, "That's a paradox!" And of either paradox we might also be inclined to say that the paradox is "real."

Concerning the private's situation, one can see what the paradox is and also its "realness." First, the paradox is that, unaccountably, the private both believes that a promise will be fulfilled, the fulfillment of which precludes the possibility of obeying the command, and also intends to obey a command the obeying of which precludes the possibility of the promise's being fulfilled. The realness of the paradox is that this preclusion is, as we shall now put it, absolute. If the promise is fulfilled then the command cannot be obeyed; and if the command is obeyed then the promise cannot be fulfilled.

This sort of "real" paradox is to be distinguished from apparent paradoxes, of which the following argument is an example:

> He who is most hungry eats most. He who eats least is most hungry.
> Therefore, he who eats least eats most.[12]

This argument paradoxically proves true what appears to be a self-contradiction. It is a syllogism in the first figure, mood AAA, and thus is valid. And yet the conclusion appears to be self-contradictory. Prima facie the argument is paradoxical, and one might explain one's calling it paradoxical by saying, "A valid argument cannot have a self-contradictory conclusion, and yet here, it seems, we have one that does." The prima facie paradoxicalness of the syllogism is removed, however, when one points out that the major premise means "He who is most hungry *will eat most*" and that the minor premise means "He who *has eaten least* is most hungry." Making these changes in the verb phrases of the conclusion as well as of the premises then eliminates the paradoxicalness of the argument, for the conclusion now reads "He who has eaten least will eat most." The paradox is thus only apparent and not real. In contrast, the paradox in the case of the private has no such resolution. One cannot eliminate it by rephrasing the statement of the situation.

Let us examine the private's case a little more closely to see what is involved in its containing a real paradox. The private both believes that the promise will be fulfilled and intends to obey the command. Now, as was brought out in the presentation of this case, the private intends to obey the command himself. He is not thinking of getting someone else to obey it for him so that while he is in town dancing with the USO girls,

---

[12]Irving Copi, *Introduction to Logic* (New York: Macmillan, 1955), p. 77.

his friend is trudging along a dark fenceline with an M1 rifle on his shoulder. Rather, what the private believes and intends must be taken to involve that it might come about that while he is in town dancing with the USO girls he is also walking his post along fenceline, that is, that one person might be in two places at once.

The immediate reaction of course is "But one person can't be in two different places at once!" And this is a way of saying that the meaning of the expression "one person" is such that it *makes no sense* to say of one person that he was in two different places at once. This may be seen if we consider what we call "counting persons." Consider this case. The commanding officer of Company B wishes to know how many of his men are on pass for the evening. He does not have the pass book with him and so asks one of his company officers to go to the USO club and another to look in at the pool hall next to the club, these being the only places outside the camp where his men take their ease. The company officers make their investigations. The first officer reports that he counted only one man from Company B at the USO club; the second officer likewise reports that he counted but one at the pool hall. The commanding officer hesitates: "But you may have counted one person twice. What time was it when you made your counts?" And what will settle it for the commander that his officers have not counted one person twice is this: that they made their counts at the same time. What is *counted* as "one person," then, is not something that can, like poverty, be in more than one place at the same time. We do not call "one person" that of which it makes sense to suggest that it is in two places at the same time.

Let us now return to the case of the private. We said of this case that if the promise is fulfilled then the command cannot be obeyed and if the command is obeyed then the promise cannot be fulfilled. We can now see why. For the promise and the command in conjunction *rule out* precisely what they *require:* they require the possibility of calling the receiver of the pass and the obeyer of the command "one person," since the person who is to receive the pass is the person who is to obey the command; and yet they rule this out as a possibility, since we do not call "one person" that of which it makes sense to suggest that it is in two places at once. Thus, the promise and the command in conjunction make no sense.

If the promise and the command in conjunction are nonsense, the paradox is that the private should believe the promise will be fulfilled and should also intend to obey the command. "How can he!" we want to exclaim. "For together the promise and the command are nonsense!" We might at this point go on to discuss the question whether it makes sense to say that one believes or intends what is nonsense. But for our purpose it is enough to have pointed out that the promise and command in conjunction are nonsense and that the paradox is that the private both believes that the promise will be fulfilled and also intends to obey the command.

Let us now return to Abraham and ask, "Is his case like that of the private? Are we to say that here too the promise and the command in conjunction are nonsense and that the paradox is that Abraham believes that the promise will be fulfilled and also intends to obey the command?" First, are the promise and the command in conjunction nonsense? One might wish to say so, for if the promise is that through Isaac Abraham's seed should be multiplied as the stars of the heaven and the command is that Isaac should be sacrificed, then the promise and command in conjunction involve that a dead boy should grow to manhood, marry, and father children. And as in the private's case we said, "One person can't be in two different places at once" in order to point out that the promise and the command in conjunction make no sense, so in the case of Abraham we might wish to say, "A dead boy cannot grow up, marry, and father children," in order to point out that here too the promise and the command in conjunction make no sense. In this latter case we might go on to explain that the very meaning of the word "dead" is "a ceasing of life processes — growth, and so forth." And so about a dead person it makes no sense to ask how much he has grown in the last six months, to inquire whether he has met a nice girl yet, to wonder whether he has a family yet, and so on. And this is true; it does make no sense.

But there is a mistake in all this. The mistake is in thinking that the promise and the command in conjunction involve the nonsense that a dead boy should grow to manhood, marry, and father children. They involve, rather, that Abraham's living son grow to manhood, marry, and father children. And how is this to be accomplished? (Abraham never asked this question. But we who want to get the logic of the situation straight must ask it.) The answer is supplied by Kierkegaard on pages 46–47 of *Fear and Trembling:* "Let us go further. We let Isaac be really sacrificed. Abraham believed. He did not believe that some day he would be blessed in the beyond, but that he would be happy here in the world. God . . . could recall to life him who had been sacrificed."[13]

This passage shows that Kierkegaard did not regard Abraham as one who was being asked to "believe" the logically impossible or the nonsensical, whatever it might mean to say of one that he believes such. There is, rather, something that we should all call fulfillment of the promise, even though the command has been obeyed. (Contrast the case of the private: there is nothing we should call fulfillment of the promise if the command is obeyed.)

But then what is Kierkegaard calling paradoxical in the case of Abraham? Is it not just what Abraham did? Is it not his believing that the

[13] Cf. Hebrews 11: 17–19.

promise would yet be fulfilled even while he obeyed a command the obeying of which rendered fulfillment of the promise impossible — *except by a miracle?* Is this not the "enormous paradox which is the substance of Abraham's life"? Is this not what Johannes de silentio cannot understand — cannot understand because it is absurd? There is little difficulty in imagining the Abraham story (not, at least, with Kierkegaard's help), but can we imagine doing what Abraham did, the while expecting what Abraham expected? But this point is best brought home by Kierkegaard himself.

At the beginning of section III of this chapter I asked the question: does the paradox of religiousness *B*, as it is exemplified in the case of Abraham, involve a logical contradiction or impossibility? If what I went on to say is correct, then we can say that, *in the case of Abraham,* the paradox does not involve a logical contradiction or impossibility. We might, however, still have doubts about the God-man paradox, which for Kierkegaard is peculiar to Christianity. For though one might argue that since both the religion of Abraham and Christianity are instance of religiousness *B*, the paradoxical religion, and the paradox in Abraham's case involves no logical impossibility, then the paradox in the case of Christianity involves no logical impossibility — the argument is very weak. I do not wish to propound it. I think, however, that its conclusion is correct. Would Kierkegaard saw off the limb he is sitting on?

SECTION FOUR

JOHN McTAGGART ELLIS McTAGGART

The Establishment of Dogma*

It is not uncommon to hear the assertion that certain religious dogmas—the personality of God, for example, or the immortality of man, or the freedom of the will—do not require proof. 'I am certain of this', some one will say, 'without argument. My conviction does not rest on argument, and cannot be shaken by it. I decline to argue. I simply believe.' A belief which does not rest upon argument, in the case of any particular person, may be said to be held by such a person immediately, since argument is a process of mediation. The assertion here is, it will be noticed, not only that the belief does not rest upon arguments—i.e. that it is immediate—but also that it cannot be shaken by arguments.

Such a position is, no doubt, impregnable from outside. If a man's belief does not rest on reasons, and cannot be shaken by them, I may believe it to be mistaken, but I should be wasting time in attempting to argue against it.

If the person who holds a belief in this manner mentions the fact to me as a reason why I should not waste his time in trying to upset it, he is acting in a perfectly reasonable manner. And it is also strictly relevant to mention it if he is writing an autobiography—for it may be an important fact in his life. Also it is relevant as a contribution to statistics. It shows that one more person has this particular conviction in this particular way.

*This selection is the major part of Chapter II of McTaggart's *Some Dogmas of Religion*, published by Edward Arnold, London, in 1906, pp. 38–76.

But it is not relevant if it is put forward for any other motive. Above all, it is absolutely irrelevant if it is put forward as a reason to induce other people to believe the same dogma. This is sometimes done. A man will assert his own immediate conviction of a dogma,[1] not as a reason for checking discussion, but as his contribution to the discussion. And here it seems certain that he is wrong.

What is the good of telling B that A has an immediate certainty of the truth of X? If B has a similar immediate certainty he believes X already, and must believe it, and, for him, A's certainty is quite superfluous. If B has an immediate certainty of the falsity of X, or of the truth of something incompatible with X, then he cannot believe X, and, for him, A's certainty is quite useless. But supposing B has no immediate certainty on the matter at all, how will his knowledge of A's immediate certainty help him? It cannot give him an immediate certainty, for, if he believes because A does, his belief rests on an argument, 'A believes this, and therefore it is true,' and so is not immediate.

But can A's immediate certainty be a valid ground for a reasoned certainty on B's part? Why, because A does believe anything, ought B to believe it? That is ultimate for A, but it is not ultimate for B. Why should B accept this fact of A's nature as decisive, or even in the least relevant, as to a truth which does not relate to A's nature, but, for example, to the existence of a personal God?

An attempt has been made to show why B should do this—an attempt which seems to rest entirely on an analogy. The people who have not this immediate certainty are compared to the blind. A blind man has no means of perceiving a balloon which floats above him in the air. Yet he would be mistaken if he disbelieved the statement of his friends that the balloon was there. Similarly, we are told, if another man has an immediate conviction of a proposition, of whose truth I am not convinced at all, I ought to supply the deficiency in my nature by taking on trust from him what he perceives immediately.[2]

But an analogy is good enough to meet an analogy. A man in delirium frequently believes that he sees assassins lurking in a corner, or rats leaping on his bed. He is as firmly convinced that he sees them as I am that I see the balloon above me. His physicians do not see them. Would they do well to believe that they were there, but that some limitation of their own faculties prevented their seeing them? They do not believe this. They do not send for the police to arrest the assassins, or for a

---

[1] I am assuming for the present that an immediate conviction is also one which cannot be shaken by arguments. We shall see later on that this is not always the case.

[2] The example I have given seems to me to do the argument more justice than the one usually taken, in which the blind man denies the existence of colour. For most people, whether blind or not, believe that colour does not exist except in the sensations of those who see. If a blind man denied the existence of colour in this sense, he would not be analogous to a person who denied the truth of the belief of others, but to a person who denied that the others had that belief.

terrier to catch the rats. And it would be generally admitted that they are right.

Now which is the more correct analogy here? When some people have an immediate conviction of the truth of some particular dogma, and others have not, are these others in the position of the blind man or of the physician? Such cases, it seems to me, are settled, outside the sphere of religious dogma, in one of two ways. Sometimes they are settled roughly by counting heads. The blind are fewer in number than those who can see. But only one man can see the assassins or the rats. Any one else who enters the room cannot see them.

If we were to decide on this plan there would be little reason for any one else to believe a dogma because of A's immediate certainty of it. People who have, or believe themselves to have, the immediate certainty of a religious dogma are always comparatively rare — much rarer than the people who believe in the dogma. Let us take, as an example, the existence of God. A great majority of the inhabitants of the United Kingdom accept this dogma. But I should say that by far the greater number of them believe in it for some reason, good or bad, — the authority of the Church, the statement of the Bible, the argument from design, or the like. The number of those who hold it because of an immediate certainty would be but small.

Moreover, the people who have such immediate convictions agree very little among themselves. Some, for example, have immediate convictions on the subjects of God, immortality, and free will. Others have them on the subject of God alone, or of free will alone, or of immortality alone. Others have them in different combinations, and others on different subjects altogether. If the sight-perceptions of mankind varied as much as this, the blind would rightly decline to put much faith in them.

But the test of counting heads, though sometimes the only possible test, is crude and unsatisfactory. We have generally better reasons. A blind man has good reasons for believing that other people have sources of knowledge which he has not. They tell him, for example, that a table is six feet in front of him. He cannot perceive this at the time, but by walking forward he can test it by touch, and he finds it correct. When this has happened several times, the hypothesis that other men have a trustworthy sense, which he has not, becomes far more consistent with his own experience than the hypothesis that they are all labouring under a delusion. When the delirious man, on the other hand, asserts that a rat has come up through a solid floor, or that he is menaced by a man who has long been dead, or who is breathing flame, the hypothesis that he sees something, to which other people are blind, would conflict with the general fabric of experience far more than the hypothesis that he is mistaken.

It is in this way that we ought to test the immediate convictions on religious dogma which we do not happen to share, before we decide whether to accept them as the basis for a reasoned, non-immediate, belief on our own behalf. But to do this is to inquire whether the existence of the object of the immediate belief harmonizes better with our experience than the nonexistence of it. And when we make this the test, we have really given up all reliance on A's immediate conviction, and are endeavouring to support our belief on the direct evidence for the truth of the proposition. A's conviction, at most, *suggests* the dogma to us, if we had not heard of it before; the ground of our belief in the dogma is no longer A's belief in it.

In the case of the blind man, the matter would be different. The perceptions of sight of those who surround him are very numerous, and when he has tested them a certain number of times he can believe in the rest without testing them. In these subsequent cases, therefore, his belief *is* based on the perceptions of others. But no man professes to have a very large number of immediate convictions on religious dogmas. It would thus be impossible to argue here that a man's immediate convictions had been proved right on so many points that they might be trusted on the rest. They can only be trusted by us in the cases in which they can be proved. And then *our* belief rests entirely on the proof, and his immediate conviction only furnishes the suggestion for us, and not the reason for our belief.

Thus, even granting that A has an immediate conviction of the truth of some religious dogma, it is quite irrelevant to me, though decisive for him. But it is by no means certain that A has an immediate conviction when he thinks he has. In many cases—though certainly not in all—it seems very probable that he has not. A man may make mistakes in judging and classifying what takes place in his own mind, just as much as he may make mistakes about other things.

For example, a man may be confused as to what it is of which he is immediately certain. He may think that his immediate certainty is of the existence of a personal God, when, in his case, it may be only that the ultimate reality is spiritual. That an ultimate spiritual reality must necessarily be a personal God may be a proposition which he believes on account of reasons—or which, perhaps, when clearly stated, he is not prepared to accept at all.

Or, again, closer analysis may convince him that the proposition, of which he supposed himself to have an immediate certainty, is really dependent for him on other propositions. If it can be proved to him that he was not justified in basing it on those other propositions—either because they are false, or because it does not properly follow from them—he will abandon the result which he had previously thought beyond the reach of argument.

So far we have assumed that a belief which is immediate—that is, which does not rest on arguments — cannot be shaken by them. But an immediate belief may rest on prejudices or tradition. (Of course, if tradition is explicitly accepted as likely to lead to truth, then it is a reason for belief, whether it is a good reason or not, and the conclusion is not immediate. But when a man believes a tradition merely because it has never occurred to him to question it, then the tradition is not a reason for belief, though it is a cause.) Now a belief of this sort, although it does not rest on arguments, may be shaken by them. For it may be shown that it is caused by prejudice or tradition, and this demonstration — though it refutes no arguments for the belief, since there were none to refute — may cause the believer to change his opinion.

The result at which I arrive is that the statement, that any man has an immediate conviction on a matter of religious dogma is one which he ought not to expect to have any relevance for others, and which he ought only to make, even for his own guidance, after careful tests have convinced him, in the first place, of what his belief really is, and in the second place, that it is not based on arguments. Even then, he ought not to consider the matter closed, unless equally careful tests have also convinced him that his immediate conviction is not to be shaken by arguments. The impotency of argument on matters of religious dogma is always to be regretted. For it is notorious that people do differ on these subjects, and, where argument is impotent, nothing can be done to promote an agreement. Where nothing can be done, the evil must, of course, be recognized. But we are bound in each case to make ourselves quite sure that the evil cannot be removed.

It is certain, no doubt, that, if we are to have any knowledge at all, we must have some immediate convictions, and that if we are to have any true knowledge at all, some of our immediate convictions must be true. For nothing can be proved unless we start from something already known, and, if we could know nothing unless it were proved, we could never start at all.

But it would not follow from this that every man must have immediate convictions on matters of religious dogma, or that he must have true immediate convictions on that subject. For it is possible to have knowledge without having immediate convictions as to religious dogmas, although it is not possible to have knowledge without immediate convictions of some sort.

Again, there is nothing to be regretted in the immediacy of our convictions as to the validity of a syllogism in Barbara, or as to the Law of Contradiction. We cannot doubt them, and we cannot prove them. But the inability to prove them is not a disaster here, because nobody denies them. Where we cannot argue, we can do nothing to remove differences of opinion. But there is no harm in this, where there are no differences of opinion to remove. With religious dogma it is different. For every religious dogma of the truth of which any man has an immediate conviction, is believed by many men to be false.

It remains to speak of the appeal, sometimes made, to leave dogmatic questions to faith. In so far as this means faith in a proposition, it presents nothing new. If the faith is asserted to be based on reason, then the question will arise whether the reasons are valid, and it becomes a question of argument. If the faith dispenses with reason, we have again the appeal to immediate conviction.

We are sometimes invited to have faith on account of the very limited amount of our knowledge, and the possible errors in it. The argument is not, I think, one which gains any importance by being advocated by thinkers of repute, but it is sufficiently popular to deserve some consideration.

The fact on which it is based is unquestionably true. We know very little, compared to what there is to be known; and what we take for knowledge is frequently error. If this were assigned as a reason for not being certain as to the truth of our conclusions—and especially of our conclusions on obscure and disputed subjects—the argument would be unquestionably legitimate. And if it were given as a reason for complete scepticism, the conclusion, though exaggerated, would not be very surprising. But it is somewhat remarkable that our want of knowledge on any subject, should be put forward as a reason for coming to a particular conclusion on that subject.

Yet this is often done. If it is suggested that there is no evidence that the universe is working towards a good end, the doubter is reminded of the limitations of his intellect, and on account of this is exhorted to banish his doubts from his mind, and to believe firmly that the universe is directed towards a good end. And stronger instances can be found. An apologist may admit, for example, that for our intellects the three facts of the omnipotence of a personal God, the benevolence of a personal God, and the existence of evil, are not to be reconciled. But we are once more reminded of the feebleness of our intellects. And we are invited to assert, not only that our conclusions may be wrong, not only that the three elements may possibly be reconciled, but that they are reconciled. There is evil, and there is an omnipotent and benevolent God.

This line of argument has two weaknesses. The first is that it will prove everything—including mutually incompatible propositions— equally well. It will prove as easily that the universe is tending towards a bad end as that it is tending towards a good one. There may be as little evidence for the pessimistic view as for the optimistic. But if our intellects are so feeble that the absence of sufficient evidence in our minds is no objection to a conclusion in the one case, then a similar absence can be no objection to a conclusion in the other. Nor can we fall back on the assertion that there is *less* evidence for the pessimistic view than for the optimistic, and that, therefore, we should adopt the latter. For if our intellects are too feeble for their conclusions to be trusted, our distrust must apply equally to their conclusion on the relative weight of the evidence in the two cases.

The other objection to the argument is that it implies that, if we cannot trust our conclusion that A is false, we have no alternative but to conclude that A is true. But there is a third alternative to being confident of the truth or confident of the falsity of A. It is to abstain from judging about A at all. And it is this which would seem to be the more reasonable alternative, supposing our intellects are as weak as they are asserted to be. If I have only taken a hasty view by twilight of my neighbour's garden, it would be rash of me to place much trust in my failure to see any lilies in it. But it would be even more rash if I proceeded from the untrustworthiness of my negative conclusion to a confident assertion that there *were* lilies in it, and that there were exactly seventeen of them.

Even in this case, however, I should not have to ignore an *a priori* conviction of the impossibility of lilies. But the argument from the feebleness of our intellects is often used as a reason why we should believe a state of things to exist which our intellects pronounce to be self-contradictory. I might as well call on you and myself to believe that in some remote corner of the universe the Law of Diminishing Returns devours purple quadratic equations. It seems to us, certainly, that a quadratic equation cannot have colour, or be eaten. But then, how inadequate are our merely human powers to limit the resources of the infinite!

But there is another form of the appeal to faith which requires more serious consideration. We are invited to have faith, not in the truth of a proposition, but in the goodness of a person. A man trusts his friends, or his political leader. He believes them to have good motives for actions whose motives he is unable to detect. He often believes them to have good motives in cases where, but for his personal faith in them, the circumstances would strongly suggest that they were actuated by bad motives. Subsequent events often — though not always — prove that he was right. Can we not, we are asked, trust God as we trust our friends?

In the first place it must be remarked that this form of faith can only have a very limited application in the establishment of dogma. It assumes, to begin with, that the dogma of the existence of a personal God has been already established. For the appeal to trust God as we trust men loses all plausibility if God is not a person. If the ultimate reality of the universe were an aggregate of atoms, or a chaos of sensations, or a substance devoid of will, intellect, and purpose, it would be futile to trust it.

Then our faith in a man does not enable us to predict his actions —

which, indeed, are often determined, as in the case of a statesman, by considerations which are inaccessible to us. All that it does is to render us confident that they will be wise and virtuous. And a corresponding faith in God will not enable us to determine whether we are immortal, whether our wills are undetermined, or similar questions of dogma. It will only give us light on one particular dogma—that the world is wisely and righteously ordered.

And even here it will not by itself enable us to say that the world *is* wisely and righteously ordered. For my faith in a man only enables me to be confident that his ends will be well chosen and pursued. They may not be attained, for that may be prevented by forces beyond his own control. All that such faith then can teach us of God is that his end is the good ordering of the universe. If we are to be certain that his end will be attained, we must, in some other manner, have established the dogma that God is either omnipotent, or at any rate so powerful as to be free from the risk of eventual defeat.

But, even with these limitations, should we be entitled to trust God as we might trust a man whose designs we could not follow? I do not think that we should. Of course, if we have convinced ourselves by direct argument that God is working towards the good and is strong enough to realize it, then we should be sure of his intentions and his success in cases where we could not divine his purpose or directly perceive his success. But this would not be the faith of which we speak. It would be demonstration. If God's nature is proved to be such that he always wills the good, then in any particular case it is clear that he does will it. The faith in God which we are now discussing is a substitute for demonstration, not an instance of it.

We do not put faith in all men, but only in some of them. Why is this? I take it that our faith is an induction from experience. If a man has always acted honourably, and now acts in a way which, viewed in itself, would seem to us dishonourable, we think it more probable that our judgement on the character of this action is mistaken, than that our mass of previous judgements on his former conduct should be mistaken, or that his character should have suffered a sudden change for the worse. We say, therefore, that we are confident that circumstances, at present unknown to us, prevent the action from being dishonourable.

Sometimes, indeed, we have faith in a man of whom we know nothing. But, after all, we know that he is a man. And our faith in this case is based on the experience of the past which tells us that men have never, or very rarely, been known to commit the particular crime or to omit the particular duty in respect of which we have faith in the man before us.

Faith in man, then, rests on an induction—an induction from the previously observed conduct of the man in question, or of men in general. Can such an induction be legitimately made in the case of God, supposing his existence as a person to be already proved? I do not think it can be. For consider how enormous is the scope of the conclusion of the inference as compared with the scope of the observations on which it can be based. What are the limits of our knowledge of what are, on this theory, God's acts? We know a very few of those which have happened on one planet for a few thousand years, together with a few isolated facts about events beyond this planet. On the strength of these we are invited to believe in a uniform law applying to all his actions for the whole universe. We know that the universe is much larger than our sphere of observation. It is perhaps even infinitely larger. Surely to conclude from so little to so much would be ineffably rash. Judas, according to the old legend, once gave a cloak to a leper. If any man who had observed this had argued that the whole of the life of Judas was one continuous succession of virtuous deeds, his conclusion would be admitted to be unfounded. Yet that action would have borne a larger proportion to the whole life of Judas, than those of God's actions which we directly know can be supposed to bear to the whole of his actions.

This objection would, I think, be fatal even if every one of the divine actions which we directly know was one which suggested a good purpose. But it is universally admitted that this is not the case, and that many of those facts of the universe which we directly know do not suggest a good design as their most obvious explanation. I will not inquire whether the facts known to us show more good than evil. It is certain that the two are so nearly balanced, that both the evil and the good have been considered, by different observers, to be the greater. Such a mixed experience as this is possibly not incompatible with the existence of a God who is working for the good and who is strong enough to succeed. But it does not form an adequate proof of his existence.

It is clear that we cannot put faith in God without reference to our knowledge of his actions, although we can, in certain cases, do this with man. We trust them from our experience of other men. But if there is a God, he is probably not one of a class of Gods, and, if he were, we should know no more of them than of him. It is true that a personal God would be included with men in the class of persons, but the difference between God and man would be far too great to justify any inference from the conduct of the one to the conduct of the other.

There are, of course, cases in which faith does not depend on induction—or indeed on any basis of reason at all. If A loves B, it is frequently the case, though by no means always, that he will decline to adopt any theory of B's action which involves blame to B, even if the facts are such that he would have adopted the theory without hesitation in the case of any person whom he did not love. It has been suggested that this is the right analogy for our faith in God. If we love him, it is said, we shall have faith in his working for good, and that faith will be justifiable.

If this is even psychologically possible, it is clear that it must be possible to love God before deciding whether he is good or not — perhaps a better expression would be, to love a being otherwise answering to the description of God, before deciding whether he possesses the remaining divine quality of goodness. For, if a belief in the goodness has to precede the love, it is clear that the love cannot be the ground of the belief in goodness.

It is, fortunately, possible to love men regardless of their wickedness. Could it be so with God? Could we love an otherwise divine being who was wicked? If he were conceived as omnipotent, or as only self-limited, I should imagine it to be impossible — though it is difficult to be certain. But if he were conceived as a finite being of limited power, working in a world of which he was not the ultimate creator, then I can see no difficulty in a man loving him, irrespective of his goodness or wickedness, as a man might be loved.

This conception of God is not, of course, a very common one. But for those who hold it the position which we are discussing is, no doubt, psychologically possible. They can love God, having satisfied themselves of his existence, with a love as ultimate and super-moral as that of friend for friend. And then, no doubt, they may be led on from this to assume his goodness when there is no evidence, or insufficient evidence, for it.

Such a position is possible, then, but is it justifiable? The analogy, at any rate, is not encouraging. For, after all, the object of any belief is to gain the truth. A belief which does not do this stands condemned. Now it is notorious that the faith in a person which is based on love for him frequently does lead to a false belief, and not to a true one. If a man's mother is convinced of his innocence when a jury is convinced of his guilt, experience shows that the jury is much more likely to be right than the mother.

Nor is faith in the goodness of the beloved essential to love, as has sometimes been maintained. It is fortunate that it is not. For there are cases where the blindest faith in a man's goodness must give way before the demonstration that he is bad. And, if faith in goodness were essential to love, then love would have to cease when this happened. But it need not cease then, and if often does not. We are better than Tennyson — or at least Guinevere interpreted by Tennyson — made us out to be. We need not love the highest when we see it. And we can love the lowest when we see it — when the lowest happens to be the person we love.

The conclusion I submit is that on matters of dogma we cannot dispense with proof, and we cannot prove anything by considering the people who believe it, or the disastrous consequences which would follow from its falsity. We must prove our dogmas more directly, if we are to continue to believe them. This will leave all questions of dogma more or less problematic, and many quite unanswered. And this is doubtless unpleasant. But unpleasant things are sometimes true.

Is there then no moral element involved in belief in religious dogma? I believe that to acquire true belief in religious dogma does require moral qualities — in almost every case — in the seeker. But they are required, not to show us what the truth is — for that purpose they seem to me as useless to the metaphysician as to the accountant — but to prevent our turning away from the truth. In the first place, a man will scarcely arrive at truth in these questions without courage. For he must seek before he can find, and at the beginning of his search he cannot tell what he will find.

And he will also need — unless he is almost incredibly fortunate — a certain form of faith. He will need the power to trust the conclusions which his reason has deliberately adopted, even when circumstances make such a belief especially difficult or painful. There are leaden days when even the most convinced idealist seems to *feel* that his body and his furniture are as real as himself, and members of a far more powerful reality. There are times when the denial of immortality seems, to the firmest disbeliever in immortality, a denial which he has scarcely strength to make.

But, whatever is true, it is quite certain that truth is not affected by incidents like these. If all reality has been proved to be spiritual, it cannot have ceased to be spiritual because to-day I am ill or over-worked. If I had no reason to believe in immortality yesterday, when other people's friends were dead, I have no greater reason to believe in it because to-day my friend has died.

If we want to know the truth, then, we must have faith in the conclusions of our reason, even when they seem — as they often will seem — too good or too bad to be true. Such faith has a better claim to abide with hope and love than the faith which consists in believing without reasons for belief. It is this faith, surely, which is sought in the prayer, 'Suffer us not for any pains of death to fall from thee.' And for those who do not pray, there remains the resolve that, so far as their strength may prevail, neither the pains of death nor the pains of life shall drive them to any comfort in that which they hold to be false, or drive them from any comfort in that which they hold to be true.

BERTRAND RUSSELL

A Free Man's Worship*

To Dr. Faustus in his study Mephistopheles told the history of the Creation, saying:

"The endless praises of the choirs of angels had begun to grow wearisome; for, after all, did he not deserve their praise? Had he not given them endless joy? Would it not be more amusing to obtain undeserved praise, to be worshipped by beings whom he tortured? He smiled inwardly, and resolved that the great drama should be performed.

"For countless ages the hot nebula whirled aimlessly through space. At length it began to take shape, the central mass threw off planets, the planets cooled, boiling seas and burning mountains heaved and tossed, from black masses of cloud hot sheets of rain deluged the barely solid crust. And now the first germ of life grew in the depths of the ocean, and developed rapidly in the fructifying warmth into vast forest trees, huge ferns springing from the damp mould, sea monsters breeding, fighting, devouring, and passing away. And from the monsters, as the play unfolded itself, Man was born, with the power of thought, the knowledge of good and evil, and the cruel thirst for worship. And Man saw that all is passing in this mad, monstrous world, that all is struggling to snatch, at any cost, a few brief moments of life before Death's inexorable decree. And Man said: 'There is a hidden purpose, could we

*From Bertrand Russell, *Mysticism and Logic.* Copyright © George Allen and Unwin 1917, pp. 46–57. Reprinted by permission of the publisher.

but fathom it, and the purpose is good; for we must reverence something, and in the visible world there is nothing worthy of reverence.'
And Man stood aside from the struggle, resolving that God intended
harmony to come out of chaos by human efforts. And when he followed
the instincts which God had transmitted to him from his ancestry of
beasts of prey, he called it Sin, and asked God to forgive him. But he
doubted whether he could be justly forgiven, until he invented a divine
Plan by which God's wrath was to have been appeased. And seeing the
present was bad, he made it yet worse, that thereby the future might be
better. And he gave God thanks for the strength that enabled him to
forgo even the joys that were possible. And God smiled; and when he
saw that Man had become perfect in renunciation and worship, he sent
another sun through the sky, which crashed into Man's sun; and all
returned again to nebula.

"'Yes,' he murmured, 'it was a good play; I will have it performed
again.'"

Such, in outline, but even more purposeless, more void of meaning, is
the world which Science presents for our belief. Amid such a world, if
anywhere, our ideals henceforward must find a home. That Man is the
product of causes which had no prevision of the end they were achieving; that his origin, his growth, his hopes and fears, his loves and his
beliefs, are but the outcome of accidental collocations of atoms; that no
fire, no heroism, no intensity of thought and feeling, can preserve an
individual life beyond the grave; that all the labours of the ages, all the
devotion, all the inspiration, all the noonday brightness of human
genius, are destined to extinction in the vast death of the solar system,
and that the whole temple of Man's achievement must inevitably be
buried beneath the débris of a universe in ruins — all these things, if
not quite beyond dispute, are yet so nearly certain, that no philosophy
which rejects them can hope to stand. Only within the scaffolding of
these truths, only on the firm foundation of unyielding despair, can the
soul's habitation henceforth be safely built.

How, in such an alien and inhuman world, can so powerless a creature as Man preserve his aspirations untarnished? A strange mystery it
is that Nature, omnipotent but blind, in the revolutions of her secular
hurryings through the abysses of space, has brought forth at last a child,
subject still to her power, but gifted with sight, with knowledge of good
and evil, with the capacity of judging all the works of his unthinking
Mother. In spite of Death, the mark and seal of the parental control,
Man is yet free, during his brief years, to examine, to criticise, to know,
and in imagination to create. To him alone, in the world with which he
is acquainted, this freedom belongs; and in this lies his superiority to
the resistless forces that control his outward life.

The savage, like ourselves, feels the oppression of his impotence
before the powers of Nature; but having in himself nothing that he

respects more than Power, he is willing to prostrate himself before his gods, without inquiring whether they are worthy of his worship. Pathetic and very terrible is the long history of cruelty and torture, of degradation and human sacrifice, endured in the hope of placating the jealous gods: surely, the trembling believer thinks, when what is most precious has been freely given, their lust for blood must be appeased, and more will not be required. The religion of Moloch — as such creeds may be generically called — is in essence the cringing submission of the slave, who dare not, even in his heart, allow the thought that his master deserves no adulation. Since the independence of ideals is not yet acknowledged, Power may be freely worshipped, and receive an unlimited respect, despite its wanton infliction of pain.

But gradually, as morality grows bolder, the claim of the ideal world begins to be felt; and worship, if it is not to cease, must be given to gods of another kind than those created by the savage. Some, though they feel the demands of the ideal, will still consciously reject them, still urging that naked Power is worthy of worship. Such is the attitude inculcated in God's answer to Job out of the whirlwind: the divine power and knowledge are paraded, but of the divine goodness there is no hint. Such also is the attitude of those who, in our own day, base their morality upon the struggle for survival, maintaining that the survivors are necessarily the fittest. But others, not content with an answer so repugnant to the moral sense, will adopt the position which we have become accustomed to regard as specially religious, maintaining that, in some hidden manner, the world of fact is really harmonious with the world of ideals. Thus Man creates God, all-powerful and all-good, the mystic unity of what is and what should be.

But the world of fact, after all, is not good; and, in submitting our judgment to it, there is an element of slavishness from which our thoughts must be purged. For in all things it is well to exalt the dignity of Man, by freeing him as far as possible from the tyranny of non-human Power. When we have realised that Power is largely bad, that man, with his knowledge of good and evil, is but a helpless atom in a world which has no such knowledge, the choice is again presented to us: Shall we worship Force, or shall we worship Goodness? Shall our God exist and be evil, or shall he be recognised as the creation of our own conscience?

The answer to this question is very momentous, and affects profoundly our whole morality. The worship of Force, to which Carlyle and Nietzsche and the creed of Militarism have accustomed us, is the result of failure to maintain our own ideals against a hostile universe: it is itself a prostrate submission to evil, a sacrifice of our best to Moloch. If strength indeed is to be respected, let us respect rather the strength of those who refuse that false "recognition of facts" which fails to recognise that facts are often bad. Let us admit that, in the world we know, there are many things that would be better otherwise, and that the ideals to which we do and must adhere are not realised in the realm of matter. Let us preserve our respect for truth, for beauty, for the ideal of perfection which life does not permit us to attain, though none of these things meet with the approval of the unconscious universe. If Power is bad, as it seems to be, let us reject it from our hearts. In this lies Man's true freedom: in determination to worship only the God created by our own love of the good, to respect only the heaven which inspires the insight of our best moments. In action, in desire, we must submit perpetually to the tyranny of outside forces; but in thought, in aspiration, we are free, free from our fellowmen, free from the petty planet on which our bodies impotently crawl, free even, while we live, from the tyranny of death. Let us learn, then, that energy of faith which enables us to live constantly in the vision of the good; and let us descend, in action, into the world of fact, with that vision always before us.

When first the opposition of fact and ideal grows fully visible, a spirit of fiery revolt, of fierce hatred of the gods, seems necessary to the assertion of freedom. To defy with Promethean constancy a hostile universe, to keep its evil always in view, always actively hated, to refuse no pain that the malice of Power can invent, appears to be the duty of all who will not bow before the inevitable. But indignation is still a bondage, for it compels our thoughts to be occupied with an evil world; and in the fierceness of desire from which rebellion springs there is a kind of self-assertion which it is necessary for the wise to overcome. Indignation is a submission of our thoughts, but not of our desires; the Stoic freedom in which wisdom consists is found in the submission of our desires, but not of our thoughts. From the submission of our desires springs the virtue of resignation; from the freedom of our thoughts springs the whole world of art and philosophy, and the vision of beauty by which, at last, we half reconquer the reluctant world. But the vision of beauty is possible only to unfettered contemplation, to thoughts not weighted by the load of eager wishes; and thus Freedom comes only to those who no longer ask of life that it shall yield them any of those personal goods that are subject to the mutations of Time.

Although the necessity of renunciation is evidence of the existence of evil, yet Christianity, in preaching it, has shown a wisdom exceeding that of the Promethean philosophy of rebellion. It must be admitted that, of the things we desire, some, though they prove impossible, are yet real goods; others, however, as ardently longed for, do not form part of a fully purified ideal. The belief that what must be renounced is bad, though sometimes false, is far less often false than untamed passion supposes; and the creed of religion, by providing a reason for proving that it is never false, has been the means of purifying our hopes by the discovery of many austere truths.

But there is in resignation a further good element: even real goods, when they are unattainable, ought not to be fretfully desired. To every man comes, sooner or later, the great renunciation. For the young, there is nothing unattainable; a good thing desired with the whole force of a passionate will, and yet impossible, is to them not credible. Yet, by death, by illness, by poverty, or by the voice of duty, we must learn, each one of us, that the world was not made for us, and that, however beautiful may be the things we crave, Fate may nevertheless forbid them. It is the part of courage, when misfortune comes, to bear without repining the ruin of our hopes, to turn away our thoughts from vain regrets. This degree of submission to Power is not only just and right: it is the very gate of wisdom.

But passive renunciation is not the whole of wisdom; for not by renunciation alone can we build a temple for the worship of our own ideals. Haunting foreshadowings of the temple appear in the realm of imagination, in music, in architecture, in the untroubled kingdom of reason, and in the golden sunset magic of lyrics, where beauty shines and glows, remote from the touch of sorrow, remote from the fear of change, remote from the failures and disenchantments of the world of fact. In the contemplation of these things the vision of heaven will shape itself in our hearts, giving at once a touchstone to judge the world about us, and an inspiration by which to fashion to our needs whatever is not incapable of serving as a stone in the sacred temple.

Except for those rare spirits that are born without sin, there is a cavern of darkness to be traversed before that temple can be entered. The gate of the cavern is despair, and its floor is paved with the gravestones of abandoned hopes. There Self must die; there the eagerness, the greed of untamed desire must be slain, for only so can the soul be freed from the empire of Fate. But out of the cavern the Gate of Renunciation leads again to the daylight of wisdom, by whose radiance a new insight, a new joy, a new tenderness, shine forth to gladden the pilgrim's heart.

When, without the bitterness of impotent rebellion, we have learnt both to resign ourselves to the outward rule of Fate and to recognise that the non-human world is unworthy of our worship, it becomes possible at last so to transform and refashion the unconscious universe, so to transmute it in the crucible of imagination, that a new image of shining gold replaces the old idol of clay. In all the multiform facts of the world—in the visual shapes of trees and mountains and clouds, in the events of the life of man, even in the very omnipotence of Death—the insight of creative idealism can find the reflection of a beauty which its own thoughts first made. In this way mind asserts its subtle mastery over the thoughtless forces of Nature. The more evil the material with which it deals, the more thwarting to untrained desire, the greater is its achievement in inducing the reluctant rock to yield up its hidden treasures, the prouder its victory in compelling the opposing forces to swell the pageant of its triumph. Of all the arts, Tragedy is the proudest, the most triumphant; for it builds its shining citadel in the very centre of the enemy's country, on the very summit of his highest mountain; from its impregnable watch-towers, his camps and arsenals, his columns and forts, are all revealed; within its walls the free life continues, while the legions of Death and Pain and Despair, and all the servile captains of tyrant Fate, afford the burghers of that dauntless city new spectacles of beauty. Happy those sacred ramparts, thrice happy the dwellers on that all-seeing eminence. Honour to those brave warriors who, through countless ages of warfare, have preserved for us the priceless heritage of liberty, and have kept undefiled by sacrilegious invaders the home of the unsubdued.

But the beauty of Tragedy does but make visible a quality which, in more or less obvious shapes, is present always and everywhere in life. In the spectacle of Death, in the endurance of intolerable pain, and in the irrevocableness of a vanished past, there is a sacredness, an overpowering awe, a feeling of the vastness, the depth, the inexhaustible mystery of existence, in which, as by some strange marriage of pain, the sufferer is bound to the world by bonds of sorrow. In these moments of insight, we lose all eagerness of temporary desire, all struggling and striving for petty ends, all care for the little trivial things that, to a superficial view, make up the common life of day by day; we see, surrounding the narrow raft illumined by the flickering light of human comradeship, the dark ocean on whose rolling waves we toss for a brief hour; from the great night without, a chill blast breaks in upon our refuge; all the loneliness of humanity amid hostile forces is concentrated upon the individual soul, which must struggle alone, with what of courage it can command, against the whole weight of a universe that cares nothing for its hopes and fears. Victory, in this struggle with the powers of darkness, is the true baptism into the glorious company of heroes, the true initiation into the overmastering beauty of human existence. From that awful encounter of the soul with the outer world, enunciation, wisdom, and charity are born; and with their birth a new life begins. To take into the inmost shrine of the soul the irresistible forces whose puppets we seem to be — Death and change, the irrevocableness of the past, and the powerlessness of man before the blind hurry of the universe from vanity to vanity — to feel these things and know them is to conquer them.

This is the reason why the Past has such magical power. The beauty of its motionless and silent pictures is like the enchanted purity of late autumn, when the leaves, though one breath would make them fall, still glow against the sky in golden glory. The Past does not change or strive;

like Duncan, after life's fitful fever it sleeps well; what was eager and grasping, what was petty and transitory, has faded away, the things that were beautiful and eternal shine out of it like stars in the night. Its beauty, to a soul not worthy of it, is unendurable; but to a soul which has conquered Fate it is the key of religion.

The life of Man, viewed outwardly, is but a small thing in comparison with the forces of Nature. The slave is doomed to worship Time and Fate and Death, because they are greater than anything he finds in himself, and because all his thoughts are of things which they devour. But, great as they are, to think of them greatly, to feel their passionless splendour, is greater still. And such thought makes us free men; we no longer bow before the inevitable in Oriental subjection, but we absorb it, and make it a part of ourselves. To abandon the struggle for private happiness, to expel all eagerness of temporary desire, to burn with passion for eternal things — this is emancipation, and this is the free man's worship. And this liberation is effected by a contemplation of Fate; for Fate itself is subdued by the mind which leaves nothing to be purged by the purifying fire of Time.

United with his fellow-men by the strongest of all ties, the tie of a common doom, the free man finds that a new vision is with him always, shedding over every daily task the light of love. The life of Man is a long march through the night, surrounded by invisible foes, tortured by weariness and pain, towards a goal that few can hope to reach, and where none may tarry long. One by one, as they march, our comrades vanish from our sight, seized by the silent orders of omnipotent Death. Very brief is the time which we can help them, in which their happiness or misery is decided. Be it ours to shed sunshine on their path, to lighten their sorrows by the balm of sympathy, to give them the pure joy of a never-tiring affection, to strengthen failing courage, to instil faith in hours of despair. Let us not weigh in grudging scales their merits and demerits, but let us think only of their need — of the sorrows, the difficulties, perhaps the blindnesses, that make the misery of their lives; let us remember that they are fellow-sufferers in the same darkness, actors in the same tragedy with ourselves. And so, when their day is over, when their good and their evil have become eternal by the immortality of the past, be it ours to feel that, where they suffered, where they failed, no deed of ours was the cause; but wherever a spark of the divine fire kindled in their hearts, we were ready with encouragement, with sympathy, with brave words in which high courage glowed.

Brief and powerless is Man's life; on him and all his race the slow, sure doom falls pitiless and dark. Blind to good and evil, reckless of destruction, omnipotent matter rolls on its relentless way; for Man, condemned to-day to lose his dearest, to-morrow himself to pass through the gate of darkness, it remains only to cherish, ere yet the blow falls, the lofty thoughts that ennoble his little day; disdaining the coward terrors of the slave of Fate, to worship at the shrine that his own hands have built; undismayed by the empire of chance, to preserve a mind free from the wanton tyranny that rules his outward life; proudly defiant of the irresistible forces that tolerate, for a moment, his knowledge and his condemnation, to sustain alone, a weary but unyielding Atlas, the world that his own ideals have fashioned despite the trampling march of unconscious power.

NORWOOD RUSSELL HANSON

The Agnostic's Dilemma*

An agnostic maintains himself in a state of perfect doubt concerning God's existence, a position I regard as unsound. The agnostic achieves his equipoise of dubiety only by shifting his ground where logic requires him to stand fast.

Is religious belief reasonable? This question pivots on reactions to the claim 'God exists'. This claim could be false. Its denial is consistent, hence the claim is synthetic. Otherwise it would be as uninformative to be told that God exists as it is to hear that bachelors are male.

Distinguishing theists from atheists, and these from agnostics, depends on there being alternative answers to the question "Does God exist?". The theist answers "Yes". The atheist answers "No". The agnostic doesn't know, or cannot decide.

There is a fund of subtle literature concerning this existence claim. Sometimes it is construed as synthetic but necessarily true. But this would make atheism impossible, which it is not. This point also cuts against 'God exists' being analytic. Again, some think the claim to be factual, yet established beyond all reasonable doubt. This makes atheism unreasonable, which it is not.

Many theologians hold the claim 'God exists' not to be central to the core of religious belief at all. In different ways, Niebuhr, Tillich, and Braithwaite have argued that the role of belief within human life re-

*This essay is published in *What I Do Not Believe and Other Essays*, ed. Stephen Toulmin and Harry Woolf, Reidel, 1972, pp. 303–308. It was originally published in *The American Rationalist* magazine of July/August 1961, and appears here by their permission.

mains fundamental whatever our decisions about the logical or factual status of the claim 'God exists'. Apparently it matters little to the reasonableness of one's religious beliefs whether or not he believes in God: indeed, it might remain reasonable for one to persist as a believer even after further thought has led him to deny God's existence.

This apologia has gained in popularity what it has lost in rationality. Clearly, a rational man will not continue to believe in what he has grounds for supposing does not exist. Nor will he maintain belief in that chain of claims which hang on a proposition he no longer thinks is true.

Hence, in this paper, 'God exists' is a synthetic claim; it could be false. Moreover, the claim could be contingently confirmed, as some theists say it already is. What have theists, atheists, and agnostics been arguing about, if not whether this existence claim is, or can be, factually established? Logically, the claim belongs in the center of our discussion. Historically, that is where it always has been. Despite the hocuspocus of theologians, the claim is also central within the lives of genuinely religious people. Surely most streetlevel believers would be affected in their religion by the disclosure that the New Testament was a forgery, or by a demonstration that God could not exist—assuming such a disclosure or demonstration to be possible.

Many theists will not be moved by these considerations. They will insist that 'God exists' is not the sort of claim that could be amenable to scientific observation, or even to logical scrutiny. Both reason and the senses fail when issues which turn on faith arise. This, of course, is a flight from reason. If neither logic nor experience can be allowed to affect our attitudes towards God's existence, then no argument and no ordinary experience can affect the theist's belief. However, it then becomes a university's function to stress that religious belief, so construed, is not reasonable. Nor is it connected with ordinary experience —since, if the latter cannot count against such belief, then neither can it count for it. A university must help young adults to distinguish positions for which there are good grounds from other positions for which the grounds are not so good. When the theist lets his appeal collapse into faith alone, he concedes that his position rests on no rational grounds at all.

The agnostic, however, cannot adopt any such theistic device. He must grant, without qualification, that 'God exists' is contingent. He feels, nonetheless, that there are no compelling factual grounds for deciding the issue one way or the other. After the atheist has exposed as inadequate all known arguments for God's existence, someone will ask, "But can you prove God does not exist?". Instead of realizing he has already done this, the atheist often hedges. This the agnostic mistakenly makes the basis for his universal dubiety.

If the argument between theists and atheists could have been settled by reflection, this would long since have been done. The theist's appeal to faith cannot settle any argument. So the agnostic adopts the only alternative, viz., that the argument concerns a matter of fact — whether or not God does in fact exist. But he remains in an equipoise of non-commitment by proclaiming that neither theist nor atheist has factual grounds for supposing the other's position to be refuted. How in detail does the agnostic argue this point?

Consider some logical preliminaries: entertain the claim 'All A's are B's'. If this ranges over a potential infinitude, then it can never be completely established by any finite number of observations of A's being B's. 'All bats are viviparous' receives each day a higher probability — but it is always less than 1, since the claim ranges over all past, present, and future bats, anywhere and everywhere.

This claim is easily disconfirmed, however. Discovering one oviparous bat would do it. Consider now the different claim: 'There exists an A which is a B'. This can never be disconfirmed. Being told that some bat is oviparous cannot be disconfirmed by appealing to everything now known about bats, as well as to all extant bats. The 'anywhere – everywhere' and 'past – present – future' conditions operate here too. However, we can confirm this claim by discovering one oviparous bat.

So, 'All A's are B's' can be disconfirmed, but never completely established. 'There exists an A which is B' can be established, but never disestablished.

'There is a God' has never been factually established. Any account of phenomena which at first seems to require God's existence is always explicable via some alternative account requiring no supernatural reference. Since appealing to God constitutes an end to further inquiry, the alternative accounts have been the more attractive; indeed, the history of science is a history of finding accounts of phenomena alternative to just appealing to God's existence.

Thus there is not one clearcut natural happening, nor any constellation of such happenings, which establishes God's existence — not as witnessing a bat laying an egg would establish 'There is an oviparous bat'.

In principle, God's existence could be established with the same clarity and directness one would expect in a verification of the claim 'some bats are oviparous'. Suppose that tomorrow morning, after breakfast, all of us are knocked to our knees by an earshattering thunderclap. Trees drop their leaves. The earth heaves. The sky blazes with light, and the clouds pull apart, revealing an immense and radiant Zeus-like figure. He frowns. He points at me and exclaims, for all to hear.

"Enough of your logic-chopping and word-watching matters of theology. Be assured henceforth that I most assuredly exist". Nor is this a private transaction between the heavens and myself. Everyone in the world experienced this, and heard what was said to me.

Do not dismiss this example as a playful contrivance. The conceptual point is that were this to happen, I should be entirely convinced that God exists. The subtleties with which the learned devout discuss this existence claim would seem, after such an experience, like a discussion of color in a home for the blind. That God exists would have been confirmed for me, and everyone else, in a manner as direct as that involved in any noncontroversial factual claim. Only, there is no good reason for supposing anything remotely like this ever to have happened, biblical mythology notwithstanding.

In short, not only is 'God exists' a factual claim—one can even specify what it would be like to confirm it. If the hypothetical description offered above is not rich or subtle enough, the reader can make the appropriate adjustments. But if no description, however rich and subtle, could be relevant to confirming the claim, then it could never be reasonable to believe in God's existence. Nor would it then be reasonable to base one's life on such a claim.

What about disconfirming 'God exists'? Here the agnostic should face the logical music—but he doesn't. What he does do, and as an agnostic must do, is as follows:

The agnostic treats 'God exists' as he should, as a factual claim the supporting evidence for which is insufficient for verification. However, he treats the denial of that claim quite differently. Now the agnostic chooses the logical point we sharpened above. No finite set of experiences which fail to support claims like 'Oviparous bats exist' and 'God exists' can by itself conclusively disconfirm such claims. Perhaps we have not been looking in the right places, or at the right things. We do not even know what it would be like to disconfirm such claims, since we cannot have all the possibly relevant experiences. But we do know what it would be like to establish that 'God exists'. Variations of the alarming encounter with the thundering God described above would confirm this claim.

The logical criterion invoked when the agnostic argues that 'there is a God' cannot be falsified applies to all existence claims. Hence, he has no grounds for denying that there is a Loch Ness Monster, or a five-headed Welshman, or a unicorn in New College garden. But there are excellent grounds for denying such claims. They consist in there being no reason whatever for supposing that these claims are true. And there being no reason for thinking a claim true is itself good reason for thinking it false. We know what it would be like to fish up the Loch Ness monster, or to encounter a five-headed Welshman, or to trap the New College unicorn. It just happens that there are no such things. We have the best factual grounds for saying this. Believers will feel that

'God exists' is better off than these other claims. They might even think it confirmed. But if they think this they must also grant that the evidence could go in the opposite direction. For if certain evidence can confirm a claim, other possible evidence must be such that, had it obtained, it would have disconfirmed that claim.

Precisely here the agnostic slips. While he grants that some possible evidence could confirm that God exists, but that it hasn't yet, he insists that no possible evidence could disconfirm this claim. The agnostic shifts logical ground when he supposes that evidence against the 'God exists' claim never could be good enough. Yet he must do this to remain agnostic. Otherwise, he could never achieve his 'perfect indecision' concerning whether God exists. For usually, when evidence is not good enough for us to conclude that X exists, we infer directly that X does not exist. Thus, the evidence fails to convince us that there is a Loch Ness monster, or a five-headed Welshman, or a New College unicorn; and since this is so, we conclude directly that such beings do not exist. These are the grounds usually offered for saying of something that it does not exist, namely, the evidence does not establish that it does.

The agnostic dons the mantle of rationality in the theist vs. atheist dispute. He seeks to appear as one whose reasonableness lifts him above the battle. But he can maintain this attitude only by being unreasonable, i.e., by shifting ground in his argument. If the agnostic insists that we could never disconfirm God's existence, then he must grant that we could never confirm the claim either. But if he feels we could confirm the claim, then he must grant that we could disconfirm it, too. To play the logician's game when saying that 'there are no oviparous bats' cannot be established, one must play the same game with 'there is an oviparous bat.' Even were a bat to lay an egg before such a person's very eyes, he would have to grant that, in strict logic, 'there exists an oviparous bat' was no more confirmed than its denial. But this is absurd. To see such a thing is to have been made able to claim that there is an oviparous bat. By this same criterion we assert today that 'there are no oviparous bats'. We take this to be confirmed in just that sense appropriate within any factual context.

The agnostic's position is therefore impossible. He begins by assessing 'God exists' as a fact-gatherer. He ends by appraising the claim's denial not as a fact-gatherer but as a logician. But consistency demands he either be a fact-gatherer on both counts or play logician on both counts. If the former, he must grant that there is ample factual reason for denying that God exists, namely, that the evidence in favor of his existence is just not good enough. If the latter, however — if he could make logical mileage out of "it is not the case that God exists" by arguing that it can never be established — then he must treat 'God exists' the same way. He must say not only that the present evidence is not good enough, but that it never could be good enough.

In either case, the conclusion goes against the claim that God exists. The moment the agnostic chooses consistency he becomes an atheist. For, as either fact-gatherer or logician, he will discover that there are no good grounds for claiming that God exists. The alternative is for him to give up trying to be consistent and reasonable, and assert that God exists in faith. But then he will have to doff the mantle of rationality which so attracted him when he adopted his original position.

The drift of this argument is not new: it is not reasonable to believe in the existence of God. Reflective people may have other grounds for believing in God's existence, but these hinge not on any conception of 'having good reasons' familiar in science, logic, or philosophy. The point is that the agnostic, despite his pretensions, is not more reasonable than the atheist or the theist. The next step for him is easy: if he chooses to use his head, he will become an atheist. If he chooses to react to his glands, he will become a theist. Either he will grant that there is no good reason for believing in the existence of God, or he will choose to believe in the existence of God on the basis of no good reason.

SECTION FIVE

JOHN HICK

Seeing-as and Religious Experience*

Much has been written during the last twenty years or so under the stimulus of Wittgenstein's remarks on religion. Indeed we have in the writings of D. Z. Phillips and others what is often referred to as the neo-Wittgensteinian philosophy of religion, according to which religious language constitutes an essentially autonomous 'language game' with its own internal criteria of truth, immune to challenge or criticism from those who do not participate in that language game. From a religious point of view it is an attractive feature of this position that it acknowledges the right of the believer to his/her beliefs and practices. On the other hand, however, in doing this it (in my view) cuts the heart out of religious belief and practice. For the importance of religious beliefs to the believer lies ultimately in the assumption that they are substantially true references to the nature of reality; and the importance of religious practices to the practitioner lies in the assumption that through them one is renewing or deepening one's relationship to the transcendent divine being. The cost, of course, of making such metaphysical claims in the secular world of today is that they inevitably provoke controversy; and a corresponding benefit of the contrary view is that such controversy is avoided. Thus when a Humanist or a Marxist tells a believer that it is foolish to pray to God, because there is no God to pray to, the neo-Wittgensteinian philosopher of religion will tell

* This essay is from *Philosophy of Religion: Proceedings of the 8th International Wittgenstein Symposium*, 1983, edited by Wolfgang L. Gombocz. Copyright © 1984 Hölder-Pichler-Tempsky, Vienna. Reprinted by permission of the publisher.

both atheist and believer that they are playing different language games and that there can therefore be no controversy between them. The believer is thus left secure in his belief, protected from outside attack, but only on the understanding that his beliefs do not depend for their validity upon the universe being structured in one way (a theistic way) rather than another (an atheistic way).

I am personally not convinced that Wittgenstein, were he alive today, would have endorsed this neo-Wittgensteinian development. I have the impression that he respected ordinary life and speech too much to accept a theory which so blatantly contradicts the normal intentions of most religious language users. To deny, for example, that the language of petitionary prayer is normally meant to presuppose the reality of a divine being who exists in addition to all the human beings who exist, is (in my view) to contradict the natural meaning of such language. Convictions about the character of the universe, and hence about the most appropriate way to live in it, are turned by this neo-Wittgensteinian analysis into expressions of emotion and attitude whose appropriateness depends upon their expressing the feelings and attitudes of the religious person rather than upon their being appropriate to the nature and structure of reality independently of human feelings and attitudes. It is true that religious people commonly use language in metaphorical ways, and indeed that religious pictures of the universe are typically mythological in character, so that their affirmations concerning God, creation, judgment, heaven and hell, and so on are generally to be construed as pointers rather than as literal descriptions. But the pointers are undoubtedly intended to point to realities transcending the metaphors and myths; and to suppress this intention is to do violence to religious speech and to empty the religious 'form of life' of its central and motivating conviction. This does not seem to me to be in the spirit of Wittgenstein. However I am not an expert on his writings and am conscious that I may be mistaken at this point. I would accordingly only say that, in my view, the neo-Wittgensteinian philosophy of religion embodies a misinterpretation of religion, and possibly also a misinterpretation of Wittgenstein's utterances on religion.

There is however another aspect of Wittgenstein's work that has, I believe, constructive implications for the philosophy of religion. This is his discussion of 'seeing as' and related topics in the second Part of the *Philosophical Investigations*. I want to suggest that this helps us to place the distinctively religious way of experiencing life on the epistemological map, as a form of what I shall call 'experiencing-as'; and helps us to understand religious faith, in its most basic sense, as the interpretative element within this distinctively religious way of experiencing life. I shall not attempt to extract a doctrine from Wittgenstein's pages, but only to show how his thought can be fruitful in ways which he himself may or may not have had in mind. I leave the question of the extent to which Wittgenstein would have approved or disapproved this suggestion to others who are more fully conversant with the Wittgenstein corpus. Such a procedure is perhaps in line with his own words in the Foreword to the *Investigations*: 'I should not like my writing to spare other people the trouble of thinking. But, if possible, to stimulate someone to thoughts of his own'.

First, then, I suggest that Wittgenstein was right in the implicit judgment, which pervades his references to religion, that what is important and to be respected here is not the conventional religious organizations and their official formulations but the religious way of experiencing and participating in human existence, and the forms of life in which this is expressed. It is in relation to this 'religious way of experiencing life and of participating in human existence' that the concept of seeing-as is relevant. Wittgenstein's Cambridge disciple John Wisdom opened a window in this direction in some informal remarks which I heard him address to the Socratic Society in Oxford around 1949. This was before the publication of the *Investigations*, although there had been a reference to the idea of seeing-as in the *Brown Book;* but in any case I presume that Wisdom's wider use of the concept had been stimulated by discussions with Wittgenstein himself.

Wittgenstein points to two senses of the word 'see'. If I am looking at a picture, say the picture of a face, in sense number one I see what is physically present on the paper — mounds of ink, we might say, of a certain shape, size, thickness and position. But in sense number two I see the picture of a face. We could say that in this second sense to see is to interpret or to find meaning or significance in what is before us — we interpret and perceive the mounds of ink as having the particular kind of meaning that we describe as the picture of a face, a meaning that mounds of ink, simply as such, do not have. The interpretative activity which is integral to seeing in this second sense, but which is absent from seeing in the first sense, is particularly evident when we are looking at a puzzle picture. As Wittgenstein says, 'we *see* it as we interpret it' (*Philosophical Investigations*, trans. G. E. M. Anscombe, Oxford 1953, p. 193). As he also puts it, in seeing-as an element of thinking is mixed with pure seeing in sense number one. When we see the duck-rabbit as a duck and then as a rabbit Wittgenstein speaks of these as aspects, and he says that 'the flashing of an aspect on us seems half visual experience, half thought' (*Ibid.*, p. 197).

We can, I suggest, immediately expand the concept of seeing-as, which is purely visual, into the comprehensive notion of experiencing-as. For the finding of meaning does not occur only through sight. We can hear a sound as that of a passing train; feel the wood as bamboo; smell the cloud as smoke; taste what is in our mouth as peppermint. In our everyday perception of our environment we use several sense organs at once; and I suggest that we adopt the term 'experiencing-as' to refer to our ordinary multi-dimensional awareness of the world. Like seeing-as (or seeing in sense number two), experiencing-as involves thought in the form of interpretation, i.e. becoming aware of our environment in terms of the systems of concepts embodied in what Wittgenstein sometimes called language games. He points out the important fact that the capacity to apply concepts to percepts is a necessary condition for having certain kinds of experience (such as seeing a particular triangle on paper as suspended from its apex) but not for having certain other kinds, such as feeling a toothache (*Ibid.*, p. 208).

The distinction between experiencing and experiencing-as, like that between seeing and seeing-as, or 'seeing' in sense number one and in sense number two, is however seldom actually exemplified. For we hardly ever experience, as distinguished from experiencing-as. Even so stark an experience as feeling pain is often linked by conceptual filaments with the systems of meaning that structure our lives. Pains can be experienced as threats to our holiday plans, or to our career, or our financial security, and so on. Perhaps, in very early infancy there is entirely unconceptualized experience. And perhaps there are kinds of aesthetic experience which are not forms of experiencing-as. But I think it is safe to say that ordinary human experiencing is always experiencing-as, always a perceiving of that which is present to us as having a certain recognizable character, which I am calling its meaning or significance. I take it that one of Wittgenstein's basic insights was that the system, or perhaps better the living organism, of meanings in terms of which we live is carried in the language of a certain linguistic community.

Wittgenstein himself seems to have been inclined to restrict the notion of seeing-as to manifestly ambiguous cases, such as puzzle pictures. It would not, he says, make sense for me 'to say at the sight of a knife and fork "Now I am seeing this as a knife and fork" . . . One doesn't '*take*' what one knows as the cutlery at a meal *for* cutlery' (*Ibid.*, p.185). On the other hand he recognises that there are occasions when I would not say '*I* am seeing this as an *x*' but when nevertheless someone else might properly say of me, '*He* is seeing that as an *x*'. And this is true, I would suggest, of the ordinary everyday seeing-as, or experiencing-as, in which we recognize familiar objects such as knives and forks. If a stone age savage is shown the cutlery he will not see it as cutlery, because he lacks the concepts, which are part of our culture but not of his, of cutlery, knife, fork, etc., together with such surrounding concepts as eating at table with manufactured implements, and so on. We could therefore say of him 'He is not experiencing it as cutlery' —but, perhaps, as something utterly puzzling or maybe as a set of magic objects. And in contrast we could say of a member of our own culture, 'He/she *is* seeing it as cutlery'.

I therefore hold that, apart perhaps from certain marginal cases, all human experiencing is experiencing-as. And I would further suggest — in general conformity, I think, with Wittgenstein's insights — that the awareness of entities as having this or that kind of significance always has a practical dispositional aspect. To experience the thing on the table as a fork is to be in a dispositional state to behave in relation to it in a certain range of ways, namely those that consist in using it as a fork. And, in general, to perceive what is before us as an x is to be in a state to treat it as an x, rather than as a y or a z.

We next have to notice that in addition to the kind of meaning exhibited by individual physical objects, such as knives and forks, ducks and rabbits, people and books, there are the more complex kinds of meaning exhibited by situations. 'Situation' is a relational notion. A situation, for X, consists of a set of objects which are unified in X's attention and which have as a whole a practical dispositional meaning for X which is more than the sum of the meanings of its constituent objects. Thus our present situation in this session this morning can be described in purely physical terms, corresponding to reports of what is seen in Wittgenstein's sense number one. Here we would describe each physical object in the room, including both human bodies and inanimate furniture, and their several shapes, sizes, positions and movements. But another kind of report is also possible, using such higher level concepts as *Gesellschaft*, philosophy, discussion, academic paper, criticism, etc. Human consciousness normally functions at this situational level, and it is here that we find the distinctively human dimensions of meaning over and above those that we share with the other animals.

These distinctively human dimensions of meaning or significance, transcending the purely physical meaning of our environment, appear to be of three kinds — ethical, aesthetic, and religious. I shall say a little about ethical meaning, very little about aesthetic meaning, and then rather more about religious meaning.

The ethical or moral meaning that we may experience a situation as having could also be called its social or its personal significance. For morality has to do with the interactions and relationships between persons. A purely physical account of a situation involving people would include a number of mobile organisms; but at the personal or ethical level we interact with these organisms as persons — as centres or consciousness, feeling, will, beings whose very existence imposes a potential moral claim upon us. For example, suppose I am present at a street accident, when someone is struck by a car and is lying in the road bleeding and in pain. If we can imagine someone experiencing this situation purely at the physical level of meaning they would observe the body and the flowing blood and hear the cries and moans; and that would be all. But as ethical beings we are also conscious in all this of a fellow human being in pain and danger, urgently needing first aid. We are perceiving the ethical meaning of the situation. We are experiencing not only in natural but also in moral terms. And the practical-dispositional aspect of this form of experiencing-as is expressed in the action which our distinctively moral awareness renders appropriate — in this case to do whatever we can to help the injured person.

Clearly, ethical presupposes natural meaning and can in this precise sense be described as a higher order of meaning. For ethical meaning is always the further meaning of a physical situation. And to experience a situation as having this or that kind of moral significance is to be in a dispositional state to behave within it in a way or ways appropriate to its having that significance. These dispositional responses may of course be weakened or cancelled out by some contrary self-regarding concern. But to be a moral, as distinguished from an amoral, being is to be conscious of moral obligations, whether or not or to whatever extent one's actions are guided by them. And to say that we are moral creatures is to say that we are liable to experience human situations as having this kind of significance.

Aesthetic meaning sometimes presupposes physical meaning (as in paintings of natural scenes and of people), but sometimes seems not to (as in much music and in abstract art). And to experience something as having aesthetic significance sometimes has a practical-dispositional aspect, affecting our attitudes, and sometimes seems not to but to be purely contemplative. The varieties and complexities here are daunting, and I do not propose to enter upon them. But to say that human beings are aesthetic as well as ethical creatures is to say that they are liable to experience aspects of their environment as having aesthetic significance.

Moving now to religious meaning, to describe man (as has often been done) as the religious animal is to say that human beings have apparently always displayed a tendency to experience individuals, places and situations as having religious meaning. Throughout a good deal of religious life individuals have been experienced as divine — usually kings, as in many primitive societies and in ancient Egypt (where the Pharaoh was divine), ancient Babylon (where the king embodied divine power), and ancient Israel (where the king was adopted at his enthronement as 'son of God'); and in Christianity Jesus of Nazareth is seen and devotionally experienced as divine. Many places have likewise been experienced as numinous and holy — hills, mountains, trees and rocks among many primitive societies, and within the great world religions such places as Benares, Bodh-Gaya, Jerusalem, Bethlehem, Mecca, Lourdes, and other places of pilgrimage. But the kind of experiencing-as that I should like more particularly to consider is situational. It is a feature of monotheistic religion that any human situation may, in principle, be experienced as one in which one is living in the unseen presence of God. For God is omnipresent, and in all that one does and undergoes one is having to do with God and God with oneself. In the case of saints this consciousness of existing in God's presence has been relatively continuous and pervasive; in the case of more ordinary believers it is occasional and fleeting. In the Hebrew scriptures a particular thread of history is described throughout in religious terms. The escape of a band of alien slaves from Egypt and their wanderings in the Sinai desert and eventual settlement in Canaan, their national consolidation and subsequent conquest and dispersion, are all presented as God's dealings with his chosen people. Their political ups and downs are seen as his encouragement of them when they were faithful and disciplining of them when unfaithful. This is often referred to as the prophetic interpretation of Hebrew history. But this interpretation is not, or not basically, a theoretical interpretation, historical schema imposed retrospectively upon the events of the past. It has its origin in the experience and then the preaching of the prophets concerning the meaning of events that were currently taking place around them. To give just one example, when in the time of Jeremiah a hostile Chaldean army was investing Jerusalem, to the prophet this was God wielding a foreign power to punish his erring people. As one well-known commentary says, 'Behind the serried ranks of the Chaldean army [Jeremiah] beheld the form of Jahweh fighting for them and through them against His own people'. Jeremiah did not, I take it, literally see the visible form of Jahweh; but he did experience what was taking place as having the religious meaning of divine punishment. And it is this kind of experience reported by the prophets that, in Jewish understanding, provides the clue to the meaning of all history.

Again, the New Testament centers upon the disciples' experience of Jesus as the Christ—which originally meant the messiah (God's anointed agent to bring in the Kingdom) but which in later Christian thought was elevated to mean the Second Person of a divine Trinity. In experiencing Jesus as the messiah the disciples were experiencing him in a way that was significantly different from that of those who perceived him, for example, as a heretical rabbi or a political agitator; and the New Testament documents reflect this apostolic interpretation of Jesus as the Christ.

This word 'interpret' can function in two senses or on two levels; and we should now distinguish these. There is the second-order sense in which an historian interprets the data, or a detective the clues, or a lawyer the evidence, or indeed in which a metaphysician may interpret the universe. This is a matter of conscious theory-construction. At this second-order level there are religious interpretations or, as we call them, theologies and religious philosophies, consisting in metaphysical theories which offer interpretations of the universe in which the data of religious experience are given a central and controlling place. Wittgenstein seems to have regarded these—rightly, in my view—as religiously much less important than the religious experiencing of life, and above all the dispositional aspect of this in attitudes of trust and acceptance and in acts of worship and service. For this second-order kind of interpretation presupposes the more basic, or first-order, interpretative activity which enters into virtually all conscious experience of our environment. In this first-order sense we are interpreting what is before us when we experience this as a fork, that as a house, and the other as a cow, or again when we experience our present situation as one of participating in a session of philosophical discussion; or yet again, when some of us might, in a moment of reflection, be conscious in and through this same situation of being at the same time in the presence of God. Interpreting in this sense is normally an unconscious and habitual process resulting from negotiations with our environment in terms of the set of concepts constituting our operative world of meaning. To interpret in this primary sense involves, as I suggested earlier, being in a dispositional state to behave in ways appropriate to the perceived meaning of our situation. Thus, in the case of the Chaldean threat to Jerusalem, the appropriate response was one of national repentance; and it was to this that Jeremiah called his fellow citizens. In the case of the disciples' experience of Jesus as the Christ, their dispositional response was one reverence and obedience, of openness to his teachings and of radical readiness to change their lives in following him.

We observe in these examples that that which is religiously interpreted and experienced is in itself ambiguous—in this respect like a puzzle picture,—in that it is also capable of being perceived non-religiously. A secular historian, describing the events recorded in the Hebrew scriptures, would speak of the rise and fall of empires, and of economic, political and cultural pressures, but would not speak of God as an agent in ancient Near Eastern history. Likewise, in addition to those who experienced Jesus as the Christ there were others who perceived him under quite other categories; so that the Jesus phenomenon was capable of being perceived in these contrary ways. One can see very clearly in such a case the hierarchy of interpretations that can occur. At the most basic level there was awareness of the physical existence of Jesus as a living organism. Superimposed upon this there was, at the human and social level of awareness, Jesus' life as a human being interacting with others in the Palestinian society of his day. And superimposed upon this there was, for the specifically Christian mode of experiencing-as, Jesus as the Christ. At this third level the Jesus phenomenon was importantly ambiguous, capable of being experienced in a number of different ways. This ambiguity is characteristic of religious meaning. On a larger scale we can say that the world, or indeed the universe, is religiously ambiguous—able to be experienced by different people, or indeed by the same person at different times, in both religious and naturalistic ways. This is not of course to say that one way of experiencing it may not be correct, in the — perhaps un-Wittgensteinian — sense of being appropriate to its actual character, and the other incorrect. But if so, the true character of the universe does not force itself upon us, and we are left with an important element of freedom and responsibility in our response to it. From a religious point of view this connects with the thought that God leaves us free to respond or fail to respond to him. I would suggest that this element of uncompelled interpretation in our experience of life is to be identified with faith in the most fundamental sense of that word. All forms of experiencing-as embody cognitive choices and are thus acts of faith; and religious faith is that cognitive choice which distinguishes the religious from the secular way of experiencing our human situation. This element of cognitive freedom in relation to God has been stressed by many religious thinkers. For example, Pascal, speaking of the incarnation, says, 'It was not right that he should in a manner manifestly divine, and completely capable of convincing all men; but it was also not right that he should come in a manner so hidden that he could not be recognized by those who sincerely seek him. He has willed to make himself perfectly recognizable by those; and thus, willing to appear openly to those who seek him with all their heart, and hidden from those who flee from him with all their heart, he so arranges the knowledge of himself that he has given signs of himself, visible to those who seek him, and not to those who do not seek him. There is enough light for those who only desire to see, and enough obscurity for those who have a contrary disposition.' (*Pensées*, No.430).

It should be noted that this account of faith as an uncompelled interpretation or mode of experiencing-as is neutral as between religious and secular understandings. The theist and the atheist might agree to this epistemological analysis of faith whilst making their own different cognitive choices, the believer trusting that the religious way of experiencing-as into which he or she has entered will ultimately be vindicated by the future unfolding of the character of the universe.

A point which Wittgenstein would, I imagine, want to stress is that the way in which we experience our environment depends upon the system of concepts that we use, and that this is carried from generation to generation in the language in terms of which we think and behave. There is thus a relativity of forms of experience to what Wittgenstein sometimes called language-games or, as I should prefer to say, cultures. This helps to explain how it is that there is not just one form of religious experiencing-as, with its own superstructure of theological theories, but a plurality, which we call the different religions. Given the concept of God — that is, the concept of the ultimate reality and mystery as personal, — and given a spiritual formation within a theistic tradition, the religious person is likely to experience life as being lived in the unseen presence of God, the world around him as God's creation, and moral claims as divine commands. Such a person may be, for example, a Jew or a Christian or a Muslim or a Sikh or a theistic Hindu. But given the very different concept of Brahman, or of the Dharma, or Sunyata, or the Tao — that is, a concept of the ultimate reality and mystery as the non-personal depth or ground or process of existence, — and given a spiritual formation within a non-theistic tradition, the religious person is likely to experience life as the karmic process leading eventually to enlightenment and the realization of reality. Such a person may be, for example, an advaitic Hindu or a Theravada or Mahayana Buddhist. Thus if we ask why it is that Christians, Buddhists, Jews, Muslims, Hindus report such different perceptions of the divine, the answer that suggests itself is that they are operating with different sets of religious concepts in terms of which they experience in characteristically different ways. This is of course a neutral account of the situation. It could be that the religions are all experiencing erroneously, projecting different illusions upon the universe. And it could on the other hand be that they are each responding to an infinite divine reality which exceeds our human conceptualities and which is capable of being humanly thought and experienced in these fascinatingly divergent ways.

My suggestion, then, is that Wittgenstein's concept of seeing-as, enlarged into the concept of experiencing-as, applies to all our conscious experience of our environment, including the religious ways of experiencing it. Such a view does justice to the systematically ambiguous character of the world, capable as it is of being experienced both religiously and naturalistically. These are radically different forms of experiencing-as. Such a view also does justice to the fact that the religious experiencing of life can itself take different forms. The world may be experienced as God's handiwork, or as the battlefield of good and evil, or as the cosmic dance of Shiva, or as the beginningless and endless interdependent process of *pratitya samutpada* within which we may experience nirvana; and so on. These are different forms of religious experiencing-as. Thus Wittgenstein's original concept can be fruitful in perhaps unexpected ways when it is brought into connection with the concrete religious forms of life.

NORMAN MALCOLM

༄

The Groundlessness of Belief*

I

In his final notebooks Wittgenstein wrote that it is difficult "to realize the groundlessness of our believing."[1] He was thinking of how much mere acceptance, on the basis of no evidence, shapes our lives. This is obvious in the case of small children. They are told the names of things. They accept what they are told. They do not ask for grounds. A child does not demand a proof that the person who feeds him is called "Mama." Or are we to suppose that the child reasons to himself as follows: "The others present seem to know this person who is feeding me, and since they call her 'Mama' that probably is her name"? It is obvious on reflection that a child cannot consider evidence or even doubt anything until he has already learned much. As Wittgenstein

---

[1] Ludwig Wittgenstein, *On Certainty*, ed. G. E. M. Anscombe and G. H. von Wright; trans. D. Paul and G. E. M. Anscombe (Oxford, 1969), paragraph 166. Henceforth I include references to this work in the text, employing the abbreviation "*OC*" followed by paragraph number. References to Wittgenstein's *The Blue and Brown Books* (Oxford, 1958) are indicated in the text by "*BB*" followed by page number. References to his *Philosophical Investigations*, ed. G. E. M. Anscombe and R. Rhees; trans. G. E. M. Anscombe (Oxford, 1967) are indicated by "*PI*" followed by paragraph number. In *OC* and *PI* I have mainly used the translations of Paul and Anscombe but with some departures.

* Reprinted from Normal Malcolm, "The Groundlessness of Belief," in *Reason and Religion*, edited by Stuart C. Brown. Copyright © 1977, the Royal Institute of Philosophy. Used here by permission of the publisher, Cornell University Press. Part IV of the version printed here appeared first in Norman Malcolm, *Thought and Knowledge*, Cornell University Press, 1977, pp. 213–216.

puts it: "The child learns by believing the adult. Doubt comes *after* belief" (*OC*, 160).

What is more difficult to perceive is that the lives of educated, sophisticated adults are also formed by groundless beliefs. I do not mean eccentric beliefs that are out on the fringes of their lives, but fundamental beliefs. Take the belief that familiar material things (watches, shoes, chairs) do not cease to exist without some physical explanation. They don't "vanish in thin air." It is interesting that we do use that very expression: "I *know* I put the keys right here on this table. They mush have vanished in thin air!" But this exclamation is hyperbole: we are not speaking in literal seriousness. I do not know of any adult who would consider, in all gravity, that the keys might have inexplicably ceased to exist.

Yet it is possible to imagine a society in which it was accepted that sometimes material things do go out of existence without having been crushed, melted, eroded, broken into pieces, burned up, eaten, or destroyed in some other way. The difference between those people and ourselves would not consist in their *saying* something that we don't say ("It vanished in thin air"), since we say it too. I conceive of those people as acting and thinking differently from ourselves in such ways as the following: if one of them could not find his wallet, he would give up the search sooner than you or I would; also he would be less inclined to suppose that it was stolen. In general what we would regard as convincing circumstantial evidence of theft those people would find less convincing. They would take fewer precautions than we would to protect their possessions against loss or theft. They would have less inclination to save money, since it too can just disappear. They would not tend to form strong attachments to material things. They would stand in a looser relation to the world than we do. The disappearance of a desired object, which would provoke us to a frantic search, they would be more inclined to accept with a shrug. Of course their scientific theories would be different; but also their attitude toward experiment, and inference from experimental results, would be more tentative. If the repetition of a familiar chemical experiment did not yield the expected result, this *could* be because one of the chemical substances had vanished.

The outlook I have sketched might be thought to be radically incoherent. I do not see that this is so. Although those people consider it to be possible that a wallet might have inexplicably ceased to exist, it is also true that they regard that as unlikely. For things that are lost usually do turn up later; or if not, their fate can often be accounted for. Those people use pretty much the same criteria of identity that we do; their reasoning would resemble ours quite a lot. Their thinking would not be incoherent. But it would be different, since they would leave room for possibilities that we exclude.

If we compare their view that material things do sometimes go out of existence inexplicably with our own rejection of that view, it does not appear to me that one position is supported by *better evidence* than is the other. Each position is compatible with ordinary experience. On the one hand it is true that familiar objects (watches, wallets, lawn-chairs) occasionally disappear without any adequate explanation. On the other hand it happens, perhaps more frequently, that a satisfying explanation of the disappearance is discovered.

Our attitude in this matter is striking. We would not be willing to consider it even as *improbable* that a missing lawn-chair had "just ceased to exist." We would not entertain such a suggestion. If anyone proposed it we would be sure he was joking. It is no exaggeration to say that this attitude is part of the foundations of our thinking. I do not want to say that this attitude is *unreasonable*; but rather that it is something that we do not *try* to support with grounds. It could be said to belong to "the framework" of our thinking about material things.

Wittgenstein asks: "Does anyone ever test whether this table remains in existence when no one is paying attention to it?" (*OC*, 163). The answer is: Of course not. Is this because we would not call it "a table" if that were to happen? But we do call it "a table" and none of us makes the test. Doesn't this show that we do not regard that occurrence as a possibility? People who did so regard it would seem ludicrous to us. One could imagine that they made ingenious experiments to decide the question; but this research would make us smile. Is this because experiments were conducted by our ancestors that settled the matter once and for all? I don't believe it. The principle that material things do not cease to exist without physical cause is an unreflective part of the framework within which physical investigations are made and physical explanations arrived at.

Wittgenstein suggests that the same is true of what might be called "the principle of the continuity of nature":

> Think of chemical investigations. Lavoisier makes experiments with substances in his laboratory and now concludes that this and that takes place when there is burning. He does not say that it might happen otherwise another time. He has got hold of a world-picture — not of course one that he invented: he learned it as a child. I say world-picture and not hypothesis, because it is the matter-of-course *(selbstverständliche)* foundation for his research and as such also goes unmentioned (*OC*, 167).

> But now, what part is played by the presupposition that a substance A always reacts to a substance B in the same way, given the same circumstances? Or is that part of the definition of a substance? (*OC*, 168).

Framework principles such as the continuity of nature or the assumption that material things do not cease to exist without physical cause, belong to what Wittgenstein calls a "system." He makes the following observation, which seems to me to be true: "All testing, all confirmation and disconfirmation of a hypothesis takes place already within a system. And this system is not a more or less arbitrary and doubtful point of departure for all our arguments; no, it belongs to the nature of what we call an argument. The system is not so much the point of departure, as the element in which arguments have their life" (*OC*, 105).

A "system" provides the boundaries within which we ask questions, carry out investigations, and make judgments. Hypotheses are put forth, and challenged, *within* a system. Verification, justification, the search for evidence, occur *within* a system. The framework propositions of the system are not put to the test, not backed up by evidence. This is what Wittgenstein means when he says: "Of course there is justification; but justification comes to an end" (*OC*, 192); and when he asks: "Doesn't testing come to an end?" (*OC*, 164); and when he remarks that "whenever we test anything we are already presupposing something that is not tested" (*OC*, 163).

That this is so is not to be attributed to human weakness. It is a conceptual requirement that our inquiries and proofs stay within boundaries. Think, for example, of the activity of calculating a number. Some steps in a calculation we will check for correctness, but others we won't: for example, that $4 + 4 = 8$. More accurately, some beginners might check it, but grown-ups won't. Similarly, some grown-ups would want to determine by calculation whether $25 \times 25 = 625$, whereas others would regard that as laughable. Thus the boundaries of the system within which *you* calculate may not be exactly the same as my boundaries. But we do calculate; and, as Wittgenstein remarks, "In certain circumstances . . . we regard a calculation as sufficiently checked. What gives us a right to do so? . . . Somewhere we must be finished with justification, and then there remains the proposition that *this* is how we calculate" (*OC*, 212). If someone did not accept any boundaries for calculating, this would mean that he had not learned *that* language-game: "If someone supposed that *all* our calculations were uncertain and that we could rely on none of them (justifying himself by saying that mistakes are always possible) perhaps we would say he was crazy. But can we say he is in error? Does he not just react differently? We rely on calculations, he doesn't; we are sure, he isn't" (*OC*, 217). We are taught, or we absorb, the systems within which we raise doubts, make inquiries, draw conclusions. We grow into a framework. We don't question it. We accept it trustingly. But this acceptance is not a consequence of reflection. We do not *decide* to accept framework propositions. We do not decide that we live on the earth, any more than we decide to learn our native tongue. We do come to adhere to a framework proposition, in the sense that it shapes the way we think. The framework propositions that we accept, grow into, are not idiosyncrasies but common ways of speaking and thinking that are pressed on us by our human community. For our acceptances to have been withheld would have meant that we had not learned how to count, to measure, to use names, to play games, or even *to talk*. Wittgenstein remarks that "a language-game is only possible if one trusts something." Not *can*, but *does* trust something (*OC*, 509). I think he means by this trust or acceptance what he calls belief "in the sense of religious belief" (*OC*, 459). What does he mean by belief "in the sense of religious belief"? He explicitly distinguishes it from *conjecture* (*Vermutung*: ibid). I think this means that there is nothing tentative about it; it is not adopted as an hypothesis that might later be withdrawn in the light of new evidence. This also makes explicit an important feature of Wittgenstein's understanding of belief, in the sense of "religious belief," namely, that it does not rise or fall on the basis of evidence or grounds: it is "groundless."

II

In our Western academic philosophy, religious belief is commonly regarded as unreasonable and is viewed with condescension or even contempt. It is said that religion is a refuge for those who, because of weakness of intellect or character, are unable to confront the stern realities of the world. The objective, mature, *strong* attitude is to hold beliefs solely on the basis of *evidence*.

It appears to me that philosophical thinking is greatly influenced by this veneration of evidence. We have an aversion to statements, reports, declarations, beliefs, that are not based on grounds. There are many illustrations of this philosophical bent.

For example, in regard to a person's report that he has an image of the Eiffel Tower we have an inclination to think that the image must *resemble* the Eiffel Tower. How else could the person declare so confidently what his image is *of? How could he know?*

Another example: a memory-report or memory-belief must be based, we think, on some mental *datum* that is equipped with various features to match the corresponding features of the memory-belief. This datum will include an image that provides the *content* of the belief, and a peculiar feeling that makes one refer the image to a *past* happening, and another feeling that makes one believe that the image is an *accurate* portrayal of the past happening, and still another feeling that informs one that it was *oneself* who witnessed the past happening. The presence of these various features makes memory-beliefs thoroughly reasonable.

Another illustration: if interrupted in speaking one can usually give a confident account, later on, of what one had been *about* to say. How is this possible? Must not one remember *a feeling of tendency to say just those words?* This is one's basis for knowing what one had been about to say. It justifies one's subsequent account.

Still another example: after dining at a friend's house you announce your intention to go home. How do you know your intention? One theory proposes that you are presently aware of a particular mental state or bodily feeling which, as you recall from your past experience, has been highly correlated with the behavior of going home; so you infer that *that* is what you are going to do now. A second theory holds that you must be aware of some definite mental state or event which reveals itself, not by experience but *intrinsically,* as the intention to go home. Your awareness of that mental item *informs* you of what action you will take.

Yet another illustration: this is the instructive case of the man who, since birth, has been immune to sensations of bodily pain. On his thirtieth birthday he is kicked in the shins, and for the first time he responds by crying out, hopping around on one foot, holding his leg, and exclaiming "The pain is terrible!" We have an overwhelming inclination to wonder, "How could he tell, *this first time,* that what he felt was *pain?*" Of course the implication is that *after* the first time there would be *no* problem. Why not? Because his first experience of pain would provide him with a sample that would be preserved in memory; thereafter he would be equipped to determine whether any sensation he feels is or isn't pain; he would just compare it with the memory-sample to see whether the two match! Thus he will have a *justification* for believing that what he feels is pain. But the *first time* he will not have this justification. This is why the case is so puzzling. Could it be that this first time he *infers* that he is in pain from his own behavior?

A final illustration: consider the fact that after a comparatively few examples and bits of instruction a person can go on to carry out a task, apply a word correctly in the future, continue a numerical series from an initial segment, distinguish grammatical from ungrammatical constructions, solve arithmetical problems, and so on. These correct performances will be dealing with new and different examples, situations, combinations. The performance output will be far more varied than the instruction input. How is this possible? What carries the person from the meager instruction to his rich performance? The explanation has to be that an effect of his training was that he abstracted the Idea, perceived the Common Nature, "internalized" the Rule, grasped the Structure. What else could bridge the gap between the poverty of instruction and the wealth of performance? Thus we postulate an intervening mental act or state which removes the inequality and restores the balance.

My illustrations belong to what could be called the *pathology* of philosophy. Wittgenstein speaks of a "general disease of thinking" which attempts to explain occurrences of discernment, recognition, or understanding, by postulating mental states or processes from which those occurrences flow "as from a reservoir" (*BB*, p. 143). These mental intermediaries are assumed to contribute to the causation of the various cognitive performances. More significantly for my present purpose, they are supposed to *justify* them; they provide our *grounds* for saying or doing this rather than that; they *explain how we know.* The Image, or Cognitive State, or Feeling, or Idea, or Sample, or Rule, or Structure, *tells* us. It is like a road map or a signpost. It guides our course.

What is "pathological" about these explanatory constructions and pseudo-scientific inferences? Two things at least. First, the movement of thought that demands these intermediaries is circular and empty, unless it provides criteria for determining their presence and nature *other than* the occurrence of the phenomena they are postulated to explain — and of course no such criteria are forthcoming. Second, there is great criticism by Wittgenstein of this movement of philosophical thought: namely, his point that no matter what kind of state, process, paradigm, sample, structure, or rule is conceived of giving us the necessary guidance, *it* could be taken, or understood, as indicating a *different* direction from the one in which we actually did go. The assumed intermediary Idea, Structure, or Rule does not and cannot reveal that because of it we went in the only direction it was reasonable to go. Thus the internalized intermediary we are tempted to invoke to bridge the gap between training and performance, as being that which shows us what we must do or say if we are to be rational, cannot do the job it was invented to do. It cannot fill the epistemological gap. It cannot provide the bridge of justification. It cannot put to rest the How-do-we-know? question. Why not? Because it cannot tell us how *it itself* is to be taken, understood, applied. Wittgenstein puts the point briefly and powerfully: "Don't always think that you read off your words from facts; that you portray these in words according to rules. For even so you would have to apply the rule in the particular case without guidance" (*PI*, 292). Without guidance! Like Wittgenstein's signpost arrow that cannot tell us whether to go in the direction of the arrow tip or in the opposite direction, so too the Images, Ideas, Cognitive Structures, or Rules that we philosophers imagine as devices for guidance cannot interpret themselves to us. The signpost does not tell the traveler how to read it. A second signpost might tell him how to read the first one; we can imagine such a case. But this can't go on. If the traveler is to continue his journey he will have to do something on his own, without guidance.

The parable of the traveler speaks for *all* of the language-games we learn and practice, even those in which there is the most disciplined instruction and the most rigorous standards of conformity. Suppose that a pupil has been given thorough training in some procedure, whether it is drawing patterns, building fences, or proving theorems. But then he has to carry on by himself in new situations. How does he know what to do? Wittgenstein presents the following dialogue: "'However you instruct him in the continuation of a pattern—how can he *know* how he is to continue by himself?'—Well, how do *I* know?—If that means 'Have I grounds?', the answer is: the grounds will soon give out. And then I shall act, without grounds" (*PI*, 211). Grounds come to an end. Answers to How-do-we-know? questions come to an end. Evidence comes to an end. We must speak, act, live, without evidence. This is so not just on the fringes of life and language, but at the center of our most regularized activities. We do learn rules and learn to follow them. But our training was in the past! We had to leave it behind and proceed on our own.

It is an immensely important fact of nature that as people carry on an activity in which they have received a common training, they do largely *agree* with one another, accepting the same examples and analogies, taking the same steps. We agree in what to say, in how to apply language. We agree in our responses to particular cases.

As Wittgenstein says, "That is not agreement in opinions but in form of life" (*PI*, 241). We cannot explain this agreement by saying that we are just doing what the rules tell us—for our agreement in applying rules, formulae and signposts is what gives them their *meaning*.

One of the primary pathologies of philosophy is the feeling that we must *justify* our language-games. We want to establish them as well grounded. But we should consider here Wittgenstein's remark that a language-game "is not based on grounds. It is there—like our life" (*OC*, 559).

Within a language-game there is justification and lack of justification, evidence and proof, mistakes and groundless opinions, good and bad reasoning, correct measurements and incorrect ones. One cannot properly apply these terms to a language-game itself. It may, however, be said to be "groundless," not in the sense of a groundless opinion, but in the sense that we accept it, we live it. We can say, "This is what we do. This is how we are."

In this sense religion is groundless; and so is chemistry. Within each of these two systems of thought and action there is controversy and argument. Within each there are advances and recessions of insight into the secrets of nature or the spiritual condition of humankind and the demands of the Creator, Savior, Judge, Source. Within the framework of each system there is criticism, explanation, justification. But we should not expect that there might be some sort of rational justification of the framework itself.

A chemist will sometimes employ induction. Does he have evidence for a Law of Induction? Wittgenstein observes that it would strike him as nonsense to say, "I know that the Law of Induction is true." ("Imag-

ine such a statement made in a law court.") It would be more correct to
say, "I believe in the Law of Induction" (*OC*, 500). This way of putting
it is better because it shows that the attitude toward induction is belief
in the sense of "religious" belief — that is to say, an acceptance which
is not conjecture or surmise and for which there is no reason — it is a
groundless acceptance.

It is intellectually troubling for us to conceive that a whole system of
thought might be groundless, might have no rational justification. We
realize easily enough, however, that grounds soon give out — that we
cannot go on giving reasons for our reasons. There arises from this
realization the conception of a reason that is *self-justifying* — something whose credentials as a reason cannot be questioned.

This metaphysical conception makes its presence felt at many points
— for example, as an explanation of how a person can tell what his
mental image is *of.* We feel that the following remarks, imagined by
Wittgenstein, are exactly right: "'The image must be more similar to its
object than any picture. For however similar I make the picture to what
it is supposed to represent, it can always be the picture of something
else. But it is essential to the image that it is the image of *this* and of
nothing else'" (*PI*, 389). A pen and ink drawing represents the Eiffel
Tower; but it could represent a mine shaft or a new type of automobile
jack. Nothing prevents this drawing from being taken as a representation of something other than the Eiffel Tower. But my mental image of
the Eiffel Tower is *necessarily* an image of the Eiffel Tower. Therefore
it must be a "remarkable" kind of picture. As Wittgenstein observes:
"Thus one might come to regard the image as a super-picture" (ibid.).
Yet we have no intelligible conception of how a super-picture would
differ from an ordinary picture. It would seem that it has to be a
super-likeness — but what does this mean?

There is a familiar linguistic practice in which one person *tells* another what his image is of (or what he intends to do, or what he was
about to say) and no question is raised of how the first one *knows* that
what he says is true. This question is imposed from outside, artificially,
by the philosophical craving for justification. We can see here the
significance of these remarks: "It isn't a question of explaining a
language-game by means of our experiences, but of noting a language-
game" (*PI*, 665). "Look on the language-game as the *primary* thing"
(*PI*, 656). Within a system of thinking and acting there occurs, *up to a
point*, investigation and criticism of the reasons and justifications that
are employed in that system. This inquiry into whether a reason is good
or adequate cannot, as said, go on endlessly. We stop it. We bring it to
an end. We come upon something that *satisfies* us. It is *as if* we made a
decision or issued an edict: "*This* is an adequate reason!" (or explanation, or justification). Thereby we fix a boundary of our language-game.

There is nothing wrong with this. How else could we have disciplines, systems, games? But our fear of groundlessness makes us conceive that we are under some logical compulsion to terminate at *those particular* stopping points. We imagine that we have confronted the self-evident reason, the self-justifying explanation, the picture or symbol whose meaning cannot be questioned. This obscures from us the *human* aspect of our concepts — the fact that what we call "a reason," "evidence," "explanation," "justification," is what appeals to and satisfies *us*.

III

The desire to provide a rational foundation for a form of life is especially prominent in the philosophy of religion, where there is an intense preoccupation with purported proofs of the existence of God. In American universities there must be hundreds of courses in which these proofs are the main topic. We can be sure that nearly always the critical verdict is that the proofs are invalid and consequently that, up to the present time at least, religious belief has received no rational justification.

Well, of course not! The obsessive concern with the proofs reveals the assumption that in order for religious belief to be intellectually respectable it *ought* to have a rational justification. *That* is the misunderstanding. It is like the idea that we are not justified in relying on memory until memory has been proved reliable.

Roger Trigg makes the following remark: "To say that someone acts in a certain way because of his belief in God does seem to be more than a redescription of his action. . . . It is to give a reason for it. The belief is distinct from the commitment which may follow it, and is the justification for it."[2] It is evident from other remarks that by "belief in God" Trigg means "belief in the existence of God" or "belief that God exists." Presumably by the *acts* and *commitments* of a religious person Trigg refers to such things as prayer, worship, confession, thanksgiving, partaking of sacraments, and participation in the life of a religious group.

For myself I have great difficulty with the notion of belief in *the existence* of God, whereas the idea of belief *in* God is to me intelligible. If a man did not ever pray for help or forgiveness, or have any inclination toward it; nor ever felt that it is "a good and joyful thing" to thank God for the blessings of this life; nor was ever concerned about his failure to comply with divine commandments — then, it seems clear to me, he could not be said to believe in God. Belief in God is not an all or

[2]Trigg, *Reason and Commitment* (Cambridge, 1973), p.75.

none thing: it can be more or less; it can wax and wane. But belief in God in any degree does require, as I understand the words, some religious action, some commitment, or if not, at least a bad conscience.

According to Trigg, if I take him correctly, a man who was entirely devoid of any inclination to religious action or conscience might believe in *the existence* of God. What would be the marks of this? Would it be that the man knows some theology, can recite the Creeds, is well-read in Scripture? Or is his belief in the existence of God something different from this? If so, what? What would be the difference between a man who knows some articles of faith, heresies, Scriptural writings, and in addition believes in the existence of God, and one who knows these things but does not believe in the existence of God? I assume that both of them are indifferent to the acts and commitments of religious life.

I do not comprehend this notion of belief in *the existence* of God which is thought to be distinct from belief *in* God. It seems to me to be an artificial construction of philosophy, another illustration of the craving for justification.

Religion is a form of life; it is language embedded in action — what Wittgenstein calls a "language-game." Science is another. Neither stands in need of justification, the one no more than the other.

Present-day academic philosophers are far more prone to challenge the credentials of religion than of science. This is probably due to a number of things. One may be the illusion that science can justify its own framework. Another is the fact that science is a vastly greater force in our culture. Still another reason may be the fact that by and large religion is to university people an alien form of life. They do not participate in it and do not understand what it is all about. This non-understanding is of an interesting nature. It derives, at least in part, from the inclination of academics to suppose that their employment as scholars demands of them the most severe objectivity and dispassionateness. For an academic philosopher to become a religious believer would be a stain on his professional competence! Here I will quote from Nietzsche, who was commenting on the relation of the German scholar of his day to religious belief; yet his remarks continue to have a nice appropriateness for the American and British scholars of our own day:

> Pious or even merely church-going people seldom realize *how much* good will, one might even say willfulness, it requires nowadays for a German scholar to take the problem of religion seriously; his whole trade . . . disposes him to a superior, almost good-natured merriment in regard to religion, sometimes mixed with a mild contempt directed at the 'uncleanliness' of spirit which he presupposes wherever one still belongs to the church. It is only with the aid of history (thus *not* from his personal experience) that the scholar succeeds in summoning up a reverent seriousness and a certain shy respect towards religion; but if he intensifies his feelings towards it even to the

point of feeling grateful to it, he has still in his own person not got so much as a single step closer to that which still exists as church or piety; perhaps the reverse. The practical indifference to religious things in which he was born and raised is as a rule sublimated in him into a caution and cleanliness which avoids contact with religious people and things; . . . Every age has its own divine kind of naïvety for the invention of which other ages may envy it—and how much naïvety, venerable, childlike and boundlessly stupid naïvety there is in the scholar's belief in his superiority, in the good conscience of his tolerance, in the simple unsuspecting certainty with which his instinct treats the religious man as an inferior and lower type which he himself has grown beyond and *above*.[3]

IV

Someone could point out that within particular religions there are beliefs that are based on evidence or to which evidence is relevant. This is indeed so. Some doctrinal beliefs about Jesus and the Holy Spirit, for example, are based on New Testament texts. Here is area where evidence and interpretation are appropriate. There are disputes between Christian sects (for example, the controversy over the authority of the Bishop of Rome)—disputes to which textual evidences are relevant.

In the present essay I have been talking not about this or that doctrinal belief but, more generally, about *religious belief.* It would be convenient if I could substitute the words "belief in God" for the words "religious belief"; but I hesitate to do so because the Buddhists, for example, do not describe themselves as believing in God, and yet Buddhism is undoubtedly a religion. Religious belief as such, not particular creeds or doctrines, is my topic.

I think there can be evidence for the particular doctrines of a faith only within the attitude of religious belief. Many people who read about incidents in the life of Jesus, as recounted in the Gospels, or about events in the lives of the Hebrew prophets, as recounted in the Old Testament, do not believe that the reported incidents actually occurred. But it is possible to believe that they occurred without regarding them as *religiously significant.* That a man should die and then come to life again is not necessarily of religious significance. That the apparent motion of the sun should be interrupted, as related in Joshua, does not have to be understood religiously. A well-known physicist once remarked to me, only *half*-humorously, that a study of the causation of miracles could be a branch of applied physics! Biblical miracles *can* be regarded as events of merely scientific interest. They can be viewed from either a scientific or a religious *Weltanschauung.* It is only from the viewpoint of religious belief that they have religious import.

---

[3]Nietzsche, *Beyond Good and Evil,* trans. R. J. Hollingdale (Penguin Classics), para. 58.

It is such a viewpoint or *Weltbild* (to use Wittgenstein's term), whether religious or scientific, that I am holding to be "groundless." I am not saying, of course, that these different ways of picturing the world do not have *causes*. Education, culture, family upbringing, can foster a way of seeing the world. A personal disaster can destroy, or produce, religious belief. Religious people often think of their own belief as a result of God's intervention in their lives.

My interest, however, is not in causes. What I am holding is that a religious viewpoint is not based on grounds or evidence, whether this is the Five Ways of Aquinas, the starry heavens, or whatever. Of course, some people do *see* the wonders of nature as *manifestations* of God's loving presence. Someone might even be able to regard the Five Ways in that light. Anselm did thank God for His gift of the Ontological Proof. But seeing something as a manifestation of God's love or creative power is a very different thing from taking it either as evidence for an empirical hypothesis or as a kind of logical proof of the correctness of religious belief.

Some readers may want to know whether my position is that people do not *in fact* seek grounds for their religious belief, or whether, as a conceptual matter, there *could not* be grounds. I hold that both things are true, even though this may shock a well-trained analytic philosopher. When you are describing a language-game, a system of thought and action, you are describing concepts, and yet also describing what certain people do — how they think, react, live. Wittgenstein reminds us that in doing mathematical calculations we do not worry about the figures changing shape after being written down; and also that scientists usually are not in doubt as to whether they are in their laboratories. That such doubts are rare is an empirical fact; yet if it were not for this kind of fact we *could not* have some of our concepts. Consider these remarks by Wittgenstein:

> Mathematicians do not in general quarrel over the result of a calculation. (This is an important fact.) — If it were otherwise, if for instance, one mathematician was convinced that a figure had altered unperceived, or that memory had deceived either him or the other person, and so on — then our concept of "mathematical certainty" would not exist (*PI*, p. 225).

> If I am trying to mate someone in chess, I cannot be having doubts as to whether the pieces are perhaps changing positions of themselves and at the same time my memory is tricking me so that I don't notice it. (*OC*, 346).

I know that some philosophers would like to have a *demonstration* that religious belief is groundless. I do not know what "demonstration" could mean here. But I will say this: it is obvious that the wonders and horrors of nature, the history of nations, great events in personal experience, music, art, the Ontological Proof, and so on — can be responded to either religiously or nonreligiously. Suppose there is a person who is untouched by any inclination toward religious belief, and another who wants to present him convincing grounds for religious belief. Can he do it? I don't see how. The first person can regard the presented "evidence" as psychologically, historically, mythologically, or logically interesting — perhaps fascinating. But even if he has an "open mind," the proffered phenomena or reasoning cannot have religious import for him unless he has at least an inclination toward a religious *Weltbild*. This is the necessary medium, the atmosphere, within which these "evidences" can have religious significance. Wittgenstein's remarks about "the language-game," namely that

> It is not based on grounds.
> It is not reasonable (or unreasonable).
> It is there — like our life (*OC*, 599).

are meant to apply to all language-games, but seem to be true in an especially obvious way of religious belief.

Belief in a God who creates, judges, and loves humanity is *one form* of religious belief. Belief in a mystical principle of causality according to which good produces good and evil produces evil is *another form* of religious belief. Those perspectives on reality are not hypotheses for or against which evidence can be marshalled. You may invite someone to see the world as a heartless mechanism or, on the contrary, as throbbing with love. Once a person has the beginnings of such a vision you may strengthen it for him by means of luminous examples. But unless he already shares that vision in some degree, he will not take your examples in the way you want him to take them. It may be that your conviction, passion, love, will move him in the direction of religious belief. But this would be speaking of causes, not grounds.

RICHARD SWINBURNE

The Nature of Faith*

So far in this book I have been concerned with propositional belief. I have analysed what it is to have a belief that so-and-so is the case, when belief is 'rational' in various senses of 'rational', when it matters what we believe, and what we ought to do about our beliefs. I claimed that it matters greatly that one should have a true belief about whether there is a God, and what he is like and what he has done. However, the virtue which the Christian religion commends is not belief but faith. What is faith, and what is its relation to belief? The faith which the Christian religion commends is basically faith in a person or persons, God (or Christ) characterized as possessing certain properties and having done certain actions; and secondarily perhaps in some of the deeds which he has done, and the good things which he has provided and promised.[1]

---

[1] In his analysis of the New Testament uses of πίστις ('faith') and πιστεύω ('believe' or 'have faith in') W. Cantwell Smith (*Belief and History*, Charlottesville, Virginia, 1977) has pointed out that the most common use is where no object of faith is specified. Faith is stated to exist or is commended, without our being told that it is faith in God or Christ or whatever. Cantwell Smith argues (p. 93) that faith is 'a quality of human living', quite independently of what (if anything) the faith is in, and he suggests that it is perhaps such a quality that is being stated to exist or being commended. I do not myself find this convincing, since the context of such occurrences would seem to imply that it is attention to God or neglect of him that is at stake. However, even Cantwell Smith (in his later work *Faith and Belief*, Princeton, N.J., 1979) seems to allow that in the early church and in its subsequent life, the faith which was commended was normally faith in some object.

* From Richard Swinburne, *Faith and Reason*, Chapter 4, Clarendon Press, Oxford, 1981. Copyright © Richard Swinburne 1981. Reprinted by permission of Oxford University Press.

Thus in the Nicene Creed, the man who pledges his allegiance before being baptised or in the course of worship, affirms (in the Latin) *credo in* ('I believe in' or 'I have faith in') '. . . one God, the Father Almighty, maker of Heaven and Earth . . . ; and in one Lord Jesus Christ . . . and in the Holy Spirit, the Lord, the Giver of Life . . . ; the Holy Catholic Church . . . the Resurrection of the Body . . .'. But there have been different views in the Christian tradition as to what this 'belief in' or 'faith in' amounts to. I shall spell these views out and show their relation to each other. We shall find that, despite appearances, advocates of the different views are not necessarily commending very different conduct or affirming very different doctrines from each other.

The Thomist View of Faith

First then, there is what I shall call the Thomist view of faith. It is a view which is found in St. Thomas Aquinas and was developed fairly explicitly by the Fathers of the Council of Trent. It is a view which has been held by many Protestants and many outside Christianity, and by many Christians long before Aquinas. Indeed it is by far the most widespread and natural view of the nature of religious faith. This is the view that, with one or two additions and one qualification which I shall state, to have faith in God is simply to have a belief-that, to believe that God exists.[2] Although to speak strictly, the object of faith is the 'first truth', God himself, to have that faith it is alone necessary that you believe a proposition, that God is.[3] The man of religious faith is the man who has the theoretical conviction that there is a God.

The first addition which Aquinas adds to this simple doctrine is that to have faith in God, you have to believe not merely that there is a God, but certain other propositions as well, and you have to believe these latter propositions on the ground that God has revealed them. If you are to have the faith of which the New Testament and Christian Church speak, you have to believe that there is a God who has the properties and has done the acts which the Christian creeds describe. Your faith must be a faith in a God of a certain kind, not just any god. The belief which is affirmed in the Nicene Creed in God as having done certain

[2]This normal interpretation of Aquinas has been denied by W. Cantwell Smith. (See his *Faith and Belief*, pp. 78–91). Cantwell Smith claims that Aquinas's *fides* and *credo* is (p. 87) 'a quality of personal life' involving commitment. Cantwell Smith's interpretation seems to me to be an interpretation of Aquinas's 'formed faith'. But Aquinas is very careful to distinguish 'faith' from 'formed faith'. For Aquinas, devils have faith (see later), and it is an intellectual act concerned with the same kinds of things as knowledge (*scientia*) and conjecture (*opinio*). He seems to me very clear on this point — see especially *Summa Theologiae*, 2a, 2ae, 2. 1 (and also 2a, 2ae, 1. 2).

[3]Aquinas adds that 'the only reason for formulating a proposition is that we may have knowledge about the real' — *Summa Theologiae*, 2a, 2ae, 1. 2, ad. 2.

things (e.g. as 'Maker of Heaven and Earth') is the belief that God did these things (e.g. 'made Heaven and Earth'); the belief in the good things which God has promised and provided (e.g. 'the resurrection of the dead') is the belief that they are or will be (e.g. 'there will be a resurrection of the dead'). Aquinas claims that unbelievers (*infideles,* e.g. presumably pagans or Muslims) may in a way believe that there is a God (*deum esse*), but because they do not believe 'in the way which faith determines', they do not truly believe *in* God (*non deum credunt*).[4] Aquinas also writes that, 'the things of faith surpass man's understanding, and so become part of his thought only because God reveals them. For some, the Prophets and Apostles for example, this revelation comes from God immediately; for others the things of faith are proposed by God's sending preachers of the faith.'[5] The First Vatican Council also taught that 'it is required for divine faith that revealed truth be believed on the authority of God who reveals it.'[6] We shall see the need for this clause in Chapter 7.

A second addition is to be found in Aquinas, but not in many others who in general follow in the Thomist tradition. Aquinas describes 'belief' as 'faith's inner act'[7] and claims that public confession is the outward act. He claims that inward belief and outward confession belong together, which seems to imply that one who did not publicly acknowledge his beliefs would not be a man of faith. However, others in this tradition seem to write as if outward confession was a work enjoined on the man of faith; but its practice was not part of having faith. In expounding the Thomist tradition in future I shall take the latter view.

The qualification on this view that faith is basically belief is, that the belief that is involved is a belief which does not in general amount to knowledge. Aquinas says that 'to believe' (*credere*) is 'to think with assent' (*cogitare cum assensione*),[8] a definition which he derives from Augustine. As Aquinas uses the terms, belief is a state inferior to, and incompatible with, knowledge. If you believe that *p*, you do not know that *p*, and conversely. I do not think that this is our modern use, where in my view and that of most philosophers who have analysed knowledge in recent years, knowledge entails belief—if you know that *p*, you believe that *p* (although of course not necessarily conversely). In this book I am using 'believe' in this modern sense. Belief which does not amount to knowledge, which alone Aquinas calls belief, I will call

---

[4]*Summa Theologiae,* 2a, 2ae, 2. 2, ad. 3.
[5]Ibid,. vol. 31 (translated by T. C. O'Brien), 2a, 2ae, 6. 1. (I replace O'Brien's translation of *cognito* as 'knowledge' by 'thought' which seems more correct, and so I am able in future to translate *scientia* as 'knowledge' without confusion.)
[6] Vatican I, *De Fide,* canon 2.
[7]*Summa Theologiae,* 2a, 2ae, 2.2.
[8]Ibid., 2a, 2ae, 2. 1.

mere belief. Aquinas holds that at least some of the beliefs (in our sense) involved in faith are mere beliefs. He holds that 'faith is midway between knowledge and opinion'[9] and thus endorses the definition given by Hugh of St. Victor that 'faith is a form of mental certitude about absent realities that is greater than opinion and less than knowledge'.[10] For Aquinas, as for many other medieval writers, men can come to *know* (by philosophical demonstration) that there is a God, although for most men, this too is a matter of mere belief. But some particularly Christian truths about God, such that he became incarnate in Christ, can only be, for all men on Earth, objects of mere belief, although belief which is justified on adequate grounds; and yet to believe some of these truths is necessary for Christian faith. The man who has 'the heavenly contemplation, the vision of supernatural truth in its own being',[11] however is no longer, according to Aquinas, a man of faith.

This view that faith is not sight does of course echo a long tradition of Christian thought, beginning with the famous Chapter 11 of the Epistle to the Hebrews, where the author describes faith as 'the assurance of things hoped for, the proving of things not seen'.[12] But do not some Christians on Earth claim to 'know' that there is a God who became incarnate in Christ? Yet if they know, how can they be men of faith, as we would be inclined to suppose? The border line between mere belief and knowledge is not always a clear one. Recent philosophical discussions of knowledge seem to indicate that if S knows that p then S has a very well justified strong true belief that p.[13] But if my belief is true, just how well justified does it have to be in order to amount to knowledge? Do I know or only believe truly that it is not yet 5.30 p.m., etc., etc.? There are too, many things which I am rightly said to know, yet which I could have been wrong about (though I am not), which I know, though not with incorrigible certainty through a means like to sight. I know that I am now writing Chapter 4 of my book — but I just could be wrong. So, even if, unlike Aquinas, we allow that there may be Christians who know the truth of all the propositions of their faith, we should, I suggest, claim that they do not know them incorrigibly with a certainty like that of those who have the beatific vision. The common Christian understanding is that faith rules out sight, and if, unlike Aquinas, we say that it does not rule out knowledge, we must neverthe-

---

[9]Ibid., 2a, 2ae, 1. 2.

[10]*De Sacramentis* 1. X. 2. Quoted by the editor of the edition of *Summa Theologiae* referred to at p. 106, n. 2, in a footnote to the passage from the *Summa* just quoted in the text.

[11]St. Thomas Aquinas, *Summa Theologiae*, vol. 31, 2a, 2ae, 5. 1, ad. 1.

[12]Heb. 11:1.

[13] Also, to meet the objection of Gettier, we must say that to amount to knowledge, the belief must be justified in a certain kind of way. See Edmund L. Gettier, 'Is Justified True Belief Knowledge?', *Analysis*, 1963, 23, 121-3; and the discussion leading to this qualification, in Keith Lehrer, *Knowledge* (Oxford, 1974), Ch. 1.

less say that it rules out the kind of knowledge which is incorrigible, analogous to that given by sight, which is more or less the point which Aquinas is making. The Blessed do not live by faith.

So then this is the Thomist view that the man of faith is a man who holds certain beliefs-that. Now in Chapter 1 I drew attention to the relativity of belief. To believe that p, I argued, is to believe that p is more probable than any alternative; and what belief amounts to depends on which alternatives are being considered. The normal alternative to a belief is its negation; and then one who believes that p believes that p is more probable than not-p. But sometimes there are alternatives, q, r, etc., other than the negation, and then to believe that p is to believe that p is more probable than q, and more probable than r, etc. Now what are the alternatives with which the propositions which Aquinas's man of faith believes are being contrasted? It is not clear. Guidance can be obtained by considering the historical circumstances in which controversies about each of these propositions took place, and by seeing with what they were being contrasted. 'There is a God' is no doubt being contrasted with 'there is no God', but some of the propositions of faith may be being contrasted with particular detailed heresies. In so far as there is uncertainty about the alternative or alternatives with which a proposition is being contrasted, it is unclear about what 'belief' that those propositions are true amounts to. In Chapter 6 I shall consider what are the alternatives with which any credal belief necessary for the practice of a religion *ought* to be contrasted.

In itself the Thomist view of faith seems to be a perfectly coherent one (although a somewhat unclear one). On this view, to have faith is basically to have certain beliefs-that, and clearly people can have those beliefs. It does however look an odd view, but this is because we tend to suppose that faith as such is meritorious (and we may even go so far as to suppose that faith alone gains salvation). Yet the Thomist man of faith may be a complete scoundrel, one who does his best to defy God.

However this is no problem for Aquinas, for he does not hold that faith as such is meritorious, and he is careful to distinguish faith from meritorious faith. Indeed he explicitly allows that devils (who have enough true beliefs about God) have faith. In support of his view he quotes St. James — 'thou believest that God is one; thou doest well: the devils also believe, and shudder'[14] and he interprets the claim about their belief as a claim about their faith.[15] However, although the devils have faith, there are, on the Thomist view, two things lacking to them, which they would need to have if their faith was to be meritorious. The

[14]Jas. 2: 19.

[15]This interpretation is prompted by the fact that *credo* is the obvious Latin translation of the Greek word for 'believe' πιστεύω, and that the natural Latin name for the state denoted by *credo* is *fides*. There was no obvious noun in medieval Latin etymologically close to *credo*, to denote 'belief'.

first thing which the faith of the devils lack, in Aquinas's view, is that it does not come into being in the right way. It is not meritorious faith, because it is not a voluntary faith. Aquinas writes that 'the devils' faith is, so to speak, forced from them by the evidence of signs. That they believe, then, is in no way to the credit of their wills.' For the devils 'the signs of faith are so evident that they are forced to believe'.[16] By contrast, Aquinas holds men can choose whether or not to have faith — the signs are not for them so evident that they have to believe; in that case, if they do believe, it is to their credit that they do. However I argued in Chapter 1 that all belief as such is a passive matter. We cannot help having the beliefs that we do at the time at which we have them. All that we can do is to set ourselves to submit them to impartial investigation or change them in less reputable ways over a period. Hence if we are to maintain that Thomist faith is a voluntary matter, we must maintain that the voluntariness of it is a matter of its resulting from investigation over a period or from our setting ourselves over a period to cultivate it. (By contrast, we could say that the faith of devils is involuntary because, whatever they do, they cannot but have that faith.) Aquinas does however seem to write as though, at any rate normally, the merit of faith resulted from one's choosing there and then to follow the dictates of reason; yet this, I have argued, cannot be. He is however aware elsewhere, as I pointed out in the last chapter, that a mistaken conscience can be the result of negligence and it would be natural for him to allow that lack of faith could result from negligence. With this caveat, the arguments of the last chapter give us reason to accept Aquinas's view that to be meritorious, Thomist faith, i.e. belief-that, has to result from religious inquiry of some sort.

However, there is another and more substantial reason why, in Aquinas's view, the faith of devils is not meritorious. This is that their faith is not 'formed by love',[17] i.e. that it is not joined to the firm purpose of bringing about the works which the love of God ought properly to bring about, which are presumably the works involved in committing oneself to God's service. The Council of Trent put the point in similar terms.[18] It was not, I think, insisting that actual good works were needed for salvation, for a man might acquire perfect love and then die before he had any opportunity to do any,[19] but only complete readiness to do them.

So, although Thomist faith by itself is a very intellectual thing, a faith of the head and not the heart, a faith which may be held without any

---

[16]*Summa Theologiae*, 2a, 2ae, 5. 2 ad. 1, and ad. 3.
[17]*Summa Theologiae*, 2a 2ae, 4. 3, 4, and 5.
[18]Council of Trent, *De Justificatione*, Decretum cap. 7, and canon 11.
[19]This is not of course a very likely situation. Normally the development of good character is a process which takes place through the doing of a lot of good actions.

natural fruit in Christian living, the meritorious faith which the Thomist commends involves the whole person. It remains to be seen just how different this view of faith is from other Christian views of faith.

The Lutheran View of Faith

The second view of faith which I shall consider is that faith involves *both* theoretical beliefs-that (Thomist faith) *and* a trust in the Living God. The man of faith, on this view, does not merely believe that there is a God (and believe certain propositions about him)— he trusts him and commits himself to him. The 'believe in' of the Creed is to be read as affirming a belief that there is a God who has the properties stated, and that the good things stated (e.g. 'the resurrection of the dead') have occurred or will occur; and also a trust in God who has the properties stated, and a trust in the means of salvation which he has provided (e.g. 'the Holy Catholic Church') as a route to the good things to come (e.g. 'the life of the world to come'). In my analysis of trust, I shall concern myself mainly with trust in God; trust in the good things would, I suggest, be susceptible of a similar but somewhat more complicated analysis.

I shall call the second view of faith the Lutheran view of faith; for Luther stressed this aspect of faith as trust[20] to such an extent that the Council of Trent was moved to declare: 'If anyone shall say that justifying faith is nothing else but trust in the divine mercy, which pardons our sins for Christ's sake, or that it is by such trust alone that we are justified, let him be anathema.'[21] Later, Lutheran theologians distinguished three parts of faith (*fides*): knowledge (*notitia*), assent (*assensus*), and trust (*fiducia*), and declared that the first two were subordinate to the trust. Trust is, on this view, the central element in faith.[22] The *notitia* is, presumably, roughly the Thomist belief-that; and the *assensus* is something like Thomas's public confession. A similar threefold division of the parts of faith occurs in the opening chapters of Barth's *Dogmatics in Outline* where, after an introductory chapter, there are three chapters on faith entitled 'Faith as Trust', 'Faith as Knowledge', and 'Faith as Confession'.[23]

[20]See his 'The Freedom of a Christian', §11, in *The Reformation Writings of Martin Luther*, translated by B. L. Woolf, vol. i (London, 1952). The Lutheran view is found in the *Book of Homilies*, commended in the Thirty-nine Articles: 'A quick and living faith is not only the common belief of the articles of our faith, but it is also a true trust and confidence of the mercy of God through our Lord Jesus Christ, and a steadfast hope of good things to be received at God's hands.' (Sermon of Faith, Part I.)

[21]Council of Trent, *De Justificatione*, canon 12.

[22]In his *Faith and Belief*, Ch. 6, and *Belief and History*, Ch. 2, W. Cantwell Smith argues that up to the seventeenth century the English word 'believe' used to mean 'trust'. The quotation from the *Book of Homilies* in note 4 on page 110 casts some doubt on this, but Cantwell Smith has accumulated many quotations to illustrate his view.

[23]Karl Barth, *Dogmatics in Outline* (London, 1948).

However, this notion of trust in God needs careful examination. To start with, what is it to put one's trust in an ordinary person? To trust a man is to act on the assumption that he will do for you what he knows that you want or need, when the evidence gives some reason for supposing that he may not and where there will be bad consequences if the assumption is false. Thus I may trust a friend by lending a valuable to him when he has previously proved careless with valuables. I act on the assumption that he will do what he knows that I want (viz. treat the valuable with care), where the evidence gives some reason for supposing that he will not, and where there are bad consequences (viz. the valuable gets damaged) if he does not. An escaping British prisoner of war may have trusted some German by telling him of his identity and asking for help. Here again, he acts on the assumption that the German will do for him what he knows that he wants (viz. provide help), when many Germans are ill-disposed towards escaping British prisoners and liable to surrender them to the police. Or again, a patient who trusts a doctor to cure him acts on the assumption that the doctor will do for the patient what he knows that he needs him to do, where there is some possibility that he may not (because attempts to cure are not always successful), and where things will stay bad unless the doctor is successful. We saw in Chapter 1 that to act on the assumption that p is to do those actions which you would do if you believed that p. The prisoner of war may not on balance believe that the German will help him; but he believes that there is some probability that the German will help, and trusting the German provides his only hope of getting out of Germany. To act on the assumption that p is to use p as a premiss in your practical inferences, whether or not you believe p. But why *should* you act on the assumption that p if in fact you do not believe p? Because you have the purpose to achieve X. You can, you believe, do so only by doing action A, and action A will achieve X only if p is true. If your purpose to achieve X is strong enough (is far stronger than your other purposes) then you will still do A even if you believe that p is not very probable. As we saw in Chapter 1, the belief that in fact guides you is the belief that there is at least a small, but not negligible, probability that p. But we can describe you as acting on the assumption that p, because you would do the same action if you believed strongly that p. Within limits, the degree of p's probability does not make any difference to your action. So a simplified description of what you are doing is 'acting on the assumption' that p. We saw that to trust a man is to act on the assumption that he will do for you what he knows that you want or need, where the evidence gives some reason for supposing that he may not, and there are bad consequences if the assumption proves false. This, it now follows, is to do those actions which you would do if you believed the stated assumption strongly, where in fact the evidence gives some reason for doubting the assumption (and there are bad consequences if it is false).

So much for trusting an ordinary person. What about trusting God? We have seen that on the Lutheran view trusting God is something additional to believing that he exists and to believing propositions about him. It is presumably to act on the assumption that he will do for us what he knows that we want or need, when the evidence gives some reason for supposing that he may not and where there will be bad consequences if the assumption is false. Yet one who believes that God exists and believes the propositions of the Christian creeds about him already believes that God will do for us what he knows that we want or need; that follows immediately from those propositions. Indeed, on some definitions of 'God' and some moral views, all this will follow from God's goodness. However, whether or not this does so follow, plausibly it is a central Christian doctrine and so one which a man of Thomist faith also believes. One who believes this will necessarily, in the primary sense distinguished in Chapter 1, act on that belief. Luther himself commended this additional *belief* (*not* just acting on the assumption).[24] He wrote: 'let no one be content with believing God is able, or has power to do great things: we must also believe that he will do them and that he delights to do them. Nor indeed is it enough to think that God will do great things with other people, but not with you.'[25] Yet one who does not believe this may still, as we have seen, act on the assumption, by doing those actions which he would do if he did believe.

The trouble with the Lutheran account of faith, as I have expounded it so far, is that it has in common with the Thomist account the feature that the perfect scoundrel may yet be a man of faith. For what you do when you act on an assumption depends on what your purposes are. One who acts on the assumption that there is money in a till and who has the purpose of stealing will break open the till; one who acts on the same assumption and who has the purpose of protecting the money will lock the room carefully. A man may act on the assumption that God will do for him what he wants or needs, with purposes good or evil. Acting on that assumption, he may try to conquer the world, believing that God will help him in his task. Shall we call such a man a man of faith? Does he not trust God? Or the antinomian whom St. Paul attacks for suggesting that men should 'continue in sin, that grace may about'?[26] Does he not trust God, to see him right?

The Lutheran, like Aquinas, may be prepared to allow that the scoundrel can be a man of faith. But historically Lutherans have wanted to claim, against Aquinas and with the historical Luther, that faith alone suffices for salvation. If the Lutheran also claims this, he seems committed to the view that the would-be world conqueror and the antino-

[24]Though whether he distinguished adequately between 'believing' and 'acting on an assumption' I have some doubt.

[25]M. Luther, *Magnificat*, in *Reformation Writings of Martin Luther*, vol. ii (London, 1956), p. 199.

[26]Epistle to the Romans 6:1.

mian are exhibiting the sort of trust which alone a man has to exhibit in order to obtain from God (unmerited) salvation. If he wishes, as he surely does, to deny that they exhibit such trust, he will have to put some further restriction on the concept of faith. He will have to say that those who act on the assumption that God will do for them what they need or want, have faith only if their purposes are good ones. A man must be ready to please God or do his duty or benefit his fellows, if his trust is to amount to faith.[27]

But if the Lutheran holds that to have faith a man must have good purposes, be ready to do good works, that means that he must have, in the Catholic sense, Love. And in that case the Reformation controversy about whether faith alone would secure salvation, would seem no real controversy about matters of substance, only a dispute resulting from a confusion about the meaning of words. The Lutheran and Catholic could agree that love was needed on top of Thomist faith, while admitting that Lutheran faith (since it included love) was sufficient for salvation. The parties only quarrelled, on this view, because they misunderstood each other's use of the word 'faith'. In so far as one thinks that the Reformation controversy was not merely a result of verbal confusion, one must think of the reformers as insisting on points implicit in the Catholic position, but not always made explicit — as denying that one's works need to be successful (i.e. that one's attempts to bring about good should come off), or that one needs to have been doing many or even any good works. What is needed for salvation (in addition to beliefs) is a basically good character, that is, a mind full of good purposes, set to bring about good results as opportunity arises, to guide the beliefs on which one acts. Failure to attempt to do good works in appropriate circumstances shows, however, the lack of such good purposes.

I shall argue in Chapter 6 that Christianity does indeed require (in addition to belief of some sort) that a man have a good character if he is to attain salvation. But I shall point out that the development of a good character often takes a long time and is achieved by attempting to do good works over a long period. I shall suggest in Chapter 6 that the good purposes involved in the good character need to become rather more specific before a man can finally attain salvation. They need to be the purposes to attain the goals of religion, i.e. salvation for oneself and others, and the rendering of due worship and obedience to God.

Luther himself was conscious of the close tie between faith and good works. In one passage he writes as though the tie was a logical one. In

---

[27]Calvin claimed that faith can 'in no way be separated from a devout disposition' and he attacked 'the Schools' for distinguishing between 'formed' and 'unformed' faith and supposing that 'people who are touched by no fear of God, no sense of piety, nevertheless believe what is necessary to know for salvation'. (J. Calvin, *Institutes of the Christian Religion,* III. 2; translated by F. L. Battles, London, 1961, vol. i, p. 553 and p. 551.)

the Preface to his commentary on the Epistle to the Romans, he writes that faith 'cannot do other than good at all times. It never waits to ask whether there is some good work to do. Rather, before the question is raised, it has done the deed and keeps on doing it. A man not active in this way is a man without faith.'[28] Elsewhere, however, he seems to write as though the tie was less strict, perhaps merely contingent. 'Faith without good works does not last', he wrote in his 'Sermon on Three Sides of the Good Life',[29] implying that for a time one could exist without the other.

So then, to summarize, the man who has Lutheran faith is a man who believes that God exists and believes certain propositions about him; and who trusts him, in the sense of acting on the assumption that God will do for him what he wants or needs, when evidence gives some reason for supposing that he may not, in which case bad consequences would follow. Belief in such things as 'The Holy Catholic Church', and 'one baptism for the remission of sins', which the Nicene Creed affirms, is a matter of believing that the Church is one, holy, and Catholic, and that remission of sins comes through a first baptism alone; and also acting on the assumption that such institutions provide the way to Heaven (when there is some reason for supposing that they do not, in which case bad consequences would follow from trying to use these institutions as providing a way to Heaven). Again belief in such things as 'the life of the world to come' is a matter of believing that there is such a life and of acting on the assumption that one can attain it (given similar qualifications to those in the last sentence). Also it is necessary, if a man is to have Lutheran faith, that he should have good purposes in his actions on these assumptions — e.g. seek remission of sins or the life of the world to come. As with Thomist faith, what the belief-that involved in Lutheran faith amounts to, depends on the alternatives with which the credal propositions are being contrasted. Again, in so far as there is uncertainty about what these alternatives are, there is unclarity about what 'belief' that these propositions are true amounts to and so as to what Lutheran faith amounts to.

The Pragmatist View of Faith

While Lutheran faith involves both belief-that (however interpreted) and trust, Luther stresses that the trust is the important thing. Is a third form of faith possible where one can have the trust without the belief-that? I think that it is and that many recent writers who stress the irrelevance to faith of 'belief-that' have been feeling their way towards

[28]*Reformation Writings of Martin Luther*, vol. ii, pp. 288 f.
[29]Ibid., vol. ii, p. 124

such a form of faith. I shall call such faith Pragmatist faith.[30] As we have seen, one can act on assumptions which one does not believe. To do this is to do those actions which you would do if you did believe. In particular, you can act on the assumption not merely that God, whom you believe to exist, will do for you what you need or want, but also on the assumption that there is such a God (and that he has the properties which Christians have ascribed to him). One can do this by doing those actions which one would do if one believed these things. In Chapter 1 I quoted Pascal who replied to a man who said 'But I can't believe' with a recipe of how to acquire belief. The recipe was that the man should act as if he believed, do the actions which believers do, 'taking holy water, having masses said', etc. and that would produce belief. Although Pascal did not hold that acting as-if it was the essence of faith, he saw it as a step on the road. But it is natural enough to develop this third view of faith according to which the belief-that is irrelevant, the acting-as-if is what matters. After all belief is a passive state; merit belongs only to actions. Surely if a man does those actions which a believer would do and for which he is to be esteemed, then the man should be esteemed whether or not he has the belief.

As we have seen, trusting God may be not just acting on assumptions; but doing so where one has good purposes. Those who have wanted to define faith in terms of trust alone would, I think, wish such a restriction to be included in the understanding of trust. So, on the Pragmatist view, a man S has faith if he acts on the assumption that there is a God who has the properties which Christians ascribe to him and has provided for men the means of salvation and prospect of glory, and that he will do for S what he knows that S needs or wants — so long also as S has good purposes. He will thus seek not his own fame, but long-term and deep well-being for himself and others. Seeking these things, he may believe that they are only to be had if there is a God who provides such well-being in this world and in the world to come. Hence he may act on the assumption that there is a God — for unless there is, that which is most worthwhile cannot be had. He will, for example, worship and pray and live a good life partly in the hope to find a better life in the world to come. He prays for his brethren, not necessarily because he believes that there is a God who hears his prayers, but because only if there is can the world be set to right. He lives the good life, not necessarily

[30]I find traces of this third view in much modern writing on the subject of faith; but, as I also find most modern writing on this subject almost unbelievably unclear, I find it very difficult to find an unambiguous expression of it in any one author. I have however called it pragmatist faith, since in 'The Will to Believe' William James seems to commend a faith which is a matter of acting-as-if. (The trouble with James, however, is that he commends this because he seems also to hold a view which I have argued to be mistaken, that all belief is simply a matter of acting-as-if — see *The Will to Believe and Other Essays in Popular Philosophy*, first published 1897; New York, 1956, p. 29 n.) Yet clearly much of

because he believes that God will reward him, but because only if there is a God who will reward him can he find the deep long-term well-being for which he seeks. He worships, not necessarily because he believes that there is a God who deserves worship, but because it is very important to express gratitude for existence if there is a God to whom to be grateful and there is some chance that there is.

The Common Structure in the Three Views

Pragmatist faith is not, however, that far distant from Lutheran faith. The man of Pragmatist faith need not believe that there is a God, but he must have certain other beliefs. He has to have moral beliefs, e.g. that any God ought to be worshipped and that he ought to help others to happiness; beliefs about his long-term well-being, e.g. that it would consist in having the Beatific Vision of God rather than living a Lotus-eater life on Earth; and beliefs about the best route to attain that well-being, e.g. by seeking a life after death or a life of service in the African jungle (though he may believe that it is improbable that even the best route leads to that well-being). And he needs the belief that there is some (maybe small) finite probability that there is a God. It is no accident that Pragmatist faith as I have described it does involve such beliefs. These could not be detached from it and anything both rational and faith-like be left. For any advocate of a way of life, such as the Christian way, which prescribes for man certain conduct and has any pretence to rational justifiability, must have a belief as to why this conduct is to be pursued (e.g. because there is some chance that it is a duty, or because there is some chance that it will lead to happiness for oneself or others here or hereafter); and a belief as to why the goal cannot be attained more easily in some other way. The difference lies not in a fact that Pragmatist faith lacks belief-that, but simply that it involves less in the way of belief-that than does Lutheran faith. You need not believe that there is a God and that in consequence you will obtain deep and long-term well-being if you do certain actions (which will bring you deep and long-term well-being if there is a God); only that there may be a God and so that you are more likely to obtain happiness by doing these actions than you are if you assume that there is no God. Some sort of creed is difficult to avoid.

---

the responsibility for the traces of this view in modern theological writing derives from Kierkegaard. Kierkegaard frequently inveighs against those whose religious 'belief' is a matter of reason and balance of probability. Thus: 'the probable is so little to the taste of a believer that he fears it most of all, since he well knows that when he clings to probabilities it is because he is beginning to lose his faith. Faith has in fact two tasks: to take care in every movement to discover the improbable, the paradox, and then to hold it fast with the passion of inwardness' (*Concluding Unscientific Postscript*, translated by David F. Swenson, Princeton, N.J., 1944, pp. 208 f.).

Also, as we have seen, Lutheran faith is not very different from Thomist 'meritorious faith' (i.e. faith 'formed' by a voluntary process and combined with a readiness to do works of love), although it is different from Thomist faith by itself. Also, as we have seen, in so far as belief (rather than assumption) is involved in faith, the faith will vary according to the beliefs with which credal propositions are being contrasted. It is by now, I hope, beginning to become clear that, on all three views of faith, the sort of faith which is meritorious involves belief of some sort and a good character, normally shown in good actions. On all these views of faith the actions which a man is ready to do include those which involve achieving good purposes, relying on the belief, or at any rate assumption, that God will do for us what we want or need. Given that the claims about God's nature and existence are not absolutely certain,[31] there is some danger that he may not. If God does not do for us what we want or need then, unless there is no God but is some other way to attain the goals of religion (to be discussed in the next chapter), such as salvation, there will be the bad consequence of our not obtaining those goals. Hence men's actions in relying on the cited belief can be described as putting trust in God. Hence faith involves trust on all three views. The real difference between kinds of faith (one which cuts across the Thomist/Lutheran division) seems to lie in just how strong the credal beliefs which faith contains have to be. This is a matter partly of whether the propositions of the Creed are believed (e.g. the belief is that God is the Father Almighty, Maker of Heaven and Earth); or whether they are simply assumptions which guide action, and so the belief is simply that our goals are most likely to be attained if we do act on the assumption that the Creed is true. The strength of belief that a proposition is true is also a matter of the alternatives with which the proposition is contrasted.

I brought out this latter point in the first chapter, and have referred to it at important points in this chapter. Here I must emphasize it again.

To believe a proposition is to believe it more probable than any alternative. So what the belief amounts to depends on what are the alternatives. The normal alternative to a proposition is its negation. To believe that p is to believe that p is more probable than not-p. But the alternatives to a proposition may be narrower than the negation. In that case to believe that p is to believe that p is more probable than each of these alternatives q,r,s, etc., but not necessarily more probable than their conjunction. It follows from this that there are really two different things which believing a creed such as the Nicene Creed might amount to. It may be a matter of believing each item of the Creed to be more

---

[31]Even on the view that the existence of God is provable with absolute certainty, what God will do for us lies within the sphere of revelation and can be known only with a high degree of probability.

probable than its negation. Thus, understanding 'I believe *in* God the Father Almighty, maker of Heaven and Earth and of all things visible and invisible' as 'I believe that there is a God who is Father Almighty, Maker of Heaven and Earth and of all things visible and invisible', we may in turn understand this as 'I believe that it is more probable that there is a God who is Father Almighty, Maker of Heaven and Earth, and of all things visible and invisible, than that there is not'. And so on for each item of the Creed. This interpretation makes it crucial just how one divides up the Creed into items. For, as we saw in Chapter 1, it does not follow from p being more probable than not-p, and q being more probable than not-q, that (p and q) is more probable than not-(p and q). Although it is to some extent clear how the Nicene Creed is to be divided up into items (for example, belief in 'God the Father Almighty' is belief in a different item from belief in 'One Holy Catholic and Apostolic Church'), it is by no means always obvious exactly where the line is to be drawn between different items. Is belief in 'God the Father Almighty, Maker of Heaven and Earth' belief in one item or belief in two separate items?

Alternatively, believing a creed such as the Nicene Creed might be a matter of believing each item of the Creed to be more probable than each of a number of specific heretical or non-Christian alternatives. A man in affirming his belief in 'the resurrection of the body' may be claiming that it is more probable that men rise embodied than that (as some other religions claimed) they rise disembodied, and so on. In affirming his belief that Christ was 'begotten, not made,' a man may only be affirming a belief that it is more probable that the pre-Incarnate Christ was brought into being *e nihilo* than that he was made from pre-existent matter. And so on. This view has the difficulty of the previous view about how the Creed is to be cut up into items, and the further difficulty of how we are to know what are the alternatives to each item. The historical circumstances of the formulation of the Creed provide guidance on the latter issue, and indeed on the former one too. By studying the reasons which led men to put a certain clause in the Creed we can see what it was designed to deny. But it remains the case that on either of these views there is very considerable uncertainty as to what believing the Creed amounts to. On the second view a man who believes a creed consisting of p, q, and r, believes p to be more probable than p_1, p_2, etc.; q to be more probable than q_1, q_2, etc., and so on. In that case he will believe his total creed to be more probable than alternative heretical or religious systems, e.g. (p, q, and r), to be more probable than (p_2, q_2, and r_2). Conversely, if he believes p-q-and-r, to be more probable than alternative religious systems (including both systems which form bases of actual religions and systems which can be constructed by combining parts of the latter), then he will have belief of the second kind. He will believe p to be more probable than p_1, p_2, etc. and so on. So the second view can be expressed by saying that a man believes a creed if he believes it to be more probable than any alternative rival system.[32] One who believes the Christian Creed on this view believes it to be more probable than the creeds of Buddhism, Islam, etc., or any amalgam of parts of such creeds. I shall call belief of the first kind in a creed a strong belief, and belief of the second kind a weak belief. Theoretically, there is a third possibility that the creed as a whole is being contrasted with its negation. On this view, to believe the creed is to believe that the conjunction of propositions which form it is more probable than the negation of that conjunction. Yet although this is theoretically possible, I find it difficult to accept that religious men have supposed that belief in a creed is as strong a thing as that. For this view carries the implication that the believer believes that it is more probable that his creed is true in all its details than that there is any mistake anywhere in it. Yet by comparison, most of us who believe complex historical or scientific claims allow the possibility of some error somewhere. So I confine myself to the two kinds of belief which a man may have in a creed and which I called strong belief and weak belief.

So the crucial issue with respect to faith is, given that meritorious faith involves good action springing from trust in God or commitment to Him, what sort of belief in the Creed is involved? Strong belief that it is true, or weak belief that it is true, or merely the belief that if one acts on the assumption that it is true, one is more likely to achieve the goals of religion (e.g. Heaven, forgiveness of sins, etc.) than if one makes any other assumption. Whichever view we take of credal belief, the results of the last chapter surely hold with regard to it. The main duty in this matter of belief is to investigate and to yield to whatever reason suggests to be true.

In both the New Testament and early Christian writing both belief-that of some kind and trust in God, involving acting on assumptions, is commended. The long sermon on faith in Hebrews 11 seems to contain an understanding of faith both as belief-that and as action on-the-assumption-that. On the one hand, 'He that cometh to God must *believe*

---

[32]If p is more probable than p_1, p_2, etc., q is more probable than q_1, q_2, etc., and r is more probable than r_1, r_2, etc., it normally holds that $(p, q, \text{and } r)$ is more probable than any other combination of p's, q's and r's, such as $(p_1, q_1, \text{and } r_1)$. There are however odd cases where it does not hold. These are cases where p, q, and r count against each other (e.g. where not all three can be true together). However, in view of the fact that religious creeds normally fit neatly together to give a coherent world-view, we may in this context ignore such cases. It also holds normally that if $(p \text{ and } q \text{ and } r)$ is more probable than any other combination of p's, q's, and r's, e.g. $(p_1, q_1, \text{and } r_1)$ that, for suitable ways of picking out the constituent propositions which make up the whole (e.g. for picking a proposition p_1, as an alternative to p rather than as an alternative to q), p is more probable than p_1 and q than q_1, etc.

that he is, and that he is a rewarder of them that seek after him.'[33] Yet on the other hand the faith of Abraham is seen in his obedience to God 'to go out into a place which he was to receive for an inheritance; and he went out, not knowing whither he went'.[34] And the faith of many other heroes of the Old Testament is seen by the writer as a matter of their doing actions in hope rather than belief.

The response required to the preaching of the Gospel by St. Peter in Acts was that his hearers should 'repent and be baptised'.[35,36]

Yet although both belief-that and acting-on-the-assumption-that are commended in early Christian thought, it seems clear to me that by far the greater number of uses of the words normally translated into English as 'faith' and 'believe in' (e.g. πίστις, πιστεύω, *fides, credo*) are better translated as 'trust' and 'put trust in' than as 'belief' and 'believe that'. In a very well documented chapter of his *Faith and Belief* [37] W. Cantwell Smith illustrates this with respect to the lectures at baptism given in the fourth century, traditionally attributed to St. Cyril of Jerusalem. He argues persuasively that the commitment involved in baptism and in the creeds originally used at baptism (by the word πιστεύω) involves doing an action (putting trust) rather than expressing a passive conviction. However, as Cantwell Smith also emphasizes, the baptisands recognized that there was a God who had certain properties and had done certain actions, and their commitment to him took for granted this background. And recognition, like knowledge, involves belief. To recognize something involves coming to believe that it is so. Cantwell Smith supposes that to say of a man that he believes something implies that he has very considerable doubt about it. That just

---

[33]Epistle to the Hebrews 11:6. In *Belief and History*, pp. 73–80, W. Cantwell Smith has argued that in this and two similar New Testament passages (Jas. 2: 19 and John 13: 9) πιστεύω is best translated 'recognize' rather than 'believe'. He claims this on the ground that the writer presupposes the existence of God and that the modern English 'believe that' does not presuppose the truth of the clause that follows it, whereas 'recognize' does presuppose the truth of the clause that follows it. That may be. But although the New Testament writers presupposed the existence of God, the verb πιστεύω (whether used by them or anyone else) does not carry this presupposition, and so I suggest that 'believe' is the better translation. But in any case 'recognize that' entails 'believe that'. The greater claim involves the lesser.

[34]Heb .11:8.

[35]Acts 2: 38.

[36]W. R. Inge in his study of the understanding of 'faith' in Bible and Church, summarized his account of the New Testament understanding by saying that 'believers' at the end of the first century AD 'were conscious that the word included moral devotion and self-surrender to Christ, a firm conviction that by uniting themselves to Him they would find remission of sins and eternal salvation, and intellectual conviction that certain divinely revealed facts are true.' (W. R. Inge, *Faith*, London, 1909, p. 23). Speaking more particularly about St. John's use of πιστεύω he wrote that 'the two meanings of intellectual conviction and moral self-surrender are about equally emphasised' (ibid., pp. 22 f.).

[37]Op. cit. pp. 70–8.

seems false, as a point about ordinary English—I believe that I am writing this on a Friday, and I have no doubt about it. Cantwell Smith seems to use 'belief' in the sense of 'mere belief'. However his discussion gives rise to a crucial question which he does not face, whether those who had mere belief were eligible for baptism. Do you have to be sure of the existence of that in which you put your trust, or is mere belief sufficient? Cantwell Smith does not explicitly consider this crucial point of just how much belief-that those to be baptised need in order to make the commitment. For those who were following other religious paths (e.g. the old pagan ways) presumably lacked both the belief that God had certain properties and had done certain actions, and the trust in him. Their conversion involved changing both their beliefs-that and the object of their trust. But how strong did their new beliefs-that need to be?

I do not think that the early Church was in the least clear about this. It had not faced the issue as a doctrinal problem. However, although it would need much historical research to substantiate my conjecture, I suggest that implicitly, in earlier centuries, men tended to assume that Christianity was being contrasted with various other religions and philosophical systems; and that in expressing belief in Christianity you are expressing a belief that it as a whole was more probable than each of those other systems. Those, like Augustine, who agonized over religious allegiance in the first centuries AD, were concerned with a choice between Christianity, Judaism, Mithraism, Manichaeism, Epicureanism, Stoicism, etc. Their concern in making a choice was with which was most likely to be true; and so among religions which offered salvation, which was most likely to provide it. There was not in those days a vast pool of 'agnostics' who owed allegiance to no system. Yet if in order to believe a system you had to believe each item of its creed to be more probable than its negation, then since you might expect most people to think that no system had all its items each more probable than its negation (although they would think that systems differed among each other in probability), you might expect most people to believe no one system and to belong to a vast agnostic pool. Religious belief then does seem to have been relative to fairly specific alternatives. In later centuries there seems to be a change. The post-Renaissance centuries saw the emergence and steady growth, among intellectuals to start with and then more widely, of a vast pool of 'agnostics'. Of course there was more than one reason for the growth of agnosticism, but many of these agnostics must have felt that one religion was more probable than others, and yet they still felt themselves unqualified for entry to it. We hear the great cry of 'I would like to believe, but unfortunately I cannot'. Clearly men supposed that there were stronger conditions for belief than those which, I have claimed, existed in early centuries. It was, I suspect, partly as a reaction to this situation, that some men developed an understanding of faith which did not involve any belief-that the propositions of the Creed were true, viz. Pragmatist understanding of faith. Yet is seems fairly clear to me that for the New Testament and the early church *some* sort of belief that the propositions of the Creed were true was required of the Christian.[38] However, although the historian may read an implicit understanding of what faith is assumed to involve in various centuries, to my knowledge the Church has never made any dogmatic pronouncements about the kind of belief which is involved in faith. In the next two chapters I shall consider on more aprioristic grounds what kind of belief is needed for pursuit of the aims of religion, and what kind of belief a church ought to demand of its adherents.

Before coming to this question, I must mention one minor matter. All the kinds of faith which I discussed involve attitudes towards, behaviour in the light of, *propositions.* They are not necessarily always so phrased, but my claim is that talk about believing in God or trusting God can without loss of meaning be analysed in one of these ways. John Hick however seems to claim that faith is not concerned with propositions. He entitles his view of faith as 'non-propositional' and claims rather that the man of faith is one who experiences the world as God's. He writes: 'faith consists of a voluntary recognition of God's activity in human history, consists in seeing, appreciating, or interpreting events in a special way'.[39] The man of faith 'sees' not merely disease, but the hand of God. But this view of faith seems easily expressible in propositional terms. The man of faith is one who sees the world and in so doing automatically and naturally *believes that* the world is God's creation; does not merely see disease, but in so doing automatically and naturally *believes that* God has brought it about. Is not to experience X as Y in this kind of case simply to experience X and in so doing automatically and naturally to *believe that* X is Y? The 'non-propositional' aspect of Hick's view of faith is simply a matter of the way in which he has expressed it.[40] There is nothing essentially non-propositional about it.

[38]Inge (*Faith*) claims this explicitly; and Cantwell Smith (*Faith and Belief*) claims that the commitment involved in faith includes 'recognition' of the existence of its object, God, with stated properties. I have argued that recognition entails belief-that things are as recognized.

[39]John Hick, *Philosophy of Religion* (Englewood Cliffs, N.J., 1963), p. 71. He is developing here ideas from his *Faith and Knowledge* (1st edn., 1957; 2nd edn., London, 1967).

[40]The same may be said about Cantwell Smith's attacks on propositional accounts of belief. See his bold claim: 'No one . . . has ever believed a proposition'—*Faith and Belief*, p. 146. Statements of belief can always be expressed as statements of belief in propositions. Aquinas saw Hick's position (see *Summa Theologiae*, 2a, 2ae, 1. 2, obj. 2) and claimed that his view was in no way incompatible with it (2a, 2ae, 1. 2, ad. 2).

ANNETTE BAIER

Secular Faith*

1. The Challenge

Both in ethics and in epistemology one source of scepticism in its contemporary version is the realization, often belated, of the full consequences of atheism. Modern non-moral philosophy looks back to Descartes as its father figure, but disowns the *Third Meditation*. But if God does not underwrite one's cognitive powers, what does? The largely unknown evolution of them, which is just a version of Descartes' unreliable demon? "Let us . . . grant that all that is here said of God is a fable, nevertheless in whatever way they suppose that I have arrived at the state of being that I have reached, whether they attribute it to fate or to accident, or make out that it is by a continual succession of antecedents, or by some other method—since to err and deceive oneself is a defect, it is clear that the greater will be the probability of my being so imperfect as to deceive myself ever, as is the Author to whom they assign my being the less powerful" (Meditation I, Haldane and Ross, tr.). Atheism undermines a solitary thinker's single-handed cognitive ambitions, as it can determine his expectation that unilateral virtue will bring happiness. The phenomenon of atheism in unacknowledged debt to theism can be seen both in ethical theory and in epistemology, and the threat of scepticism arises in a parallel manner.

*From the *Canadian Journal of Philosophy*, Volume X, No. 1, March 1980, pp. 131–148. Reprinted by permission of the author and publisher.

In a provocative article, David Gauthier[1] has supported the charge
made two decades ago by Anscombe,[2] that modern secular moral philosophers retain in their theories concepts which require a theological
underpinning. "The taking away of God . . . in thought dissolves all,"
said Locke, and Gauthier agrees that it dissolves all those duties or
obligations whose full justification depends upon a general performance of which one has no assurance. He quotes Hobbes: "He that
would be modeste and tractable and perform all he promises in such
time and place where no man els should do so, should but make himself
the prey to others, and procure his own ruin, contrary to all Lawes of
Nature, which tend to Nature's preservation" (*Leviathan*, chap. 15).
The problem arises not merely when "no man els" does his[3] duty, but
when a significant number do not, so that the rest, even a majority,
make themselves prey to the immoral ones, and procure their own
exploitation, if not their own ruin. The theist can believe, in his cool
hour, that unilateral, or minority, or exploited majority morality will
not procure his ultimate ruin, that all things work together for good,
but what consolation can a secular philosopher offer for the cool
thoughtful hour, in the absence of God? If Gauthier is right, either false
or insufficient consolation. He says that in those modern theories which
preserve some vestige of a duty to do what others are not known to be
doing, or known to be failing to do, "God is lurking unwanted, even
unconceived, but not unneeded."[4]

I shall suggest that the secular equivalent of faith in God, which we
need in morality as well as in science or knowledge acquisition, is faith
in the human community and its evolving procedures—in the prospects for many-handed cognitive ambitions and moral hopes. Descartes
had deliberately shut himself away from other thinkers, distrusting the
influence of his teachers and the tradition in which he had been
trained. All alone, he found he could take no step beyond a sterile self
certainty. Some other mind must come to his aid before he could
advance. Descartes sought an absolute assurance to replace the human

---

[1]"Why Ought One Obey God, Reflections on Hobbes and Locke," *Canadian Journal of
Philosophy* 7 (1977), pp. 425–46.

[2]G. E. M. Anscombe, in "Modern Moral Philsophy," (*Philosophy*, 1958, pp. 1–18,
reprinted in *The Definition of Morality*, ed. Wallace and Walker, London) 1970 claimed
that all deontological moral concepts are empty words unless there is a divine lawgiver
and duty-determiner. Gauthier's thesis concerns not *all* moral laws and duties, but only
those involving "moral convention," where mutual benefits depend upon general observance. I accept his assumption that all moral duties require some rational basis, that
we do not simply intuit moral absolutes.

[3]Throughout this paper I use 'his' to mean 'his or her' and sometimes use 'man' to
mean 'person'. This is especially regrettable in a paper about justice, but needed allusions to the words of Hobbes and other sexists dictated my usage. I am not, it seems,
willing to make the sacrifices in communication needed to help gain as much currency for
'the one just woman' as already gained for the one just man.

[4]Gauthier, op.cit., p. 428.

reassurance he distrusted, and I suggest that we can reverse the procedure. If we distrust the theist's absolute assurance we can return to what Descartes spurned, the support of human tradition, of a cross-generational community. This allows us to avoid the narrow and self-destructive self seeking which is the moral equivalent of solipsism. But Gauthier's challenge is precisely to the reasonableness of community-supportive action when we have no guarantee of reciprocal public-spirited or communally-minded action from others. Not only may we have no such guarantee, we may have evidence which strongly *disconfirms* the hypothesis that others are doing their part. We may have neither knowledge nor inductively well based belief that others are doing their part. Faith and hope I take to involve acceptance of belief on grounds other than deductive or inductive evidence of its truth. Faith is the evidence of things unseen. It will be faith, not knowledge, which will replace religious faith. I shall try to make clear exactly what that faith is faith in, and what it would be for it to be (a) ill–founded or unreasonable, (b) reasonable, but in vain. I shall be defending the thesis that the just must live by faith, faith in a community of just persons.

2. Faith: the substance of things hoped for

Faith, not knowledge, was and is needed to support those "plain duties" whose unilateral observation sometimes appears to procure the dutiful person's ruin. But faith, for rational persons, must appear reasonable before it can be attained. If it is to be reasonable, it must not fly in the face of inductive evidence, but it may go beyond it, when there are good reasons of another sort to do so. We may have such good reasons to hope for an empirically very unlikely but not impossible eventuality. Reasonableness is relative to the alternative beliefs or policies one might adopt, or be left with, if one rejected the candidate for the status of reasonable belief. One of the chief arguments for the moral faith I shall present is the great unreasonableness of any alternative to it. The *via negativa* which leads to secular faith has been clearly indicated in Hobbes' description of the state of nature, the state of persons without the constraint of justice. Hobbes' modern commentators, including Gauthier, have underlined the futility of the alternatives to morality. Yet if everyone insisted on knowing in advance that any sacrifice of independent advantage which they personally make, in joining or supporting a moral order, will be made up for by the returns they will get from membership in that moral order, that order could never be created nor, if miraculously brought about, sustained. Only by conquest could a Hobbesian *Leviathan* ever be created, if the rational man must have secure knowledge that others are doing likewise before he voluntarily renounces his right to pursue independent advantage.

How, except by total conquest, could one ever know for sure that other would-be war makers will lay down their arms when one does so?

In fact Hobbes' first Law of Nature requires every man to endeavor peace, not when he has certainty of attaining it, but "as fare as he has *hope* of attaining it" (*Leviathan*, chap. 14, emphasis added). Hope had been previously defined as "appetite with opinion of attaining" (op.cit., chap. 6) and opinion is contrasted with science (op.cit., chap.7), which alone is the outcome of correct reckoning or calculation. It is then, for Hobbes, a Law of Nature, or a counsel of rational prudence, to act on hope when what is at stake is escape from the Hobbesian state of nature.

Faith, Hobbes tells us "is in the man, Beleefe both of the man and of the truth of what he says" (ibid.). It is faith in its Hobbesian sense, in men, not merely belief in the truth of what they say which I shall argue is the only 'substance' of the hoped-for cooperation which avoids the futility and self destructiveness of its alternatives. Faith, in a non-Hobbesian sense, that is a belief which runs beyond the inductive evidence for it, when it is faith in the possibility of a just cooperative scheme being actualized, is the same as that hope whose support is trust "in the man."

Trust in people, and distrust, tends to be self-fulfilling. Faith or lack of faith in any enterprise, but especially one requiring trust in fellow-workers, can also be self-fulfilling. Confidence can produce its own justification, as William James[5] persuasively argued. The question whether to support a moral practice without guarantee of full reciprocity is, in James' terminology, live, momentous, and forced, and the choice made can be self-verifying whichever way we choose. Every new conversion to moral scepticism strengthens the reason for such scepticism, since, if acted on, it weakens the support of moral practices and so diminishes their returns to the morally faithful. Similarly, every person who continues to observe those practices provides some reason for belief that they are supported, and so strengthens the foundation for his own belief that their support is sufficient, and provides some justification for his own dependence on that support. *Some* justification, but not enough, surely, to be decisive, since he is unlikely to be the critical straw to save or break the camel's back. The case for the self-confirmation of moral faith is less clear than for the self-confirmation, the band wagon effect, of moral scepticism. Immorality breeds

[5]William James, "The Will to Believe," in *The Will to Believe and Other Essays in Popular Philosophy* (New York and London, 1897). In this paper I am really saying no more than James said about moral faith. I suppose the justification for saying it again, and adapting it to a Hobbesian context, is the perennial character of the issue. I have benefited from discussion with Richard Gale on James' position, and from his comments on an earlier version of this paper.

immorality, but need moral action, especially if *unilateral*, breed more of the same? The sense in which the exemplary unilateral act *does* provide its own support, even if the example it gives is not followed by one's contemporaries, will be explored later. For the moment the best one can say for the reasonableness of willing to belief in the value of (possibly) unilateral moral action is that the alternative, giving up on that crucial part of the moral enterprise which secures cooperation, must lead eventually to an outcome disastrous to all, although those with a taste for gun-running may make a good profit before doomsday dawns. There are different styles of shoring fragments against one's ruin, and some choose to exploit the presumed failure of morality, while others or even the same ones, retreat into a narrow circle where virtues can still be cultivated. But when, even granted the badness of its alternatives, would it be unreasonable to keep faith in the moral enterprise, in particular in the attempt to achieve a fair scheme of human cooperation? I turn next to consider the coherence of the ideal of justice.

3.   More or less just societies

When would an actual cooperative scheme between persons be a just one, one which gave its participants the *best reasons* to support it? When the goods, for each, gained by cooperation outweigh the individual advantage any sacrificed, and where all partakers in the benefits make their fair contribution, pay their dues, observe the rules which ensure production and fair distribution of benefits. Even in a society where this was true, there would still be a place for a descendant of Hobbes' *Leviathan,* to enforce rules, since there may still be persons who act irrationally, and who have a perverse taste for bucking the system, whatever the system. A stable, efficient, equitable[6] and democratic scheme of cooperation would give its conforming members security, delectation, non-exploitation and freedom, but some may still try to get a free ride, or to break the rules out of what Hobbes called "the stubbornness of their passions." His fifth Law of Nature commands "compleasance," that every man strive to accommodate himself to the rest, and unilateral breach of this rule is contrary to Hobbesian reason whose dictates include the laws of nature, since it calculates that the individual can count on preserving himself only if steps are taken to ensure the conservation of men in multitudes, and so to ensure peace.

[6]It is not an easy matter to formulate an acceptable criterion of the equitable, but I have assumed that we can get a stronger test for justice than that provided by Hobbes— "What all men have accepted, no man can call unjust." If we cannot, then maybe only the fool says in his heart that there is more to justice than fidelity to possibly forced agreement. If the ideal of the equitable or fair is empty or incoherent, then the more inclusive ideal of justice in a strong sense, which I am invoking, will also be empty or incoherent.

"He that having sufficient security, that others observe the same laws towards him, observes them not himself, seeketh not peace, but war; and consequently the destruction of his own nature by violence" (*Leviathan*, chap. 15, immediately following the passage quoted by Gauthier, which points out the folly of unilateral conformity to the laws of nature).

Both unilateral conformity and unilateral non-conformity are, according to Hobbes, contrary to reason, but man's natural intractability inclines him to the latter. In any state of affairs short of perfect and perfectly secure justice such intractability provides a healthy challenge to an imperfect *status quo*, but if a satisfactory form of cooperation were attained such a character trait would serve no useful function. And even if Hobbes is wrong in claiming that one who refuses to do his part thereby irrationally seeks his own violent destruction, his claim that only a fool believes he can profit by breaking the rules his fellows keep is plausible to this extent, that if those rules were just in a stronger sense than any Hobbes can provide, then however attractive the promised gains of a free ride, or of exploiting others, only a fool would believe that he has more to gain by risking the enmity of his fellows by such a policy than by cultivating a taste for the pleasures of cooperation and regulated fair competition. It may not be positively irrational to break the fifth Law of Nature, especially in a would-be totalitarian Leviathan state, but it would be against reason to think one would do better by breaking the rules of a decent just scheme of cooperation. There is no reason *not* to be sociable in a decent society, and nothing to be gained there by non-irrational unsociability, by going it alone, by entering into a state of war with one's fellows. But some will act contrary to reason, "by asperity of Nature," and be "Stubborn, Insociable, Forward, Intractable." Such stubbornness is perversity, not superior rationality, when the rules are just. We could define a perfectly just society as one where it takes such intractability to motivate disobedience.

How do we measure how close an actual society is to the adequately just society? Unless we can do this it would seem impossible ever to judge a society so unjust that its institutions merit disrespect, or to have confidence that any change made in existing institutions is a change for the better. Yet there are grave problems in establishing any coherent measure of comparative justice. These problems arise because of the tension between two ways in which an existing state of things may approximate the just society. In one sense an institution is just to the extent that it *resembles* one we expect to be part of the adequately just society. In another sense an institution is better to the extent that it is instrumental in moving the society closer in time to that adequacy. But the institutions a society needs, to change itself, may be quite other than those it needs, once improvement is no longer needed. Yet if we opt for this dynamic measure of relative justice, and say that institutions are good to the extent that they facilitate movement towards adequate justice, we run up against the possibility, explored by Hegel and developed by Marx, that historical movement towards a social ideal may be dialectical, that the institutions which best facilitate movement towards an ideal may be ones which least embody that ideal.

The ideal of *justice*, however, is one which cannot generate a sense of 'more just than' in which intolerable exploitation is counted more just than a lesser degree of exploitation, merely because it is more likely to precipitate rebellion and change. Those who advocate making things worse in order, that they may get better cannot claim that what their strategies increase is justice. Is justice then an ideal which is committed to a perhaps groundless liberal faith in progress, faith in its own gradual attainment by moves, each of which represents *both* an increase in qualitative approximation to the ideal, and *also* a step closer, historically and causally, to its attainment? If these two measures of approximation are both proper, yet can come apart, can come into irresolvable conflict with one another, then the ideal of justice may be confused and incoherent,[7] may rest on a faith which is false. I think there is a genuine issue here, but it is not one which I shall discuss further. Social science, not philosophy, would shore up the liberal's faith, or show it to be false. If it is false, if there is no coherent measure of relative justice, then the modern moral philosophy Gauthier criticises is in even worse straits than he claims. But I shall proceed within the limits of the comforting liberal faith with I take Gauthier to share, faith that some institutions can be judged less just than others, and that improving them can count as progress towards a just society. It is worth pointing out that this is part of the *faith* the just live by, but it is not that part of it which is controversial to Gauthier and those he criticises, none of whom embrace the radical moral scepticism to which the Marxist argument leads, nor the new non-moral revolutionary faith which can fill the vacuum it creates.

Where else does faith enter into the motivation to act, in a less than fully just society, for the sake of justice, to conform to more or less just institutions which not all conform to, or to act, possibly unilaterally to reform salvageable institutions, and to protest corrupt ones? What must the just person believe, which must turn out to be true if his action is not be to pointless or futile? Before we can discuss the question of whether and when personal advantage is pointlessly sacrificed, we must

---

[7]As has been pointed out by a reader for this journal, coherence could be preserved by letting one test apply on some occasions, the other on others, whenever the two tests would give conflicting decisions if both were applied. This would preserve only a weak formal coherence, unless some clear principle could be formulated which selects which test is applicable, and unless this principle itself expressed some component element in our hazy intuitive idea of justice.

first discuss the nature and varieties of advantage and personal good. I shall in this discussion adopt a hedonist terminology, to stay as close as possible to the Hobbesian point of departure.

4. Goods: secure and insecure

Hobbes speaks not of advantage but of *power*, namely "present means to obtain some future apparent good." Advantage strictly is advantage over, or against, others, and Hobbes' emphasis on man's "diffidence" or need to assure himself that there is "no other power great enough to endanger him" (op.cit., chap. 13) turns power-seeking into the attempt to attain advantage, competitive edge, a position superior to one's fellows, since even in civil society he believes that men "can relish nothing but what is eminent" (op.cit., chap. 17). I shall keep the term 'advantage' for this competitive good, superiority over others, and use Hobbes' word 'power' for the more generic concept of possession of present means to obtain some future, apparent, possibly noncompetitive, good. (I think that when Gauthier speaks of 'advantage' he is using it in a looser way, more equivalent simply to 'good', that is to a combination of possession of present good and power or present means to attain a future good, whether or not these goods are scarce and competed for.)

Hobbes says that prudence, the concern for power rather than for immediate good, is concern for the future, which is "but a fiction of the mind" (op.cit., chap. 3), and moreover is based on an uncertain presumption that we can learn, from the past, what to expect in the future. "And though it be called Prudence, when the Event answereth our Expectation; yet in its own nature is but Presumption" (ibid.). Hobbes is surely correct in pointing out the risks inherent in prudence. One may invest in a form of power which turns out to be a passing not a lasting one. Hobbes (op.cit., chap. 10) catalogs the many forms power takes, and it is fairly obvious that accidents of chance and history may add to, and subtract from, this list, as well as determine the relative importance of different items on it. Even if one's choice of a form of power to obtain is a lucky one, one may not live into that future where the power could be spent in delectation, or even in misery-avoidance. At some point, in any case, the restless pursuit of power after power must end in death, so *some* future good for which the prudent person saved is bound, if he remains prudent to the end, not to be enjoyed by him. In theory one might, when imminent death is anticipated, make a timely conversion to imprudence, cash one's power in for delectation and die gratified and powerless, but persons with Hobbesian, or with our actual, psychology are not likely to be capable of such a feat. One may have advantage, and have power, which is no good to one, or no longer any good to one, if to be good it must be cashed in delectation.

How are we to judge what is and what is not good to a person? Must good, to be such, be converted, eventually, from apparent good into real indubitable good, and from future into present good? These are hard questions, and it would take a full theory of the good of a person, the place in it of pleasure, interest, power, advantage, to answer them. I have no such theory,[8] and will offer only a few remarks about the complexity of all goods other than present simple pleasures. In all human motivation, other than the gratification of current appetite, there is a potential multi-tier structure. In the case of action designed to make possible the gratification of future desires, that is in prudent action, the good for the sake of which one acts is the expected future gratification, but usually also, derivatively, the present satisfaction of feeling secure, of believing that one has taken thought for the future, secured its needs. So even if the prudent investor does not live into that future for which he provided, he may still enjoy a sense of security while he lives. Prudence, like virtue, may be, and sometimes has to be, its own reward. It is possible, but unlikely, that prudent persons take no present satisfaction in their prudent action, that they develop no taste for a sense of security. The normal accompaniment of prudence is the pleasure of a sense of security. I shall call such pleasures, which make reference to other, possibly non-present pleasures, 'higher' pleasures (Hobbes' "pleasures of the mind"). By calling these pleasures 'higher' I do not mean to imply that they should necessarily be preferred to lower ones. The special class of them which makes reference to future pleasures are power-derivative higher pleasures (Hobbes' "glory"). Such pleasures can coexist with regret that the cost of prudence was renunciation of a present available lower pleasure, and even with doubt whether such costs were unavoidable, and whether one will live to enjoy the future for which one has saved. It would be incorrect to say that the prudent person trades in present lower pleasure for higher pleasure — the higher pleasure is merely a bonus which can come with the power for which the lower pleasure was traded. But hedonic bonuses count for *something*, when the rationality of the action is to be judged.

When one acts for the sake of some good for others, be that good pleasure or power, present or future, there is a similar immediate bonus or "glory" possible, the pleasure of believing that someone else's present or future is improved by one's action. Persons who perform

---

[8]Although in what follows I try to depart as little as possible from the hedonism of Hobbes and Locke (not because I agree with it, but because of the context of the present discussion), I do however depart very significantly from Hobbes in accepting, as rational motivation, not only self preservation of the natural man, or "nature's preservation" but also preservation, not of Leviathan, but of a moral community, and of the very idea of such a community. A special 'pleasure of the mind' would have to be added to Hobbes' list to accommodate such Kantian motivation.

such altruistic acts usually do develop a taste for altruism, a fellow-feeling whereby they share in the good they do others. Just as the sense of personal security usually pleases the prudent person, the awareness of others' pleasure and the sense of their security usually pleases the altruist. It may be possible to do good to others because the moral law is thought to require it, without thereby getting any satisfaction for oneself, but such bonus-refusing psychology seems neither likely nor desirable. It is best if virtue is at least *part* of its own reward, and a waste if it is not.

5. Artifices to secure the insecure

To be a normal human person is to be capable of higher pleasures, both self-derived and other-derived, to be able to make the remote in time and the remote from oneself close enough in thought and concern not merely to affect present action but to give present pleasure. Hume explored the mechanisms whereby concern for the remote, both from the present, and from oneself and one's family, can be strengthened by its coincidence with concern for the contiguous, so that the "violent propension to prefer the contiguous to the remote," (*Treatise*, p. 537) may be combatted, its unfortunate and sometimes violent effects avoided. These mechanisms include not merely psychological ones, imagination and sympathy, which turn the useful into the also agreeable, and the agreeable for others into the agreeable for oneself also, but also social practices of training and education, and social artifices. Such artifices — promise, property, allegiance — turn the useful for people in general into what is useful for oneself, and this requires both convention, or agreement between people as to *what* the artifice is, and general conformity to its constitutive rules. Convention requires both communication and coordination. Hume believed, perhaps wrongly, that all of justice was in this sense artificial and that only with respect to the artificial virtues did a person risk being "the cully of his integrity" (*Treatise*, p. 535) if he acted unilaterally, without assurance that others were similarly virtuous. Since the actions of a kind or a generous person do the good they do, to individual others, case by case, whereas just or honest actions *need* do no good to any specified individual, and do what good they do, for people in general, for the public interest, only when they are supported by other just acts, it is an easy but false move from this valid contrast between the ways the natural and the artificial virtues do good, to a contrast at the level of motivation for the agent, and to the claim that an individual always has good reason to display a natural virtue whether or not others do, while one has no reason to display an artificial virtue, unless others are displaying the same version of it. Non-violence, or gentleness, is a natural virtue, but non-violence toward the violent can be as self-destructive as unilateral promise-keeping. Moreover, the higher pleasure of knowing that one's attacker has not suffered at one's hands is not merely insufficient to outweigh the loss of life or limb, it will also be lessened by the awareness that, when violence is the rule, the good to the violent man done by one's own non-violence is shortlived and insignificant, unless it inspires others to non-violence.

The natural virtues can, in individual cases, lose most of their point if the degree of non-virtuousness of others is great enough. They still contrast with the artificial virtues, however, in that their good-promoting power will vary from case to case, given the same degree of general conformity. When there is general conformity to non-violence, one may still have reason not to trust individual persons, if there is reason to believe that those ones reciprocate non-violence with violence. When there is general violence, one may still have reason to expect a non-violent response to non-violence in selected cases, so that isolated pockets of gentleness and mutual trust can grow up within a climate of general violence. The same is true, up to a point, of the artificial virtues, in that respect for property rules, or promise keeping, or allegiance, may be dependable within a restricted circle — say among members of the mafia — although they do not observe rules outside the group. The artificial virtues differ from the natural ones, however, in that there is never excuse for *selective non-observance,* within a generally conforming circle, as there can be reason for selective non-observance of non-violence, generosity, helpfulness. A debt owed to a vicious man, a miser, a profligate debauchee, or a dishonest man, is still owed. "Justice, in her decisions never regards the fitness or unfitness of objects to particular persons, but conducts herself by more extensive views. Whether a man be generous, or a miser, he is equally well receiv'd by her, and obtains with the same facility or decision in her favor, even for what is entirely useless to him" (Hume, *Treatise,* p. 502). To grant that the conformity of others does affect the value of the natural as well as the artificial virtues is not to deny Hume's point here, that selective non-observance, based on "fitness or unfitness of objects to particular persons," is reasonable with natural but not with artificial virtues. "Taking any single act, my justice may be pernicious in every respect; and 'tis only on the supposition, that others are to imitate my example; that I can be persuaded to embrace that virtue; since nothing but this combination can render justice advantageous or afford me any motives to conform myself to its rules" (op.cit., p. 498).

6. *The pleasures of conformity*

One must suppose, then, that enough others will imitate one's just action if a just act is to be "advantageous," is to advance any interest or give anyone, however altruistic or public-spirited, rational motive to perform it. When the supposition or faith is reasonable, then there will be a new higher pleasure obtainable by virtuous persons, the satisfaction of knowing that they have contributed to the preservation of the condition of general conformity needed for justice to deliver its utility. This higher pleasure of conformity will be obtainable not only from acts conforming to established more or less just artifices, but also from acts displaying those natural virtues whose full point requires the reasonable expectation that others will not return vice for virtue. The higher pleasure of conformity can, in those latter cases, be added to those of altruism and prudence, and it exceeds them in 'height'. As prudence and altruism facilitate delectation, so conformity facilitates prudence and altruism, as well as extending their range through artifices.

There are, then, a series of hedonic bonus pleasures which we can enjoy, if we cultivate our spiritual palates and develop a relish for them, as Locke puts it (*Essay,* Bk. II, 21, 69). They can accompany the non-hedonic goods which are powers, the non-self directed goods, and conformity to those artifices which create public "powers" to increase the powers and pleasures of individuals. Such present occurrent pleasures, once obtained, cannot be taken away from the prudent man, the altruist, or the conformist, even if the non-present or other-dependent good *in* which the pleasure is taken does not eventuate. Bonus pleasures are non-negligible contributors to the goodness of a life. As pains are indicators of other ills, these pleasures are indicators, not guarantees, of other presumed goods, and they add to them as well as indicate them. But the indication may be false, the glory may be vainglory. Only insofar as one can reasonably hope for the success of one's prudent policy, altruistic project, or for the successful achievement of *general* conformity to an institution, can one derive a higher pleasure from prudent, altruistic or conforming action. Should the hopes on which they were, reasonably, based become later known to be false, the already obtained bonus pleasures may be devalued. They cannot be cancelled, but they may count for less, perhaps count negatively, in the person's proper assessment of the goodness of the life. If hopes turn out to have been what Hobbes calls vain "presumptions," the pleasures dependent on them may come to have been vainglory. If, on one's deathbed, one were persuaded that the person whose apparent love and devotion had given one much pleasure had really been uncaring, perhaps even had despised one, it would not, I think, be reasonable to react with the thought 'thank God I didn't know till now'. False pleasures, pleasures based on what comes to be seen as a lie, can, if the lie is serious and has reverberating implications for many of one's concerns, be worse than the absence of pleasure. Better no glory than vainglory.

Would the prudent man's bonus pleasure of feeling secure come to have been, like the friend's trusting pleasure, fool's gold, if he comes to realize that he will not live into the future for which he saved? If the bonus pleasure had been pleasure in the anticipated spendings of his savings, it would certainly be degraded by realization that he will not spend it, but to the extent that his bonus pleasure in his sense of security was in that which freed him from anxiety about his future, that bonus pleasure is not devalued by any knowledge he may acquire about his imminent early death. The power he had was a good, even if not exercised, because its absence would have been an ever present felt evil. One might say, of the trusting friend, that his trust that his love was reciprocated was a good similar to the prudent man's security, in that its absence would have been an evil for him. But could the evil of suspicion or distrust, or of the absence of affection, be as great as the evil the friend suffers if he bases his life on a false trust? The difference, I think, lies in the fact the unnecessarily prudent man is not *betrayed* by events, as the friend is by the false friend. The prudent man saves, because of the *possibility* that he may live long, but the friend loved in the confidence that love was returned. Prudence is, and knows itself to be, a reaction to risk and uncertainty, so its goods are not devalued if the possibility the prudent man provided for does not come about. But friendship does not, typically, see itself as content with the mere *possibility* of returned trust and love.

Can the man who acts for the sake of justice, when he knows or suspects that others are *not* conforming, get any bonus pleasures which are not fool's gold? We need to distinguish the cases where most but not all others are conforming from the cases where the conformists are in a minority, and, within the latter class, between the few who are trying to *inaugurate* a needed practice, and the few who are clinging to a once accepted but now imperilled institution. The last case, of fidelity to a once supported practice, faces less severe problems than those of the moral innovator, who must both get agreement on *what* should be conformed to, and also try to get sufficient conformity to it to secure the rewards of conformity. At least the moral conservative, the would-be supporter of a once established practice, does not face what have been called[9] the isolation and coordination problems, he faces only the problem of assurance of compliance. I shall not discuss the problems, faced by Hobbesian natural men, of simultaneously achieving communication, agreeing on what institutions are desirable (what coordination scheme to adopt) and also getting assured compliance to them. Let us, optimistically, assume that we have got, by the fact of past established conventions, their later reform, and their agreed need for specific further reforms, a solution to the isolation and coordination problems, that is, we have agreement on how we *should* all be acting. The compli-

---

[9]Kurt Baier, "Rationality and Morality," *Erkenntnis* 11 (1977), p. 197, where the 'isolation', 'coordination', and 'assurance' problems are distinguished.

ance problem then arises—namely whether to act as we all should if we all are to get the best state of things for us, when there is no assurance that the rest of us are going to comply. If I comply and the rest of you don't, then the main good, for the sake of which that cooperative scheme was seen to be acceptable, will not be fully obtained, by any of us. To the extent it is partially attained it will be attained by non-compliers as well as compliers. I will have been the cully of my integrity. So, it seems, the pleasure of conformity is fool's gold unless others do in fact conform in sufficient numbers.

One thing which might save those pleasures from becoming false is the psychological taste of the individual for conformity. Not everyone can enjoy gun-running. Just as the prudent man who doesn't live to enjoy his savings may nevertheless have been saved by his prudence from unpleasant anxiety, so conformity to the old ways may soothe the timid who would be alarmed, not gratified, by the immoralists' life style.

But suppose I *could* develop a relish for gun-running, would it be irrational for me to decide to stick by, not to abandon, the threatened moral practices? Can unilateral, (or minority-wide) conformity to just, or potentially just, institutions have any genuine lure for me?

7. The higher pleasure of qualifying for membership in the kingdom of ends

Hume's point, a valid one, is that only a fool supports widely unsupported institutions whose only good depends on their getting wide support. But support from whom? My contemporaries and only them? It is fairly evident, I think, that the support of the majority of his contemporaries is not *sufficient* to guard the conformist from being taken in by fool's gold, especially when the institution is one which *conserves* goods for future generations. Whole generations can be retroactively made into cullies of their joint integrity by later generations' waste and destruction. What I want to stress is that conformity by the majority of one's contemporaries is not *necessary* to save the moral man from having been a fool.

Here, at last, I turn to the obvious source of a reply to Gauthier: Kant. He spelled out more clearly than any other modern philosopher the wholly secular basis for a strong set of plain duties. It is wholly secular, and it is also faith-requiring.

Kant says that although a rational being, when he acts on the maxim he can will as a universal law, "cannot for that reason expect every other rational being to be true to it; nor can he expect the realm of nature and its orderly design to harmonize with him as a fitting member of a realm of ends which is possible through himself. That is, he cannot count on its favoring his expectation of happiness. Still the law: Act according to the maxims of a universally legislative member of a merely potential realm of ends, remains in full force, because it commands categorically. And just in this lies the paradox, that merely the dignity of humanity as rational nature without any end or advantage to be gained by it, and thus respect for a mere idea, should serve as the inflexible precept of the will. There is the further paradox that the sublimity and worthiness of every rational subject to be a legislative member in the realm of ends consists precisely in independence of maxims from all such incentives" (Kant, *Foundation of the Metaphysics of Morals*, trs. Lewis White Beck). In this remarkable passage Kant appears to be claiming that the willingness to act *as if* one were a member of an actual kingdom of ends, when one knows that one is in fact a member of a society which falls short of this ideal, alone makes one worthy to be a legislating member of an actual kingdom of ends, or just society. But unless there can be such sublime and worthy persons, no just society is possible. The kingdom of ends is "possible through oneself." The existence of persons with the ability to act from respect for that "mere idea," is, then, the condition of the idea's actualization. Apparently just institutions would not guarantee a just society, if those persons living under them fail Kant's motivational test. A just society must be comprised of just men whose lives are ordered by just institutions.

On this account, apparently futile unilateral and possibly self-sacrificing action is neither futile nor unilateral. Not futile, because it keeps alive the assurance of the possibility of qualified members for a just society. Not unilateral, because the one just man has a 'cloud of witnesses,' all those others whose similar acts in other times kept alive the same hope. The actions of individuals who, unsupported by their contemporaries, act for the sake of justice do not necessarily hasten the coming of a just society, but they do rule out one ground on which it might be feared impossible. In this very modest way the just man's actions confirm his faith, demonstrate that *one* condition of the existence of a just society can be met, that human psychology can be a psychology for sovereigns. And the one just man is not alone, his isolation problem is solved if he recalls that enough others have already acted as he is acting. Thus every action in conformity to a just but threatened institution or in protest against an unjust but supported one, furthers the cause, keeps the faith. The highest pleasure or 'relish' of all is that of qualifying for membership in the kingdom of ends.[10] It is not just a priggish pleasure if the demonstration that there are and can be

---

[10]I have not discussed the question, raised by Gauthier's example of unilateral abstention from preemptive nuclear strike, of what should be done when the decision taken may commit others besides the decision-maker to the higher pleasures of martyrdom for a good cause. This is the *really* difficult question.

qualified members has the role which Kant as I interpret him claimed for it. (The blood of the martyrs is the seed of the church.)

8. *The faith the just live by*

The secular faith which the just live by is, then, a faith in the possibility of a society for membership in which their just action theoretically qualifies them. They believe, in part, because of the previous demonstration that there can be such qualified members, so they join a movement already started. Each new member gives other potential members new assurance that the faith is not in vain, and it also confirms the faith of that new member himself, in that, after his act, the club of which he is an 'honorary' member is the larger by one, and its point depends on the size and persistence of its membership.

The qualified, so honorary, member of the kingdom of ends, usually hopes that some actual society, perhaps long after his death, will embody the kingdom of ends on earth, that the possible will become actual. Such a society would, in general intention, honor all those who acted for the sake of justice, who qualified for membership but did not survive to be members. They would be participants in the secular variant of the communion of the saints. This higher pleasure is a variant of that pleasure of imagination, delight in the prospect of posthumous recognition, which even Hobbes allows as a real pleasure. "Though after death there be no sense of the praise given us on earth, as being joys that are either swallowed up in the unspeakable joys of heaven or extinguished in the extreme torments of hell, yet is not such fame vain; because men have a present delight therein from the foresight of it and of the benefit that may redound thereby to their prosperity, which, though they see not, yet they imagine; and anything that is pleasure to the sense, the same is also pleasure in the imagination" (*Leviathan*, chap. 11). Hobbes would not be content with anonymous recognition —presumably only the foresight that one's name will live on, preserved on some honor roll, could give Hobbesian man this pleasure of imagination. Fame is one thing, membership in the faceless communion of the saints quite another for one who values nothing but what is eminent. Still, the qualification for praise and recognition by a posterity to whom benefits redound is at least part of what the Hobbesian can glory in, and for a Kantian it suffices for glory.

Does this pleasure of imagination require expectation that posterity *will* benefit? Does the faith the just live by include confidence that some society on earth will some day actually be just? As already acknowledged, the ideal of justice includes a demand, which may be Utopian, that its historical approximation coincide with its qualitative approximation. In addition to this demand, which the just person must, for the moment at least, merely *hope* can be met, there is another more serious difficulty in the idea of an actual just society which would meet the Kantian requirements. This is that, to the extent that there *is* conformity among one's contemporaries to apparently just practices, to precisely that extent none of the conformers can be assured that they, each of them, qualify for membership in the kingdom of ends. If they are acting, not for a mere idea, but in support of an actual practice, they cannot be sure they meet Kant's paradoxical test for qualification for membership in a just society, that is they cannot be sure how they *would* act if there were not general conformity. But the apparently just conforming society will not *be* just, in Kant's sense, if its sovereign-subjects are not qualified to be members. Kant's paradox is real, and so, once again, the ideal of a just society threatens to become incoherent. The threat, this time, is not one which can be allayed by sociological and historical findings, but is more fundamental— a *necessary* conflict between the criteria for qualification as the just society comprised of qualified members, and the criteria for its actualization.

Must the just man then conclude '*credo quia absurdum est?*' He might—as he might develop a relish for acting for necessarily lost causes—but he can keep his faith from being the absurd hope for the impossible, by acceptance of the fact that one can live without certainty. As the just man *now*, in an unjust world, has no certainty, only faith and hope, that there really can and will be a just society of the living, so, in any apparently attained just society, that is in one with just institutions, its members will rely on the faith and hope that they could if necessary act for a mere idea, and so that they really qualify for membership. A new variant of Hobbesian faith in man will be needed. Both in the absence and in the presence of an actual just society, then, the just will live by faith.[11]

---

[11]I have tried, throughout this paper, to evoke some Biblical echoes, to show how the secular faith I describe parallels its theological forerunners. The effort to speak both the language of Hobbes and that of the King James Bible has resulted in a style which some readers have found obscure. This I regret, but I do want to keep, for those in a position to recognize them, allusions to, e.g., St. Paul's Epistle to the Hebrews chaps. 10 and 11.

BIBLIOGRAPHY

Since faith is the subject of a vast literature, both philosophical and religious, this bibliography must be very selective and fragmentary. It consists of suggested further readings on the themes and writers represented in the text or singled out for mention in the Introduction, and is divided accordingly. The annotation (B) indicates that the work listed contains a valuable bibliography.

Faith in the Bible

Buber, M. 1961. *Two Types of Faith.* Trans. N. Goldhawk. New York: Harper.

Bultmann, R., and Weiser, A. 1968. "pisteuo." In *Theological Dictionary of the New Testament,* Vol. VI. Ed. G. Kittel and G. Freidrich, trans. G.W. Bromiley; pp. 174–228. Grand Rapids: Eerdmans.

"Faith." 1955. In *Encyclopedia of Religion and Ethics,* Vol. 5. Ed. Hastings, pp. 689–697. Edinburgh: Clark.

Findlay, G., and Shires, H. 1955. "Faith." In *Hastings' Dictionary of the Bible,* rev. ed., pp. 288–290. Edinburgh: Clark.

Fison, J.E. 1957. *The Faith of the Bible.* Harmondsworth, Middlesex: Penguin.

Minear, P.S. 1951. "Paul the Apostle." In *The Interpreter's Bible,* Vol. VII, pp. 200–213. Nashville: Abingdon. (B)

Taylor, V. 1951. "The Life and Ministry of Jesus." In *The Interpreter's Bible,* Vol. VII, pp. 114–144. Nashville: Abingdon. (B)

Wright, G.E. 1952. "The Faith of Israel." In *The Interpreter's Bible,* Vol. I, pp. 349–389. Nashville: Abingdon. (B)

Classical Works

A. AQUINAS

Copleston, F.C. 1955. *Aquinas*. London: Penguin.
Mascall, E.L. 1943. *He Who Is*. London: Longmans.
————. 1949. *Existence and Analogy*. London: Longmans.
Summa Contra Gentiles, translated as *On the Truth of the Catholic Faith*. 1955. Book I, Chapters 1–8. New York: Doubleday.
Summa Theologiae, Secunda Secundae (Part II of Part II), Questions 1–16. 1974, 1975. Latin text with English translation in Volumes 31 and 32 of the Blackfriars edition. London: Eyre and Spottiswoode.
Truth, Vol. 2, Question 14. 1952. Trans. J.V. McGlynn. Chicago: Regnery.

B. LUTHER

Bainton, R. 1950. *Here I Stand*. Nashville: Abingdon.
————. 1952. *The Reformation of the Sixteenth Century*. Boston: Beacon.
Dillenberger, J., (ed.). 1961. *Martin Luther: Selections from His Writings*. New York: Doubleday.
Dillenberger, J., and Welch, C. 1954. *Protestant Christianity*. Chapters II and IV. New York: Scribners.
Watson, P.S. 1950. *Let God Be God*. Philadelphia: Muhlenberg.

C. PASCAL

Hazelton, R. 1974. *Blaise Pascal: The Genius of His Thought*. Philadelphia: Westminster.
Krailsheimer, A. 1980. *Pascal*. Oxford: Oxford U.P. (Past Masters Series).
Patrick, D. 1947. *Pascal and Kierkegaard*, Vol. 1. London: Butterworth.
Pensées. 1966. Trans. A. Krailsheimer. London: Penguin.
  On the Wager argument, see particularly the following:
Flew, A. 1960. "Is Pascal's Wager the Only Safe Bet?" In *Rationalist Annual*. London: Watts.
Hacking, I. 1975. *The Emergence of Probability*, chapter 8. New York: Cambridge U.P.
Penelhum, T. 1983. *God and Skepticism*, chapters 4 and 5. Dordrecht: Reidel.
Rescher, N. 1985. *Pascal's Wager*. Indiana: Notre Dame.
Swinburne, R. 1981. *Faith and Reason*, pp. 88–99. Oxford: Clarendon Press.

D. BUTLER

The Analogy of Religion. 1736. In *The Works of Bishop Butler*. 1900. Ed. J.H. Bernard, 2 vols. London: Macmillan.
Broad, C.D. 1953. "Bishop Butler as a Theologian." In *Religion, Philosophy and Psychical Research*, pp. 202–219. London: Routledge.
Penelhum, T. 1985. *Butler*. London: Routledge.

E. ROUSSEAU

Foxley, B., trans. 1957. *Emile*. New York: E.P. Dutton.

"Letter to Voltaire on Providence," translated in P. Edwards (ed.), *Voltaire*, Macmillan, N.Y. 1989.

Grimsley, R. 1957. *The Philosophy of Rousseau*. New York: Oxford U.P.

———. 1968. *Rousseau and the Religious Quest*. Oxford: Clarendon Press.

Hendel, C.W. 1962. *Jean-Jacques Rousseau: Moralist*, 2nd ed. New York: The Library of Liberal Arts.

Jimack, P. 1983. *Rousseau: Emile*. London: Grant and Cutler.

Mossner, E.C. "Deism." In *Encyclopedia of Philosophy*, Vol. 2. Ed. Paul Edwards, pp. 326–336. New York: Macmillan.

F. KIERKEGAARD

The Concept of Anxiety. 1980. Trans. R. Thomte. Princeton: Princeton U.P.

Concluding Unscientific Postscript. 1941. Trans. D. Swenson and M. Lowrie. Princeton: Princeton U.P.

Fear and Trembling and Repetition. 1983. Trans. H.V. Hong and E.G. Hong. Princeton: Princeton U.P.

Philosophical Fragments and Johannes Climacus. 1985. Trans. H.V. Hong. Princeton: Princeton U.P.

Pojman, L. 1984. *The Logic of Subjectivity*. Alabama: Alabama U.P.

Thomas, J.H. 1957. *Subjectivity and Paradox*. Oxford: Blackwell.

G. OTHER IMPORTANT CLASSICAL WORKS

Bayle, P. 1965. *Historical and Critical Dictionary*. Selections trans. and ed. Richard Popkin. Indianapolis: Bobbs-Merrill.

Calvin, J. 1960. *Institutes of the Christian Religion*, 2 vols. Trans. F.L. Battles. Philadelphia: Westminster.

Chadwick, O. 1983. *Newman*. Oxford, Oxford U.P. (Past Masters Series).

Collins, J. 1967. "Newman." In *Encyclopedia of Philosophy*, Vol. 5. Ed. Paul Edwards, pp. 481–485. New York: Macmillan.

Fey, W.R. 1976. *Faith and Doubt: The Unfolding of Newman's Thought on Certainty*. Shepherdstown: Patmos Press. (B)

Kant, I. 1956. *Critique of Practical Reason*. Trans. L.W. Beck. Indianapolis: Bobbs-Merrill.

———. 1960. *Religion within the Limits of Reason Alone*. Trans. T. Greene and H. Hudson. New York: Harper.

Labrousse, E. 1983. *Bayle*. Trans. D. Potts. Oxford: Oxford U.P. (Past Masters Series).

Newman, J.H. 1985. *Essay in Aid of a Grammar of Assent*. Ed. I.T. Ker. Oxford: Clarendon Press.

Paley. W. 1838. *Evidences of Christianity*. London: Longmans.

Webb, C.C.J. 1926. *Kant's Philosophy of Religion*. Oxford: Oxford U.P.

Wood, A.W. 1970. *Kant's Moral Religion*. Ithaca: Cornell U.P.

Critiques of Faith

Flew, A. 1966. *God and Philosophy.* London: Hutchinson.
————. 1984. *God, Freedom, and Immortality.* New York: Prometheus.
Gaskin, J.C.A. 1978. *Hume's Philosophy of Religion.* New York: Barnes and Noble.
Hume, D. 1957. *The Natural History of Religion.* Ed. H.E. Root. Stanford: Stanford U.P.
————. 1963. *Dialogues Concerning Natural Religion.* Ed. N.K. Smith. New York: Barnes and Noble.
Kenny, A. 1979. *The God of the Philosophers.* Oxford: Clarendon Press.
Martin, C.B. 1959. *Religious Belief.* Ithaca: Cornell U.P.
Nielsen, K. 1971. *Contemporary Critiques of Religion.* London: Macmillan.
————. 1973. *Scepticism.* London: Macmillan.
Russell, B. 1957. *Why I am Not a Christian and Other Essays.* Ed. P. Edwards. New York: Simon and Schuster.

Some Twentieth-Century Studies

Anscombe, G.E.M. 1981. "Faith." In *Ethics, Religion, and Politics: Collected Papers*, Vol. Three, pp. 113–122. Minneapolis: University of Minnesota Press.
Ebeling, G. 1961. *The Nature of Faith.* Trans. R.G. Smith. London: Collins.
Geach, P.T. 1977. *The Virtues*, chapter 2. Cambridge: Cambridge U.P.
Hick, J. 1966. *Faith and Knowledge*, 2nd ed. Ithaca: Cornell U.P.
————. 1967. "Faith." In *Encyclopedia of Philosophy*, Vol. 3. Ed. P. Edwards, pp. 165–169. (B)
Mavrodes, G. 1970. *Belief in God.* New York: Random House.
Mitchell, B. 1973. *The Justification of Religious Belief.* London: Macmillan. (B)
Penelhum, T. 1971. *Religion and Rationality.* New York: Random House.
————. 1983. *God and Skepticism.* Dordrecht: Reidel.
Plantinga, A. 1967. *God and Other Minds.* Ithaca: Cornell U.P.
Sutherland, R. 1984. *Faith and Ambiguity.* London: SCM.
Tillich, P. 1952. *The Courage to Be.* New Haven: Yale U.P.
————. 1957. *The Dynamics of Faith.* New York: Harper.

The Nature of Belief and its Relation to the Will

Helm P. 1973. *The Varieties of Belief.* London: Allen and Unwin.
Passmore, J. 1977. "Hume and the Ethics of Belief." In *David Hume: Bicentenary Papers.* Ed. G. Maurice, pp. 77–92. Edinburgh: Edinburgh U.P.
Penelhum, T. 1981. "Faith and Uncertainty." *Scottish Journal of Religious Studies*, II: 28–37.
Pojman, L.J. 1986. *Religious Belief and the Will.* London: Routledge. (B)
Price, H.H. 1954. "Belief and Will." In *Proceedings of the Aristotelian Society*, Supplementary Volume 28, pp. 1–26. Published for the Aristotelian Society, by Harrison & Sons, London.
————. 1969. *Belief.* London: Allen and Unwin.

Stevenson, J.T. 1975. "Doxastic Responsibility." In *Analysis and Metaphysics.* Ed. Keith Lehrer. Dordrecht: Reidel.

Williams, B.A.O. 1973. "Deciding to Believe." In *Problems of the Self*, pp. 136–151. Cambridge: Cambridge U.P.

On the "Will-to-Believe" Controversy, see the following:

Clifford, W.K. 1879. "The Ethics of Belief." In *Lectures and Essays.* Ed. L. Stephen and F. Pollock. London: Macmillan. Reproduction in R. Ammerman and M. Singer, 1970, *Belief, Knowledge and Truth*, New York: Scribners.

James, W. 1897. "The Will to Believe." In *The Will to Believe and Other Essays.* London: Longmans. Reproduction, 1956, New York: Dover.

Kauber, P., and Hare, P. 1974. "The Right and Duty to Will to Believe." *Canadian Journal of Philosophy*, 4:327–343.

Wernham, J.C.S. 1987. *James' Will-to-Believe Doctrine.* Kingston and Montreal: McGill-Queen's Press.

Wittgenstein and Religion

Cupitt, D. 1980. *Taking Leave of God.* London: SCM.

———. 1982. *The World to Come.* London: SCM.

Hudson, W.D. 1975. *Wittgenstein and Religious Belief.* London: Macmillan.

Keightley, A. 1976. *Wittgenstein, Grammar and God.* London: Epworth.

Moore, G.E. 1959. "Certainty." In *Philosophical Papers*, pp. 226–251. London: Allen and Unwin.

Nielsen, K. 1967. "Wittgensteinian Fideism." *Philosophy*, 37:191–209.

Phillips, D.Z. 1965. *The Concept of Prayer.* London: Routledge.

———. 1970. *Faith and Philosophical Enquiry.* London: Routledge.

———. 1976. *Religion Without Explanation*, Oxford: Blackwell.

Wittgenstein, L. 1953. *Philosophical Investigation.* Trans. G.E.M. Anscombe. Oxford: Blackwell. (See especially pp. 193–229.)

———. 1966. *Lectures and Conversations on Aesthetics, Psychology and Religious Belief.* Ed. C. Barrett. Oxford: Blackwell.

———. 1969. *On Certainty.* Trans. G.E.M. Anscombe and G.H. von Wright. Oxford: Blackwell.

The Basic Belief Apologetic

Alston, W.P. 1986. "On Perceiving God." *Journal of Philosophy*, 83: 655–665.

Kenny, A. 1983. *Faith and Reason.* New York: Columbia.

Penelhum, T. *God and Skepticism*, chapter 7. Dordrecht: Reidel.

Plantinga, A. 1982. "Rationality and Religious Belief." In *Contemporary Philosophy of Religion.* Ed. S. Kahn and D. Shatz, pp. 255–277. New York: Oxford U.P.

Plantinga, A., and Wolterstorff, N. (eds.) 1983. *Faith and Rationality: Reason and Belief in God.* Indiana: Notre Dame U.P.

Runzo, J., and Ihara, C. (eds). 1986. *Religious Experience and Religious Belief.* University Press of America.

Faith and the Plurality of Religions

Hick, J. 1973. *God and the Universe of Faiths.* London: Macmillan.
————. 1985. *Problems of Religious Pluralism.* London: Macmillan.
Smith, W.C. 1964. *The Meaning and End of Religion.* New York: Mentor.
————. 1977. *Belief and History.* Charlottesville: U.P. of Virginia.
————. 1977. *Faith and Belief.* Charlottesville: U.P. of Virginia.
————. 1981. *Towards a World Theology.* London: Macmillan.

The question of the suitability of the concept of faith for the understanding of non-Western traditions can only be approached through some acquaintance with the teachings of those traditions. Analogies are closest, perhaps, in the case of the *bhakti* tradition in Hinduism, and the "Pure Land" tradition in Mähayana Buddhism. The most famous *bhakti* scripture is, of course, the *Bhagavad-Gita*, which can be read in R.C. Zaehner's edition, Oxford, 1969. For a revealing study of a startling likeness between the Pure Land and Protestant Christianity, see J. Ishihara, "Luther and Shinran," *Japanese Religions*, Vol. 14, pp. 31–54, NCC Center for the Study of Japanese Religions, Kyoto, 1987. See also Alfred Bloom: *Shinran's Gospel of Pure Grace*, University of Arizona Press, Tucson, 1965.